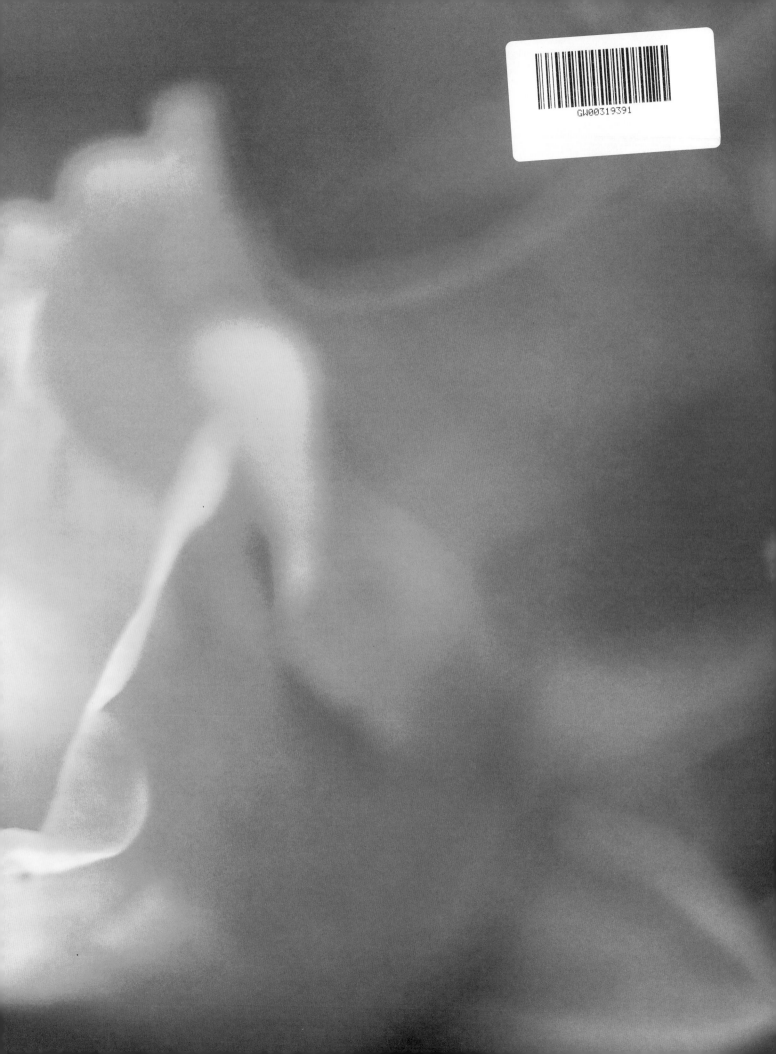

05-23

Just **Flowers**

Pamela Westland

Photography by David Loftus

Hamlyn

Contents

Many thanks to the following for their help and assistance:
Ocean Home Shopping Ltd, The Pier
Locations: Brett and Elizabeth Gosper, Nicky Hillier

First published in Great Britain in 1998
by Hamlyn, an imprint of Reed Consumer Books Limited,
81 Fulham Road, London, SW3 6RB

A CIP catalogue record of this book is available from the
British Library

ISBN 0 600 59473 4

Printed and bound in China

Publishing Director: Laura Bamford

Creative Director: Keith Martin
Design: Mark Winwood, Ruth Hope

Executive Editor: Simon Tuite
Project Editor: Jane Royston

Introduction

A vibrant, hand-tied bunch of mixed berries and brilliant blossoms; a trio of spectacular flowers presented minimalist style; a handful of country-garden flowers clustered together in a teapot – whatever style comes closest to expressing your mood of the moment, you will find creative inspiration for it here.

The concept behind this book is that imagination, flair and even a little courage bring more exciting rewards than time and money; that purpose-made containers and specialist floral equipment have their uses, but are not indispensable.

From cover to cover the floral designs show, reassuringly, that pressure of time is no barrier to creating imaginative displays for a dining or dressing table, windowsill or alcove.

As you become more confident, you could explore the decorations towards the end of the book, the ones that are not stop-watched and second-counted. Spend a little more time emulating the medley of colours, textures and forms that characterize the flower paintings of Dutch Old Masters, or creating a colourful floral wreath that traditionally symbolizes welcome and friendship.

Above all, take time, even if it can only be seconds, to notice each flower. Appreciate beauty through simplicity: the effect of water sprinkled over leaves and petals; the tactile contrasts of spiky seedheads against soft-petalled flowers; and the reflected glory of perfect blooms against harsh, shiny metals. These experiences can be an even greater pleasure than to have time on your hands.

Pamela Westland

In 5 minutes

Crystal clear

What you need...

- Florist's scissors
- Rectangular clear-glass vase

Plant material
- Blue delphinium
- Pastel pink and white lisianthus

...and some tips!

- **Highly polished**
Before arranging the flowers, check your vase for marks and,
if necessary, polish it with window-cleaning fluid and a soft cloth.

- **Lasting freshness**
Flowers positioned underwater will fade more quickly. Lift the stems and pick off these flowers, changing the water at the same time.

- **Seasonal variation**
Long, straight stems of yellow-flowered forsythia blended with tulips would make an equally attractive grouping in springtime.

Tall stems of ice-blue delphinium contrast pleasingly here with the supple, gently curving lines of lisianthus in pastel pink and white.

Basic outline

1 Cut the delphinium stems into almost equal lengths. Strip off any leaves that would come below the water line, but leave on a few of the lowest flowers as these will create an interesting underwater effect. *Arrange the stems in the vase in a criss-cross pattern, forming a 'mesh' to hold the lisianthus in place.*

Creating 'movement'

2 Add approximately two-thirds of the lisianthus flowers, positioning them so that they nestle among the framework created by the delphinium flowers and distributing the colours randomly to create a natural appearance. From the remaining lisianthus, select some of the most attractive-looking flowers, cut their stems fairly short and then carefully arrange them just above the rim of the vase.

The curving lisianthus stems give 'movement' to this design. With its harmonious blend of colours and soft-petalled flowers, the arrangement will look best viewed against a cool light – a table in front of a north-facing window would be ideal.

1

Simply elegant

What you need...

- Plain ginger-jar-type vase
- Metal pin-holder (optional; available from florists)
- Florist's scissors

Plant material
- 3 stems of bird-of-paradise (*Strelitzia*)
- 1 or 2 sprays of hypericum berries

...and some tips!

- **Balancing act**
In a 'minimalist' arrangement, when only a few flowers are used and each one is seen in isolation, an uneven number of stems – three, five or more – generally gives a more pleasing balance to the eye.

- **Seasonal variation**
A trio of white arum lilies in a rounded, plain vase would make an equally striking composition in spring or summer.

A trio of spectacular bird-of-paradise flowers combined with berries makes for a group that is elegant in its simplicity.

A stem-holder

1 Unless the aperture of your chosen container is narrow enough to hold the flower stems firmly, it is advisable to start by placing a metal pin-holder in the vase: with its heavy metal base and stout pins, this will steady the top-heavy flowers in the arrangement. *A pin-holder like this one can be re-used and should last a lifetime.*

Height variation

2 Stand one of the bird-of-paradise flowers against the vase to judge where to cut the first, and longest, stem. Cut at a sharp angle so that it will be able to take up water more readily (this is especially important with thick flower stems such as these – see also pages 132–3). *To achieve a good visual balance and avoid a clash of flowerheads, cut the second stem shorter, and the third stem shorter still. Position the three stems in the vase.*

Front cover

3 With the three principal flowers in place, finish off by adding one or two short sprays of hypericum berries around the rim of the vase. *Keep these stems short – so that the foliage justs rests on the rim – to fill in the aperture without detracting from the simplicity of the group.*

Presented in a cluster of glasses at the table centre, or as a single splash of colour at each place, roses are ideal for a celebration.

Pink champagne

What you need...

- Florist's scissors
- Wineglasses or glass tumblers (these need not match)
- Craft knife

Plant material
- Roses in a variety of pastel colours (one for each glass)

...and some tips!

- Room for expansion
Check that the glasses or tumblers that you have chosen are wide enough to hold the flowers easily, without squashing them.

- Optical illusion
Hand-blown glass, with its integral pattern of bubbles, is especially effective for this type of presentation – it seems to turn the water into sparkling wine!

- Seasonal variation
Glasshouse carnations are available all year round and, like roses, will take kindly to total immersion. To achieve the best effect, pick off any buds that detract from the simplicity of a single bloom.

Preparation and immersion

1 Cut the rose stems so that the immersed flowerheads will sit just below the rims of the glasses, and strip away all the leaves. Taking each stem in turn – and holding the flower facing away from you – use the craft knife to strip off the thorns, then cut a slit in the end of the stem. Cutting the stem in this way exposes a larger area of plant tissue to water, and so will keep the flowers fresh for longer (see also pages 132–3).

Partly fill each wineglass or tumbler with water and gently press a rose into it. Hold the flowerhead below the water for a few seconds so that the spaces between the petals fill up. *You will be able to create different effects by totally or only partially submerging the flowers – refraction plays pretty visual tricks.*

Just for fun

What you need...

- Soft, dry cloth
- Florist's scissors
- Skewer (optional)
- Florist's clay (optional)

Plant material
- 3 medium-sized aubergines
- 5 small sunflowers or rudbeckia

...and some tips!

- A firm base
A dab of florist's clay under the aubergines will hold them steady.

- Seasonal variation
In the autumn you could substitute small marrows, pumpkins or other squashes for the aubergines, decorating them with any large, colourful flowers – dahlias or chrysanthemums would be ideal.

You don't need a container – just a sense of fun – to create this table decoration that picks up on today's trend for informal entertaining.

Measuring up and making way

1 Wash the aubergines if necessary, and polish them with the soft cloth until they shine. Decide on the angles that the stems of the sunflowers or rudbeckia will take, and measure each one against the vegetables before cutting. Allow for at least 4 cm (1½ in) of each stem to be pushed into the aubergine – if you are unsure, err on the long side, as you can trim them later if necessary. Use a skewer (or a stiff, woody plant stem) to pierce holes in the skin of the aubergines. *Piercing the aubergines in this way will avoid putting pressure on the flower stems, and therefore the risk of breaking them.*

Getting it together

2 Push the sunflower or rudbeckia stems into the ready-made channels in the aubergines. Stand back to assess the effect and, if necessary, re-cut the stems a little shorter. *If the aubergines appear at all unstable, insert a small strip of florist's clay beneath each one.*

Light fantastic

What you need...

- Long-stemmed wineglass
- Tall, waisted glass vase (or similar)
- Florist's scissors
- Natural-coloured raffia
- 2 frosted-glass bottles (optional)

Plant material
- 2 or 3 bunches (depending on vase size) of freesias in mixed colours

...and some tips!

- Special affinity
Frosted-glass, plastic and resin holders of all kinds look very effective with flowers such as freesias, lilies and iris, whose petals have a slight sheen.

- Seasonal variation
In spring, you could pair an arrangement of tulips in the larger container (positioning their stems so that they will curve gently outwards) with a posy of miniature tulips in the wineglass.

Positioned so that the daylight floods through, glass containers filled with freesias and arranged with frosted bottles make a very pleasing still-life composition.

Using the shape

1 Begin by selecting the straightest freesia stems to make the posy for the wineglass (otherwise it may be difficult to balance), and set these aside. Place the remaining freesias in the vase, creating an airy design so that each one may be viewed separately – this treatment works particularly well with these different-coloured flowers.

The outward-curving rim of the blue vase used here dictates a design with freedom of movement, the flower stems curving this way and that to form a circular outline.

An even bunch

2 Gather the reserved freesias loosely into a small bunch and then cut the stem ends level.

When forming the bunch, carefully arrange each of the flowers so that none is crushed or crowded.

A free-standing posy

3 Tie the stems with raffia and then splay out their ends slightly so that the posy stands up securely when you place it in the wineglass.

Position the containers where the daylight will pass through them, adding the frosted-glass bottles to complete the display if you wish.

A group of flowers floating in cool, clear water and left to twist and turn in the breeze makes for very therapeutic viewing on a hot summer's day.

Tranquil pool

What you need...

- Large, shallow stoneware bowl
- Rock chippings or small pebbles (or glass nuggets)
- Florist's scissors

Plant material
- Purple-and-white Singapore orchids or white roses

...and some tips!

- Economy-wise
Floating Singapore orchid flowers in this way need not be as extravagant as it seems. For example, if you are arranging some long-stemmed Singapore orchids in a tall container you will probably want to cut off the lowest flowers on the stems, in which case these are the ones to use in your rock pool.

- Single option
An individual flower floating in a shallow bowl beside each place setting makes a lovely decoration for a dinner table.

- Seasonal variation
In the spring months, single, semi-double or double camellias – with their rose-like outline and waxy petals – would look extremely effective presented like this.

Natural texture

1 Partially fill the bowl with water and add a handful of the rock chippings or pebbles – scattering them randomly – to give the table decoration an added natural dimension.

If the occasion calls for more sparkle, you could use glass nuggets instead, choosing either clear glass or colours to tone with the flowers.

Floating flowerheads

2 Cut the flowers from their stems (if using roses, you will also need carefully to pull off any petals that are damaged or discoloured). Then simply float the flowers on the water.

There is little point in trying to arrange the flowers in a pattern as the slightest movement or breeze will scatter them in all directions – but that is part of the attraction.

Reflected glory

What you need...

- Florist's scissors
- Tall metal vase
- Protective gloves (optional)
- Small glass vase

Plant material
- 5 red gerberas
- About 8 stems of bear grass

...and some tips!

- **Monochromatic**
The use of a single type of flower, in a single bright colour, emphasizes the simplicity of this design and lends oriental overtones.

- **Seasonal variation**
Several white spider chrysanthemums or lime-green 'Tokyo' chrysanthemums, arranged with slender iris leaves, would make a very striking display in the late summer or autumn.

Two contrasting containers, five red gerberas and a handful of bear grasses combine here to create a simple group that has more than usual impact.

Height variation

1 Cut four of the gerbera stems to slightly varying lengths, and place them in the metal vase.

Bear in mind that the composition will have greater 'movement' and visual interest if the flowers face in different directions so that they will be seen from varying aspects.

Gentle curves

2 Always handle the stems of bear grass with great care (or wear a pair of protective gloves to be absolutely safe), as they have painfully sharp edges. Wind the grasses around your hand and hold them there for a few moments; when you release them, they will spring into graceful arcs.

When stored in a shop these grasses tend to flatten out, but winding them around your hand is an easy way to restore their curves and create a natural-looking arrangement.

Double value

3 Add the grasses to the metal vase. Cut short the fifth gerbera stem and place it in the smaller vase, then position the containers so that the single flower is reflected in the metal.

Positioning the two vases in this way will produce two images instead of just one; trailing the strands of bear grass over the smaller vase will serve to unify the composition.

1

Optical illusion

What you need...

- Large, shallow stoneware dish
- Florist's scissors

Plant material
- Trails of vine
- Nasturtiums
- Courgette flowers (if available) or cream mimulus

...and some tips!

- Ground level
It should appear as though the flowers are actually growing, not floating in a pond, so be fairly restrained with the amount of water in the dish.

- Well supported
If some of the larger vine leaves subside into the water and look rather squashed, support them underneath with a few concealed pebbles.

- Seasonal variation
In the early summer, a tangle of clematis stems – complete with some of their flowers and whorls of seedheads – would make another very good subject for this type of treatment.

These nosegays of nasturtiums create the illusion that they are growing among the vine tendrils, producing a very natural effect.

Gentle ties

1 To make each posy, gather together six or eight nasturtiums and tie the stems loosely with a vine tendril; trim the stem ends if necessary.

Vine tendrils are ideal here, as they will hold the delicate nasturtium stems without cutting into them.

All bunched up

2 Pour a little water into the dish and arrange the trails of vine in the base, letting some leaves overlap the rim. Tuck the completed posies and a few individual nasturtiums and courgette flowers (or mimulus) among the vine trails, making sure that the stem ends are immersed in the water

For a natural look, arrange the posies and flowers randomly – just as you would find them growing in the wild – rather than in a neat circle or in straight lines.

Celebrate the height of summer with a cluster of gold and lemon sunflowers arranged in a classic vase; this is a design that will look good on any surface.

Summer sun

What you need...

- Round, narrow-necked vase
- Florist's scissors

Plant material
- Sunflowers (quantity will depend on vase aperture)
- Trail of hop, vine or ivy

...and some tips!

- Conditioning
If you are able to cut your sunflowers from the garden, you must be sure to condition them as soon as you bring them indoors (see pages 132–3).

- Tying time
If the container that you plan to use has a wide neck, compose the sunflowers into a bunch in your hand, tie the stems with raffia and then lower them into the vase.

- Seasonal variation
To create a similarly bold and beautiful effect in the spring or early summer, you could use orange and yellow crown imperial lilies or day lilies.

Low level

1 Position the sunflowers that have the shortest stems around the rim of the vase. As you gradually fill in the aperture in this way, the taller stems to be added at the centre will be well supported.

When using a single flower type like this, placing some of the flowerheads so that they are viewed in profile will give the design a feeling of 'movement' and added interest.

Long trail

2 Add more sunflowers to fill in the centre of the group, then add a single trail of foliage to curve across the vase. *If your foliage stem does not have a natural curve, wind it around your hand and leave it there for a minute or so. When you unwind the stem, it should gently curve to complement the roundness of the vase.*

Milky-white roses and lisianthus contrast here with variegated foliage that spans the colour scale from lime green to pale lemon, for a look that is sharp and refreshing for summer.

Cool and white

What you need...

- Clear-glass jug with straight sides
- Florist's scissors

Plant material
- White roses
- White lisianthus
- Ice-plant
- Green (unripe) poppy seedheads
- White phlox
- Variegated pineapple mint
- Feverfew
- Carrot leaves or fern fronds
- Small variegated hosta leaves

...and some tips!

- Keeping up appearances
Change the water every day, to ensure that it remains clear. Hold the stems gently in one hand as you pour away the water, let them settle back into place and then pour in fresh water.

- Seasonal variation
In early spring you could create a lovely arrangement using white tulips, cream and pale green parrot tulips; white narcissi and white bluebells, together with ferns, variegated ivy and a few sage leaves.

Basic framework

1 Put the choicest two or three roses aside. Make the framework for the design by arranging some of the longest stems – the lisianthus and roses – to criss-cross at right angles from opposite sides of the container.

Seen through clear glass, the stems are high-profile: let them reach all the way down to the base of the container, as if the finished arrangement could be free-standing.

Stem support

2 Cut the ice-plant stems to varying lengths and arrange them in a cluster in the centre, then position more roses around them.

You will find that the network of stems made inititally will hold these later additions firmly in place.

Colour and texture

3 Position poppy seedheads and phlox flowers among the central cluster, angling some of the stems backwards (away from you). Take the roses that you set aside at the start and position them at the centre front, where they will act as the focal point of the design. To complete the arrangement, fill in the gaps with pineapple mint and add a few stems of feverfew (not too many, or their bright yellow centres will be dominant). Finally, add the frondy carrot leaves or ferns at the back of the container and the small, solid hosta leaves at the sides.

When using a limited colour range of plant materials, it is important to emphasize the contrasting shapes and textures in the arrangement so as to create visual interest.

Dancing flames

What you need...

- Florist's scissors
- Squat, round cooking pot (or similar)

Plant material
- Pinky-orange lilies
- Orange and red gerberas
- Cream roses
- Pampas-grass leaves

...and some tips!

- Handle with care
Pampas-grass leaves have sharp edges, so it is best to wear gloves when handling them, or to do so with great care. Never run the leaves through your hand in order to bunch them up.

- Lighting up
An arrangement like this, with its blend of pale tints and deep shades, should be seen in a good light to be appreciated.

- Seasonal variation
In the spring, orange-centred daffodils, cream narcissi and orange tulips would make an equally 'warm' composition. In the late summer, you could combine bronze and gold chrysanthemums or dahlias with rowan or hawthorn berries.

Brightly coloured lilies and gerberas arranged with cool cream roses in a terracotta pot create a design that makes just the right accompaniment for a kitchen or barbecue party.

Stem preparation

1 Pull off almost all the leaves from the lily stems, leaving (if you wish) only those that will sit above the water level and be visible.

Removing the leaves from the lower part of the stems will help to keep the water fresh and free from algae.

Good proportions

2 Cut the stems of the lilies so that the lowest flowers rest only just above the rim of the pot as you put them in, then start to intersperse the orange and red gerberas.

Forget anything that you have ever heard about the ideal proportion of plant material to container being in a ratio of two to one – in this case, colour and compactness rule!

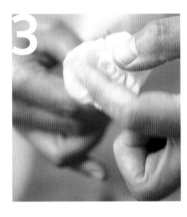

Good proportions

3 If you would like your roses to be more showy more quickly, gently open out the petals: start at the outside of each flower and work towards the centre. Add the roses to the arrangement, recessing some of them close to the pot's rim, then add the pampas-grass leaves in a cluster to one side.

By almost hiding the roses among the lilies, the gerberas' strong colours will be seen in dramatic silhouette.

A frame of cinnamon sticks resting on the rims of these containers serves to hold the flower stems in place, as well as adding a hint of spice.

Spice is nice

What you need...

- Tumblers and high-ball glasses
- Cinnamon sticks, each approximately 45 cm (18 in) long
- Natural-coloured raffia
- Florist's scissors

Plant material
- Blue scabious
- Magenta gerberas
- Purple-and-cream Singapore orchids

...and some tips!

- **The rustic look**
For a more informal display, you could make the triangular frames in the same way but using either straight twigs or lengths of bamboo.

- **Seasonal variation**
A composition using iris and ranunculus would make an attractive springtime group; later in the year, pale green tobacco plant and pansies would be a pretty alternative.

Making the frames

1 To make each frame, break the cinnamon sticks into three equal pieces about 15 cm (6 in) long. Bind two of the lengths together with raffia, about 4 cm (1½ in) from the ends. Position the third stick to form a triangle, and bind the sticks at the remaining two crossing points.

You can vary the size of the frames, and of the triangular spaces in the centre, according to the size of your containers; the frames are re-usable, so you may like to build up a small collection of them in varying sizes.

Bunching up

2 Gather together a small bunch of scabious and gerbera, and cut the stems level. Place one of the frames over a tumbler or high-ball glass and push the stems through the hole.

If you would like the flowers to be more upright – as if the stems had been tied – push the raffia ties inwards along the sticks to make the central hole a little smaller.

Dual purpose

3 Long-stemmed flowers such as the Singapore orchids used here are especially suited to this type of display. Unless your glasses are colourless, pick off any flowers that would otherwise be submerged in water before you use them, as coloured glass may distort rather than enhance their colour.

There is no need to waste the low-level flowers – which will be the largest along the orchid stems – that you have removed, as you can float them in a stoneware or glass bowl to beautiful effect (see pages 20–2).

To arrange stems vertically in a wide container, you will need to include florist's foam to hold them securely. Here, the ferns used to line the tank conceal the foam – and they look good, too.

Vertical take-off

What you need...

- Wide, rectangular glass tank (or similar)
- Block of florist's foam
- Kitchen knife
- Bowl
- Florist's scissors

Plant material
- 'Hard-shield' (*Polystichum aculeatum*) ferns (or similar)
- 2 purple gladioli
- 2 blue agapanthus
- 2 sprays of sea holly (*Eryngium*)
- 1 lime-green 'Tokyo' chrysanthemum

...and some tips!

- Washing up
If the ferns have gathered any dust in the wild, swish them in warm, soapy water and rinse well before arranging them.

- Moisturizer
Keep the florist's foam permanently moist to prolong the life of the arrangement by topping it up with water each day.

- Seasonal variation
In the springtime, an arrangement of white star-of-Bethlehem (Ornithogalum), green iris and clusters of yellow-leaved ivy will have great impact.

Preparation

1 Using the kitchen knife, cut the foam block to fit the tank, allowing space all around it to insert the ferns. Soak the foam in a bowl of water for about 20 minutes (or until it sinks to the bottom), then place it in the tank. *Slide the ferns between the foam and the glass, and you will see the character of the tank transform into that of a damp forest!*

The principal flowers

2 Cut the stems of the gladioli (one slightly longer than the other) and agapanthus at sharp angles. Arrange the gladioli vertically, with the taller stem slightly behind the shorter one, and place the agapanthus on either side of the composition. *Used in this way, the round-headed agapanthus will provide a sense of balance and perfectly complement the spear-shaped gladioli.*

Diagonal line

3 The sea holly is lighter in colour and more wayward than the other flowers: position the two sprays diagonally, so that they trail over the tank rim at the front and back of the design. Finally, place the 'Tokyo' chrysanthemum just in view at the back. *Including a 'surprise element' in a flower arrangement is often highly effective; here this is achieved with the sharp lime-green colour of the 'Tokyo' chrysanthemum.*

Fruitful idea

What you need...

- Kitchen knife
- Grapefruit knife
- Florist's scissors
- Plate or dish (for display)

Plant material
- Oranges
- Variegated pineapple mint
- Purple gladioli
- Orange montbretia
- Purple and cream passion flowers
- Orange marigolds

...and some tips!

- Paintbox colours
Blue and yellow flowers in lemon shells, or red and sharp yellowy-green flowers in lime shells, would also be good.

- Future use
Once the flowers are over, you can freeze the orange shells for use another time.

- Seasonal variation
Orange miniature tulips arranged in orange shells with grape hyacinths and purple anemones would make a bold and colourful statement in the spring.

Scooped-out orange shells make dramatic containers for a cluster of contrasting flowers. Display them individually or in groups – either way, they are sure to be a talking point.

Container preparation

1 It is not often that foliage and flowers get to drink orange juice, but in this composition they do! Cut a thin slice from the top of one orange (and a sliver from the base if necessary so that the fruit will stand steady), and then use the grapefruit knife to scoop out the flesh from the centre. Insert a spray or two of pineapple mint.

Starting with the pineapple mint in this way will help you to define the height of the arrangement.

Adding colour

2 Using a downward movement, carefully pull some of the lower flowers from a stem of gladiolus and arrange it at the front of the orange. Reinforce the line of the pineapple mint with the montbretia stems, add a passion flower, and then fill in the gaps with marigolds and pineapple mint.

Repeat the whole process with the remaining oranges, and arrange them as you wish for display.

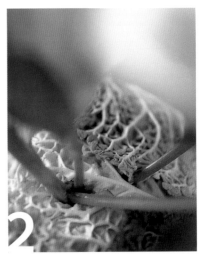

Cabbage patch

What you need...

- Kitchen knife
- Florist's scissors
- Decorative plate or dish (for display)

Plant material
- Savoy cabbage
- 2 'Star Gazer' lilies

...and some tips!

- Conditioning
The cabbage will not provide the lilies with a moisture source, so leave them in water for as long as you can before arranging them. After the event, put them in water again – it will take only moments to re-create the decoration another time.

- Show-time
If you wish to use flowers other than the 'Star Gazer' lilies, choose large, showy blooms – clusters of small flowers would look insignificant against the heavily textured cabbage.

- Seasonal variation
A red cabbage (having been stripped of any discoloured outer leaves) would make a dramatic and unusual container for pink and green hellebores, or for pink bearded iris.

Whatever your choice of dishes for an informal gathering, put cabbage on the menu in this highly unusual way.

Initial preparation

1 Cut a sliver from the base of the cabbage so that it will stand steady on the plate or dish. Cut one lily stem a short distance below the lowest flower, and strip off the lower leaves (if kept in the arrangement, these would wilt more quickly than the flowers).

This is more than ever a design that encourages freedom of expression, so there is no 'ideal' length for the displayed stems; however, remember that they will make the decoration top-heavy if left extra-long.

Flower decoration

2 Cut the discarded piece of stem to a sharp angle at one end, and use it to pierce holes in the cabbage. *Carefully push the cut lily stem into a ready-made hole – you will find that the cabbage is more receptive to the stem than you might imagine.*

Extra texture

3 Cut the lowest flowers from the second lily stem and insert these stemlets around and below the central stem. You can insert them at any angle – even sloping downwards. *If you wish, cluster together a trio of leaves and insert them behind the main stem to add textural variety.*

Checking out

What you need...

- Florist's scissors
- Round, bulbous, checked jug

Plant material
- 5 or 6 cream Brompton stocks
- Cream, pale pink, mauve and purple lisianthus (quantity required will depend on size of jug)
- 3 bright pink roses

...and some tips!

- Colour balance
Blending flowers as contrasting in colour as the cream and purple of this jug can be very difficult, but 'halfway' tones and tints such as the pinks and mauves used here will help to bridge that gap.

- Seasonal variation
In the spring you could substitute blue or white bluebells for the long-stemmed Brompton stocks, and place pale and vibrant ranunculus around them.

The blue-and-white design of a boldly chequered jug is echoed – and then diluted – by a selection of flowers that includes lisianthus in a range of four co-ordinating shades.

Hand-held

1 Cluster the stocks in one hand. Arrange the various colours of the lisianthus around the stocks, keeping these flowerheads slightly lower than the tips of the central flowers; then add the three pink roses in a cluster, with their stems shortest of all.

Composing an arrangement in the hand like this is a quick and easy way to achieve a 'free', natural look in a wide-necked container.

More of the same

2 Continue adding lisianthus around the posy in your hand. Hold the posy against the jug for check it for height, then cut the stems level.

Hold the stems gently but firmly, being sure not to crush any of the flowers as you trim the ends.

Letting go

3 Place the posy in the jug, with the roses at the front. Release the stems from your hand and allow them to settle into place.

Stand back to assess the arrangement and, if necessary, use both hands to ease the flowers very gently so that none of them is squashed or sitting at an awkward angle.

Daisy shapes

What you need...

- Florist's scissors
- Goldfish bowl (or similar)

Plant material
- Trails of hop, vine or ivy
- Approximately 12 yellow gerberas
- 1 red gerbera

...and some tips!

- **All change**
Change the water in the bowl if it becomes cloudy. Re-cutting

the stem ends of the gerberas at the same time will considerably prolong their life.

- **Seasonal variation**
In winter, try making an arrangement of yellow, silver and deep green foliage – including glossy evergreens such as laurel, bay and elaeagnus – with some lavender and cotton lavender for contrast. One or two waxy-textured flowers – such as hellebores or camellias – tucked in among the stem-holding foliage would make a very pretty finishing touch.

Long trails of hop wound inside this bowl act as natural stem-holders for the daisy-shaped gerberas; vine or ivy leaves can just as easily be used instead.

Making a base

1 If necessary, wash the foliage in warm, soapy water and then rinse it thoroughly. Cut off any thick or 'woolly' stems that would cloud the water. Wind the hop, vine or ivy stems around the inside of the bowl.

As you wind the foliage, ease out some of the largest leaves so that they are clearly visible against the glass – any squashed leaves will look ugly.

Building in height

2 Arrange short stems of the yellow gerberas around the edge of the bowl, allowing some of them to droop over its rim for a natural effect.

Build up the height of the arrangement with longer stems in the centre, to create a domed shape.

Helping hands

3 Tuck in the red gerbera among the yellow flowers. Continue building up the arrangement with yellow gerberas, placing longer stems at the centre to create the attractive domed effect.

Once you have added all the flowers, ease them gently into place and re-position any stems that have not stood firm among the foliage trails.

Greeny-pink hydrangea heads need little in the way of embellishment here, with the exception of a few greenish-yellow fennel seedheads.

All the greens

What you need...

- Florist's scissors
- Craft knife
- Round basket with water-holding inner container

Plant material
- Green-and-pink hydrangea
- Fennel seedheads

...and some tips!

- Aromatherapy
The fragrance of the fennel seedheads will enhance this composition; dill and caraway are other options. Just to touch these seedheads is to enjoy them!

- Everlasting
After use, dry the hydrangeas for long-lasting decorations: stand them in a dry container in a warm place, or stand in 5 cm (2 in) of water at room temperature and leave to dry.

- Seasonal variation
In late summer or autumn, you could achieve a similar domed effect using either mop-head chrysanthemums or dahlias, arranged with achillea.

Measuring and cutting

1 Strip away the lower leaves from the hydrangea stems (you could use these separately in another arrangement). Measure the height of the stems against the basket, and cut them at an angle. Using the craft knife, slit the ends and scrape off the woody bark. *When measuring the stems against the basket, remember that you want the flowers to form a rounded dome shape – not a flat surface.*

In-filling

2 Position the hydrangea stems in the basket so that they overlap its rim in places, and then arrange the fennel seedheads to fill in any gaps. *Check to make sure that the inner container is not visible from any viewpoint – even through the basket handles – and, if necessary, add more seedheads to conceal it.*

1

Token of love

What you need...

- Craft knife
- Florist's scissors
- Natural-coloured raffia, or ribbon

Plant material
- Asters in mixed colours
- White roses
- Pink thistle flowers
- Purple lisianthus

...and some tips!

- Water shortage
Give all the flowers a long drink of cool water and keep them in a cool place before you arrange them.

- Flower meanings
To make your posy more meaningful, you could use flowers that in Victorian times carried a particular message, as found in 'flower-language' dictionaries. Asters, for instance, meant 'a variety of emotions', while white roses said 'I am worthy of you'.

- Seasonal variation
Flowers available all year round – such as glasshouse-grown carnations and spray carnations – mixed with ferns and ivy leaves would make a very pretty posy. Deep red carnations signify true love; ferns mean sincerity; and ivy, fidelity.

A small posy of delicate pastel flowers tied to a bedpost, placed on a pillow or hung in a doorway will evoke more than a hint of Victorian romance and welcome.

Preparation

1 Strip the lower leaves from the asters and all the leaves from the rose stems, using the craft knife to remove any thorns.
Removing the leaves will give the finished posy a neat appearance.

Head height

2 Gather in one hand a cluster of pink thistle flowers (these will be the longest in the posy), and begin to add the asters. Add more and more rings of asters, the heads of each new layer slightly below those in the previous one. Make sure that the flowers are not too crowded, or crushed. You could compose the bunch in colour order – forming a ring of pink flowers, then a ring of blue, and so on – but a random approach will have greater spontaneity. It will help to 'fluff out' the flowers with your hand as you compose the bunch,and to loosen the stems slightly if your grip seems too tight. Add the purple lisianthus

at the sides of the posy, where they will define its shape, and position the white roses in a cluster at the centre front. Cut the stems of all the flowers level, then tie them neatly with a length of raffia or ribbon.
Hang the posy wherever you like: above a door it would signify a welcome to party guests; tied to a bedpost it will perhaps have a more personal significance.

Floral fruit bowl

What you need...

- Wide, deep pottery dish
- 4 or 5 water-holding flower phials (available from florists)
- Florist's scissors
- Craft knife

Plant materials
- Yellow and white roses (quantity will depend on size of dish)
- Greengages
- Lady's mantle

...and some tips!

- Improvisation
Instead of flower phials, you could use small plastic pillboxes or tiny bottles with holes pierced in the lids to insert the rose stems. Alternatively, simply give the flowers a good drink of cool water and then wrap their stems in damp tissues.

- Seasonal variation
Small green apples – arranged with orange zinnias, and clusters of rowan berries and rose hips – would make a striking winter table decoration.

Fruit and flowers are made for one another in this simple partnership of greengages and roses; they are also given a soft trim of lady's mantle.

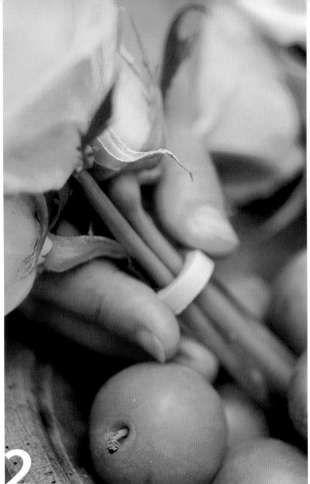

Hidden assets

1 Partially fill the flower phials with water. Cut short the rose stems, use the craft knife to strip off any thorns and push two or three stems into the hole in each phial cover.

Carefully adjust the roses, using your fingers, so that the flowerheads are at varying levels and do not crush one another.

Adding colour

2 Partially fill the dish with greengages and then press the flower phials down among the fruit, angling them this way and that.

Arrange at least one of the flower clusters so that it overlaps the rim of the dish and visually 'breaks up' its hard outer edge.

Adding substance

3 Fill up the dish with the remaining greengages so that the flower phials are completely hidden; finish off by tucking a few stems of lady's mantle in a cluster around one flower group.

The soft, blurred outline of this mass of tiny flowers will make a pleasing shape and texture contrast to the roundness of the greengages and the smooth rose petals.

Moody blues

What you need...

- Natural-coloured raffia
- Florist's scissors
- Round, wide-necked vase

Plant material
- Orange and pink antirrhinum
- Dark blue larkspur
- Purple lisianthus
- Peach and orange roses
- Blue hydrangeas

...and some tips!

- Revivalist tactics
Hydrangea flowers will benefit from the hot-water treatment. Immediately after cutting the stems, immerse the ends in boiling water for a few seconds (be sure to protect the flower-heads from steam with a cloth), and then stand them in cold water to revive.

- Seasonal variation
In the summer, you could fill the front of a design similar to this one with clematis flowers, using lupins and polygonum in mixed colours to provide height, and perennial cornflowers and pyrethrum for the 'rounds'.

A hand-tied bunch of flowers in a mix of complementary colours is blended here with rich blue hydrangea heads to flatter a wide-necked vase.

Hand-made

1 Cut a piece of raffia long enough to fit around all the flower stems in a loop, and put it aside. Arrange the antirrhinum and larkspur stems in a group in one hand, interspersing the lisianthus (with their heads positioned a little lower), and adding the roses in a ring around the bunch.

Your aim is to compose a bunch with the flowerheads becoming gradually lower towards the front – just as they might grow in a flower border.

Height check

2 When you have formed the bunch to your satisfaction – turning it around in your hand to check that the finished design will look equally good from whatever angle it is seen – take up the pre-cut length of raffia in your free hand, then loop and tie it around the flower stems. Hold the bunch up against the vase and check it for height before cutting the stems.

You will want the lowest flowers to be only slightly higher than the hydrangeas, so think about this before you cut the stems.

Final composition

3 Place the tied bunch in the vase, carefully easing out the stems with your fingers so that the flowers are free-standing. Add the hydrangeas to fill the front of the vase.

Stand back to assess the completed arrangement, making any minor positioning adjustments as necessary.

The 'Tokyo' chrysanthemum is a wonderfully showy flower, and is 'planted' here in a pot with small, contrasting-coloured blooms to create a *faux* topiary.

Flower tree

What you need...

• Flower pot and water-holding container to fit inside
• Florist's clay (available from florists), or modelling clay
• Small metal pin-holder (optional)
• Florist's scissors
• Craft knife

Plant material
• 1 lime-green 'Tokyo' chrysanthemum
• 2 or 3 stems of lime-green miniature spray chrysanthemums
• Purple lisianthus

...and some tips!

• Suitable material
When selecting flowers to display in this way, choose those with straight, sturdy stems that will best represent the 'tree-trunk' effect.

• Container-wise
Experiment with containers made of various materials to create widely differing results. Aluminium flower pots, frosted-glass pots, and others that have been painted and/or stencilled will all alter the character of the presentation.

• Seasonal variation
In the early summer, a large, ball-shaped geranium flower in red, pink, peach or white would make a delightful centrepiece surrounded by pink and white daisies or cornflowers.

A secure base

1 To secure the principal flower – the 'Tokyo' chrysanthemum – so that it has a moisture source, press a strip of florist's clay (a material that stays in position, even in water) to the underside of the pin-holder and then press this into the inner container. *Alternatively, as the chrysanthemum will last reasonably well out of water, you can simply secure the stem in a ball of modelling clay pressed into the container before filling it with water. The main stem will then not be able to take up water, but the other flowers will do so.*

Blossoming out

2 If the chrysanthemum is not fully open, ease it to a fuller shape by gently pressing the petals outwards with a thumb and forefinger. Measure the flower against the pot for height, cut the stem and 'plant' it in the pot. *Once you have cut the stem to length, use the craft knife to split it if you are going to put it in water.*

Mix and match

3 With the chrysanthemum firmly in place, surround it with short stems of spray chrysanthemums. *These lime-green sprays match the colour of the 'Tokyo' chrysanthemum perfectly, forming a visual link.*

Colour contrast

4 One by one, carefully add the purple lisianthus flowers around and between the spray chrysanthemums. *The finished decoration resembles a neatly clipped evergreen tree rising from a colourful bed of flowers.*

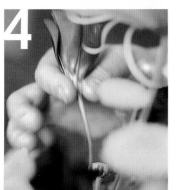

Salad days

What you need...

- Knife
- Citrus-fruit zester
- Glass plate (or similar moisture-proof holder)

Plant material
- 1 cucumber
- Sprays of rowan berries
- Red geraniums
- Trails of Russian vine
- Maidenhair fern

...and some tips!

- Vegetable craft
Experiment with cutting away the cucumber skin to make other patterns, such as hearts, diamonds, daisy-shaped flowers or any other simple shapes. A craft knife will be best suited to this task.

- Seasonal variation
Bright red poppies and sweet peas – with golden leaves such as oregano or thyme – would make a stunning presentation in the height of summer.

Chunks of cucumber have all it takes to display flowers and foliage: an interesting texture, plenty of moisture and the all-important element of surprise.

Container preparation

1 Cut off the ends of the cucumber. Cut the remainder into three unequal lengths, and then scrape the zester firmly down the length of each section to make ridges all around it.

There is no need to keep the ridges even: in fact, you may find irregular light and dark stripes on these cucumber 'vases' more attractive.

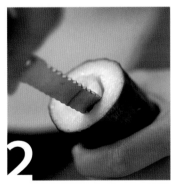

At the ready

2 Using the knife scoop a hole in the top of each cucumber section. Check, too, that the bottoms are flat and that the 'vases' will stand straight. Fill each of the 'vases' in turn with a mix-and-match selection of bright scarlet rowan berries and geranium flowers, contrasted with dainty Russian vine trails and maidenhair fern leaves. Allow some of these materials to trail over the sides of the containers, as this will make the decorations look more natural and therefore more visually appealing.

You can arrange the filled cucumber sections either in a cluster as a table-centre decoration, or individually – perhaps using one at each place setting around the table.

1

Country casual

What you need...

- Florist's scissors
- Pottery jug in a bold colour

Plant material
- Lady's mantle
- Peach, pale pink and dark pink roses
- Blue delphinium
- Mauve lisianthus
- Lime-green spray chrysanthemums
- Light-coloured and variegated pineapple mint

...and some tips!

- Extending vase life
When blending a mix of flowers that have different lasting properties – here, for instance, the roses are likely to go over most quickly – you should discard any that fade and replace them with fresh ones.

- Seasonal variation
As a springtime alternative, bring together pale pink and white daffodils, apricot tulips, blue and white lilac, grape hyacinth and variegated ivy to make a beautiful arrangement with quite a different feel.

At the height of summer, this colourful collection of country-garden flowers will bring a hint of nostalgia to any setting.

Trimming down

1 Begin by preparing all the materials, trimming the stem ends and removing any leaves low down the stems. *Trimming will only be approximate at this stage, but be careful not to cut stems too short – measure them first against the height of the jug.*

Networking

2 Arrange the lady's mantle stems from either side of the jug so that they criss-cross just below the rim and form a 'mesh' to hold other materials in place. Start to add the other flowers, beginning with the roses and spacing them evenly within the 'mesh'. *The misty effect of the tiny lady's mantle flowers will soften the outline of the finished design, and appear to tone down the stronger colours.*

Colour build-up

3 Add the remaining roses, and the delphinium and lisianthus, distributing the stronger colours evenly. Arrange stems of light-coloured and pineapple mint to trail down over the jug's rim. *The arrangement should look random and natural, as if you had gathered the flowers one by one from a garden. Trailing the pineapple mint will separate the stronger tones and 'break up' the solid colour of the jug, unifying the flowers and their container.*

Beads of colour

What you need...

- Glass container for mixing
- Bowl
- Blue food colouring
- Old spoon
- Water-retaining crystals (available from garden centres and specialist outlets)
- Glass vase
- Florist's scissors

Plant material
- Bird-of-paradise flowers (*Strelitzia*)

...and some tips!

- **Storage and re-use** *Store any unused coloured water in a lidded container. As the plant stems draw water from the gel, you can then top it up with additional coloured water in order to keep it moist and to prolong the life of the flowers.*

- **Seasonal variation** *In winter, one or two bright red poinsettias would make a striking presentation, perhaps supported by crystals tinted with green food colouring.*

Water-holding crystals are normally used in planted tubs and hanging baskets. In a glass jug, they can be coloured blue – or any other shade – to create the brightest stem-holding material you are likely to see.

Colouring crystals

1 Fill the glass container with cold water, and stir in a few drops of food colouring. Spoon some of the crystals into the bowl and then pour on some coloured water. The crystals can absorb several hundred times their own weight of water and, as they do so, will swell into soft, round beads. *Gradually stir in more water from the container until the gel is thick enough to support the flower stems. Transfer the coloured gel to the vase.*

Flower arranging

2 Cut the bird-of-paradise stems at a sharp angle and to slightly different lengths, and then arrange them in the holding material.

Cutting the stems at an angle will enable them to take up more water; arranging them at different heights will give the design a greater feeling of 'movement' and variety, and also means that the beaks of the bird-like flowers are less likely to clash.

Victorian style

What you need...

- Plain china jug
- Florist's scissors

Plant material
- Blue delphiniums
- Mauve, red and pink asters
- Pink Peruvian lilies
- Peach and red geraniums
- Orange and bronze zinnias
- Scented geranium leaves
- Sprays of viburnum foliage

...and some tips!

- Colour choices
An arrangement in an all-white or cream jug will look best if at least one flower group is pale to medium in tone; an all-dark composition in a container of this colour would look top-heavy and unbalanced.

- Seasonal variation
Gather together a medley of forsythia, ranunculus, tulips and lilac to make a scented springtime arrangement.

Blue and mauve, red and pink, peach, orange and bronze: this composition presents a medley of bright, vibrant colours in the true Victorian tradition.

Colour concentration

1 Arrange the delphinium stems in a ring around the back of the jug, where they will define the height of the arrangement. Gather a handful of mauve asters, followed by some of the pink Peruvian lilies, and add these in bunches. Continue in this way with the red and pink asters and with more lilies.

Adding the flowers in this way, colour by colour, emphasizes the gradual progress through the arrangement from the blue and purple shades on to the pinks and reds. This helps to create a natural yet ordered effect, characteristic of the Victorian approach.

Colour build-up

2 Position the geranium flowers close to the front rim of the jug, and then arrange the zinnias singly among the vibrant colours of the asters. Lastly, tuck in individual geranium leaves and sprays of viburnum.

Arranging the darker-coloured zinnias separately among clustered groups works well here (using pastel-coloured flowers in this way could have produced a 'spotted' look).

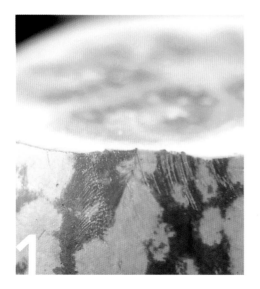

Natural beauty

What you need...

- Kitchen knife
- Florist's scissors

Plant materials
- 1 watermelon
- Magenta dahlias
- Freesias in mixed colours

...and some tips!

- Toning up
However casual a decoration, it will be more effective if one of the flower types tones with the colour of the holder – in this case, with the pinky flesh of the fruit.

- Keeping fresh
Although the flowers will have a moisture source, the watermelon will not keep fresh for many days at room temperature. Remove the flowers at night and put them in water, cover the melon with plastic wrap and put it in the refrigerator – and then re-arrange the flowers in the morning.

- Seasonal variation
A pumpkin burgeoning with bronze chrysan- themums or dahlias, cream roses and orange rowan berries could take centre stage at any autumn- harvest celebration or Thanksgiving supper.

Watermelon is not only visually attractive and highly refreshing to eat – it can also make one of the prettiest flower containers you are ever likely to use.

Standing securely

1 Using the knife, cut a thin slice from the top of the watermelon and, if necessary to make it sit securely, cut a sliver from the base as well.

If you cut a piece from the base of the melon, you will obviously need to stand it on a waterproof base in order to protect your furniture.

Changes of direction

2 Cut the dahlia stems to varying lengths and press them into the top of the melon, with the flowers facing in different directions.

As the sliced top of the watermelon is so pretty, make sure that you don't hide it beneath a mass of flowers.

Working in clusters

3 With the dahlias in position, arrange a cluster of purple freesias on one side of the melon, then add another group of freesias in mixed colours opposite and towards the back.

Concentrating the colour in one of the flower groups in this way will give even more impact to your fun and informal decoration.

Kumquats floating in a decorative glass vase act as unofficial stem-holders, and make an interesting study of colour and texture beneath the flowers.

Floating fruit

What you need...

- Florist's scissors
- Tall glass vase

Plant material
- Orange Peruvian lilies
- Sprays of hypericum berries
- Orange and bronze zinnias
- 1 yellow lily
- Kumquats

...and some tips!

- Keeping fresh
Change the vase water frequently (as soon as it starts to look cloudy): it must be kept sparkling for an arrangement like this to look effective.

- Seasonal variation
Pale green gooseberries floating in a clear glass vase, arranged with long spires of bells of Ireland, yellow antirrhinum and yellow marigolds, would make a very attractive design to celebrate the arrival of spring.

Preparation

1 Partially fill the vase with kumquats, then pour on some water. Prepare all the plant materials: strip the lower leaves from the Peruvian lilies, cut the hypericum and zinnia stems to varying lengths, and cut the yellow lily stem fairly short (this will sit at the front). *Measure the stems against the vase height before cutting; if necessary, you can then make additional adjustments as you arrange them.*

Stem formation

2 Arrange some of the Peruvian lilies from either side so that their stems cross below the level of the fruit. Arrange hypericum stems at different heights among the lilies, angling some of the stems forward to give the arrangement depth, and add more lilies as required. Arrange the zinnia stems in twos and threes throughout the group. Lastly, position the yellow lily close to the vase rim, where it will become the focal point.
Although the lily is a key feature of the composition, when you place the arrangement on a table or on a windowsill do not feel that this flower must face directly forward – it can be better to avoid the obvious.

Tea blending

What you need...

- Natural-coloured raffia
- Florist's scissors
- Plain teapot

Plant material
- Purple and mauve verbena
- Scented geranium leaves
- Peony foliage
- Pink Peruvian lilies
- 1 yellow lily
- Pink-flowering ice-plant

...and some tips!

- **Colour opposites**
In order to create the strongest colour contrasts, you can blend together any two colours that sit opposite each other on an imaginary six-section colour wheel. Mauve – a blend of primary red and blue – is opposite primary yellow, which is why the verbena posy looks so striking in this yellow teapot.

- **Seasonal variation**
In spring, the yellow teapot could blossom with yellow ranunculus and mauve and purple lilac, while an orange teapot would look at its most vibrant filled with orange-centred daffodils and narcissi, bluebells and grape hyacinth.

A posy of purple and mauve verbena is blended with pastel-coloured lilies in an arrangement that contains elements of both the traditional and the modern; a sunny yellow teapot makes the perfect container.

Exploiting colour

1 Gather the purple and mauve verbena into a posy, and back it with scented geranium leaves. Tie the stems with raffia and cut them level. Position a peony leaf at the back of the teapot – where it will frame the flower group – and add some of the (less open) Peruvian lilies, followed by the yellow lily, placing this at the front of the teapot and just above its rim. *Keeping the small verbena flowers in a cluster will concentrate the strong, vibrant colour in one area. In contrast, the sharp colour of the lemon-yellow lily almost merges with the container, and in turn gives greater prominence to the more delicately coloured lilies.*

Textural contrast

2 Arrange a cluster of fully opened Peruvian lilies at the centre of the teapot, with the ice-plant flowers around them. Insert the verbena posy at the front of the design. *The almost bead-like texture of the ice-plant heads will complement the soft outlines of the Peruvian lilies in their similar colours.*

This combination of soft fruit and summer flowers in strawberries-and-cream colours makes for a table centrepiece that is quite irresistible.

Strawberry fair

What you need...

- Glass tumbler
- Footed glass bowl
- Florist's scissors

Plant material
- Strawberries
- Cream Brompton stocks
- Cream, peach, pale pink and deep pink roses
- Cream and pink lisianthus
- Cream scabious
- Pink godetia
- Bear grasses

...and some tips!

- **Perfect balance**
Aim to keep the overall impression of the flower group light and airy, or the completed arrangement may look out of balance.

- **Seasonal variation**
When soft fruit is out of season, consider other materials: small duck's eggs and quail's eggs blended with sea holly (Eryngium) and globe thistles; coloured pebbles or shells with a group of statice, sea lavender and strawflowers; or mixed nuts polished until they shine.

Setting up

1 Carefully place the tumbler in the centre of the glass bowl, and then fill the tumbler with water.

Make sure that the tumbler is firmly balanced, and not likely to wobble.

A firm base

2 Partly fill the space between the two containers with whole strawberries.

The fruit will not only give interest and colour to the arrangement, but also helps to keep the glass tumbler steady and secure.

Clusters of colour

3 Establish the height of the flower group with three stems of cream stocks. Keeping the deep pink roses to one side, arrange groups of the remaining roses and the lisianthus colour by colour, keeping the flower-heads well below the height of the stocks. Cut the scabious so that you can arrange the flowers in a 'ribbon' through the design.

Selecting the pale-coloured stocks to be the tallest in the group will prevent the design from looking top-heavy, while the neutral tone of the scabious will separate the other pale tints and highlight each one.

Side interest

4 Carefully insert a cluster of the deep pink roses on one side of the arrangement.

These roses – which provide the strongest colour of all – will have a much greater impact when grouped together in this way.

Balancing act

5 Arrange the pink godetia – again, in a cluster – on the opposite side of the arrangement to the roses.

This second flower group – which is also strong in colour – balances the effect of the roses, with the combination providing visual weight at the base of the arrangement.

Gentle curves

6 Gather together several stems of bear grasses, measure them against the decoration and then cut them to length. Insert the stems at one side of the tumbler, adjusting their position so that they fan out prettily.

To enhance the natural shape of the bear grasses, wrap them around your hand and hold them there for a few moments to restore their curves.

1

A silver-coloured wire basket arranged with creamy-white flowers is worthy of a special family celebration such as a wedding or a baptism.

Precious metal

What you need...

- Oval wire basket with handle
- Water-holding container to fit inside basket
- Florist's scissors

Plant material
- Long ivy trails
- Variegated sage
- White scabious
- White roses
- White lisianthus
- Lady's mantle

...and some tips!

- A new look
For a completely different look, fill the space between the basket and the water-holding container with crumpled tissue paper in white or another soft shade.

- Seasonal variation
For a celebration in the spring months, you could create a similar arrangement using pale green hellebores, white tulips, daffodils and bluebells, with a base of variegated ivy.

Filling the basket

1 Wind ivy trails to fill the gap between basket and inner container, then wind more trails to fill the container and form a natural stem-holder.

Survey the basket from all angles to make sure that the container is completely hidden.

Gradual build-up

2 Tuck in short sprays of the lime-green sage among the ivy to make a lighter base, and then add short stems of scabious to form a ring that defines the outer rim of the basket. Cut the rose stems short, and add these and then the lisianthus within the existing oval outline.

Your aim here is to achieve a gradual build-up of height towards the centre of the arrangement, thus creating a shallow dome shape.

Sharp contrast

3 Fill in the design with short sprays of lady's mantle, allowing some of this to spill over the basket rim.

The misty sprays of tiny lime-green flowers will separate the white blooms, emphasizing the contrasting textures of each one.

1

utes

Flower rings

What you need...

- Round bowl or dish
- Transparent adhesive tape
- Florist's scissors
- Florist's watering can, or funnel

Plant material
- Yellow gerberas
- Blue scabious
- 1 lime-green 'Tokyo' chrysanthemum

...and some tips!

- Old-fashioned style
You could compose an arrangement to resemble a Victorian posy, by making a larger number of concentric rings of small flowers in contrasting colours.

- Seasonal variation
An arrangement on a smaller scale – consisting of pansies, buttercups and daisies in a shallow glass dish – would make a charming composition in the early spring.

For this bright concoction the container is arranged with rings of contrasting flowerheads, which are cleverly supported using a well-hidden framework of adhesive tape.

The framework

1 Working from one side of the bowl or dish towards the centre and then across to the other side, cut and stick strips of adhesive tape parallel to one another and approximately 3 cm (1¼ in) apart.

Complete the criss-cross framework by sticking more strips from side to side of the bowl or dish, at right-angles to the first set of strips.

Watering holes

2 Using a watering can with a long, narrow spout (or a funnel), partially fill the bowl or dish with water.

Pour the water carefully: if you keep the structure dry, you will be able to re-use it indefinitely.

Outer ring

3 Cut the gerbera stems so that the ends will come below the water level when you arrange the flowers. The stems shown are about 7.5 cm (3 in) long, but the appropriate length will depend on the depth of your bowl or dish. Arrange the gerberas in a ring around the bowl, pushing the stems through the holes in the 'frame'.

The flowers should overlap the container rim and just touch one another, edge to edge – any gaps would give away the secret of their clever support system!

Colour contrast

4 Cut the scabious stems to a uniform length and arrange these flowers edge to edge in a ring inside the circle of gerberas.

Once again, make sure that there are no gaps between the flower-heads as this will spoil the effect.

Flower centre

5 For the finishing touch, position the 'Tokyo' chrysanthemum at the centre of the arrangement.

If the flower is not yet fully open, gently ease out the petals with your fingers and thumbs to make it into a more rounded shape.

Hand-tied bunch

What you need...

- Craft knife
- Green twine
- Florist's scissors
- Purple or mauve tissue paper
- Clear Cellophane
- Wide purple ribbon
- Narrow mauve ribbon
- Bucket or other dry container

Plant material
- Ruby and pink roses
- Purple freesias
- Sea holly (*Eryngium*)
- Sprays of viburnum
- Hypericum berries
- Whitebeam (*Sorbus*) berries

...and some tips!

- Practice run
Composing a hand-tied bunch is easy when you know how, but you may like to practise initially with some inexpensive flowers and foliage before embarking on a special gift posy.

- Seasonal variation
A hand-tied bunch composed of a single flower type – even in a single colour – can be as good as any medley of form and texture. In the spring, tulips and parrot tulips arranged with a few of their leaves and slender bear grasses look especially pretty presented in this way.

Say it with flowers in perhaps the prettiest way of all, with a hand-tied posy that anyone would be thrilled to receive. After a little practice, you will find this very easy to make.

Conditioning

1 Prepare all the plant materials with special care (see pages 132–3), as they may be out of water for several hours. Using the craft knife, strip off all the rose thorns and pull away the lower leaves; scrape the bark from the ends of woody stems and slit them. *If any of the flowers (or foliage) start to wilt, revive them by immersing the ends in boiling water for a few seconds, then give all the materials a good long drink in cold water, in a cool place, away from strong light. Care taken at this stage will really pay dividends later.*

Starting point

2 Arrange the flower and foliage stems in groups so that you can easily pick up each one without getting them into a tangle. Have the twine ready for tying. Take two roses in one hand so that their stems cross. Give them a quarter-turn in your hand, then add two more roses, one facing to the left and the other to the right. Add more stems, beginning with the freesias. *This is the method to follow all the way through: a quarter-turn, two more stems crossing in opposite directions and another quarter-turn, followed by more stems, and so on.*

Colour variation

3 Add more stems in the same way, contrasting colours and textures all the time. Purple freesias and sea holly will, in their different ways, contrast strikingly with the velvety roses, and whitebeam and hypericum berries introduce yet more textural interest. *Arrange the flowerheads or foliage tips of each layer only slightly lower down than the previous layer: the finished bunch should be gently rounded, not rising to a high dome.*

Finishing touches

4 Tie the stems with twine, then cut the stem ends level. Place two sheets of tissue paper on your worksurface and then place the bunch diagonally across the paper, with the stem ends towards the centre. Draw up the corners and wrap the paper carefully around the bunch; then, in exactly the same way, overwrap the bunch with a sheet of Cellophane.

Using Cellophane over the paper not only creates a highly professional finish, but also adds sparkle.

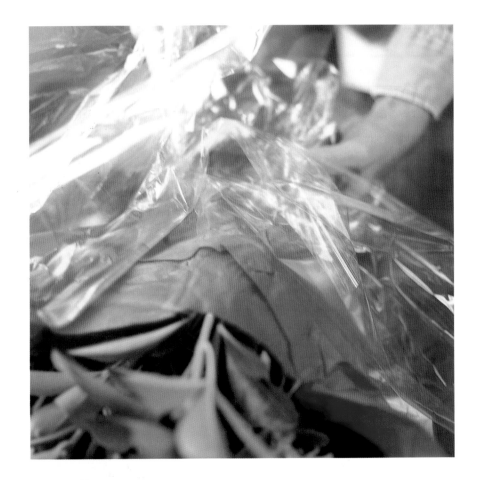

In waiting

5 Shape the wide ribbon into a four-loop bow. Hold the bow at the centre with your thumb and forefinger, and then tie around the centre with the narrow ribbon. Tie this around the bunch and trim the ends into an attractive 'V' shape.

At this stage, you will not be able to put the flowers in water – nor even spray them – as the dye in the tissue paper would run. Instead, stand the bunch in a dry container such as a bucket, and keep it in a cool, dark place until needed.

Blackberry brambles bring a little of nature indoors in this unusual decoration. Arranged around a fluted baking ring, the brambles make a compact network that holds all the other plant stems very securely.

The wild look

What you need...

- Baking ring (gugelhof pan)
- Florist's scissors
- Craft knife

Plant material
- Fruiting blackberry stems
- Purple sage
- Sweet marjoram flowers
- Mauve scabious
- Blue lisianthus
- Lime-green 'Tokyo' chrysanthemums
- Light pink and dark pink everlasting pea
- Lime-green miniature spray chrysanthemums

...and some tips!

- Container option
If you do not have a baking ring, use an ordinary round metal cake tin with a water-holding inner liner.

- Seasonal variation
You could combine yellow-berried holly stems with variegated sage and bay leaves, decorating them with sea holly (Eryngium) and yellow and mauve dahlias, for an attractive late-autumn decoration.

1

Forming a network

1 Arrange the blackberry stems around the baking ring so that the tips overlap the inner and outer rims at intervals, then cut off some of the leaves and re-arrange these among the stems.

Make sure that the blackberry stems criss-cross each other all the way around the ring to form a complex network, as this will make your task much easier as you add all the other plant material.

Complementary colour

2 Tuck sprays of purple sage among the blackberries so that some also overlap the outer edge of the ring. Arrange the marjoram flowers, scabious and lisianthus around the ring, distributing the textures, shapes and colours to best advantage.

Avoid putting many strong-coloured flowers together: a concentration of the deep blue lisianthus, for example, might resemble a dark hole in the arrangement.

Cluster of interest

3 Use the craft knife to split the 'Tokyo' chrysanthemum stems so that they can take up water, then arrange them in a cluster, where their sharp green colour will become the focal point. Position short sprays of the miniature chrysanthemums opposite and around these chrysanthemums. *The miniature chrysanthemums will help to provide colour balance and create a unified appearance.*

Finishing touches

4 Finally, use sprays of light and dark pink everlasting pea to fill in any gaps. *The untidy growth of this wild-looking flower is well suited to informal arrangements – in this case, to one that begins with brambles!*

Rich harvest

What you need...

- Wooden basket
- 2 white candles of different heights
- Florist's clay
- Plastic prongs
- Florist's scissors
- Water-holding phials (optional)

Plant material
- Selection of vegetables such as butternut squash, aubergines, peppers, courgettes, chilli peppers and small pattypan squash
- Sunflowers
- Trails of hops
- Clematis stems with flowers and seedheads
- Passion flowers

...and some tips!

- In hot water *Sunflowers especially will benefit from proper conditioning before you start to arrange them (see pages 132–3).*

- Seasonal variation *Orchard fruits – rosy apples and pears – would make an attractive harvest-time group. Passion fruit and lychees would also look eye-catching if combined with roses and some trailing ivy.*

A wooden basket loaded with richly coloured and textured vegetables, bright sunflowers and trailing hops is transformed into an eye-catching harvest-time candleholder.

Candle power

1 Fix the candles securely to the wooden basket, with space between them, by pressing a strip of florist's clay on to two plastic prongs and fitting these into the bases of the candles. Arrange the vegetables all around the candles.

Make sure that both the basket and candles are completely dry before using the clay, or it will not adhere.

Water source

2 Condition the sunflowers if necessary (see opposite). Cut the stems to varying lengths – some so short that they will rest on top of the vegetables, and at least one much longer so that it will appear to grow out of them. Push the stems into water-holding phials.

For a short-term decoration you can arrange the sunflowers just as they are, but using the phials will prolong the life of the composition.

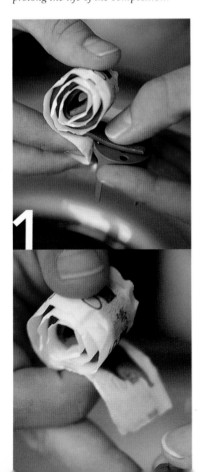

Concealment

3 Press the sunflower stems (in the water-holding phials) among the vegetables, and re-arrange the squash, peppers and so on as necessary to conceal the water holders.

You can angle the phials in any direction – even horizontally – as the hole in the cap closes tightly around each stem and will prevent seepage.

Natural curves

4 Add trails of hops and clematis stems to ramble over the vegetables, around the base of the candles and across the rim of the wooden basket. You can also fit these stems into water phials but, if you are not using these, the stems will simply dry out naturally and still look attractive.

As you add these elements to the decoration you will see that gradually the vegetables play a less important part, and eventually just form a colourful background for the flowers, hops, foliage and seedheads.

Finishing touches

5 Lastly, add the passion flowers. These will benefit from a moisture source so, if you don't have phials, fill small plastic pillboxes or tiny bottles with water and pierce a hole in each lid to hold the stems.

Notice how the intricate colouring of the passion flowers links all the different hues of the vegetables, from the reddish-purple of the aubergines right through to the creamy-yellow of the butternut squash.

Berry bright

What you need...

- Block of florist's foam (to fit inside the basket)
- Bowl
- Rectangular basket with moisture-proof inner container
- Florist's scissors
- Kitchen knife

Plant material
- Peony leaves (or similar large foliage)
- Sprays of rowan berries
- 1 globe artichoke
- Pink and orange Peruvian lilies
- Hypericum berries
- Orange and bronze zinnias

...and some tips!

- Preparing stems
You will need to condition the woody rowan stems before you arrange them (see pages 132–3).

- Maintenance
Remember to keep the florist's foam permanently moist by topping it up with fresh water each day: there are a lot of thirsty stems in this arrangement!

In a porch, on the floor, in the corner of a room or in an alcove: wherever you decide to put this bright decoration, it will help to herald the arrival of winter.

1

Preparation

1 Soak the florist's foam in a bowl of water for about 20 minutes (or until it sinks), and then place it in the moisture-proof container in the basket. Begin the arrangement by positioning the peony leaves (or similar foliage) to make a fan shape across one end of the basket. *While the florist's foam is soaking, condition the woody rowan stems (see pages 132–3).*

Vegetable 'flower'

2 Cut the stem of the globe artichoke at a very sharp angle, so that you can easily press it into the foam without breaking it up. *As you are using the artichoke in place of a large, focal-point flower, show it to advantage by gently opening it up with your fingers to reveal its more colourful inner leaves.*

A straight diagonal

3 Position long sprays of rowan berries diagonally across the basket. *Adding the sprays of shiny berries in this way helps to create extra textural and directional interest.*

Working in clusters

4 Arrange clusters of Peruvian lilies within the outline created earlier with the peony leaves, and fill in any gaps with sprays of hypericum berries. *As you insert the lilies you will appreciate the contribution of the berries – their colour picks up the dark flashes in the lily petals, while their texture contrasts well with the softness of the flowers.*

Closing the gaps

5 Finish off the arrangement by positioning the bright zinnias in a ring around the artichoke head. *Turn the basket around and check that the florist's foam is completely hidden from every aspect. Although the foam does serve an invaluable purpose in an arrangement of this type, it is very ugly to look at!*

Gift posies

What you need...

- Shallow bowl
- Colourless Cellophane, cut into 20-cm (8-in) squares
- Transparent adhesive tape
- Scissors
- Glass vase
- Wineglasses (optional)

Plant material
- Selection of flowers and foliage such as delphiniums, Brompton stocks, roses, lisianthus, ice-plant, green (unripe) poppy seed-heads, variegated sage, carrot leaves or fern fronds and variegated ivy

...and some tips!

- Colour change
Have fun with colour: wrapping posies in coloured Cellophane (for instance, yellow flowers and foliage in red cellophane) will create an intriguing illusion of floral colours that do not exist in nature.

- Seasonal variation
This is an idea for all seasons, and you can use it with numerous combinations of flowers and foliage – the only restrictions being what you can find and what works well.

Tiny posies of romantically pretty flowers and pale pastel foliage are beautifully wrapped, and would make charming gifts – perhaps as mementoes of a family celebration.

1

Colour balance

1 Make your selection of flowers and foliage to compose the first posy, gathering the materials up in your hand so that you can assess the effect of the varying colours and textures. For a vibrant posy full of interest, you will want to contrast flowers borne on short spires with fully rounded ones, and solid colours with variegated ones. Place all the ingredients for the posy crosswise in the centre of a Cellophane square. Re-adjust the stems so that none of the flowers will be obscured, and then carefully wrap the Cellophane to form a loose cone around them.

Secure the overlap of Cellophane with a strip of adhesive tape, keeping this as unobtrusive as possible.

Water course

2 Cut off the end of the Cellophane cone and then place the posy in the bowl of water in a cool, dark place. *The posy will spend the rest of its life out of water, so it is important to keep it fresh for as long as you can.*

Looking cool

3 Make up as many more posies as required, each time putting them into water to keep fresh.

To compose an all-green posy that contrasts with the more colourful ones, select materials with striking texture and shape contrasts. Here, green poppy seedheads, lady's mantle flowers and umbrella-shaped heads of ice-plant are blended with carrot leaves and variegated herbs, making a posy to prove that colour does not always rule – although care in selecting the plant materials is essential.

Underwater

4 Press one of the posies below the water level in the display vase and see how it shimmers! Arrange more posies in the vase, facing this way and that, and check that all the flower and foliage stems reach into the water. *Another idea – in addition to the vase – is to flatter each guest around a party table by placing a single posy in a wineglass beside each setting. Choose a combination of plant materials to match or tone with the table setting or as a reflection of a larger centrepiece, or use flowers that are specially meaningful to you.*

The full circle

What you need...

- 20-cm (8-in) florist's-foam ring
- Sharp knife
- Shallow bowl
- Florist's scissors
- Skewer
- Plate or dish (for display; optional)

Plant material
- Small-leaved ivy
- Orange marigolds
- Orange, bright pink and yellow roses
- Variegated pineapple mint
- Green poppy seedheads
- Ice-plant
- Delphinium buds
- Chives
- Lady's mantle

...and some tips!

- Aftercare
On completion, mist the flowers with cool water. Remove the wreath to a water-resistant surface and spray it at least once a day, or twice in hot weather. Keeping the foam ring moist will also prolong the life of the arrangement.

- Seasonal variation
For a Christmas or Thanksgiving wreath, cover the foam ring with mixed ever-greens such as juniper, ivy and bay, and decorate it with small red and bronze spray chrysanthe-mums and rose hips.

A floral wreath – traditionally a symbol of hospitality and welcome, but often confined to Christmas – is used here to make a long-lasting table decoration; it could also be hung on a wall or a door.

Sizing down

1 Some pre-formed foam rings have unnecessarily thick bases. If you wish to cut down your ring to a more manageable size, use the sharp knife to slice through the base. There is also a practical reason for this, as it will take considerably less foliage and flowers to conceal the foam structure. Soak the ring in cold water for 20 minutes. Meanwhile, prepare all your flower materials by cutting the stems short – to approximately 6 cm (2½ in) – and putting them in a shallow bowl of water.

At this stage you may find it helpful to arrange the flowers in colour groups, as you will be using them.

Foliage first

2 Arrange curving trails of ivy over and around the sides of the foam ring until you have almost covered it. *The leaves not only provide a natural framework against which the flowers will be viewed, but also go a long way towards concealing the foam.*

Block of colour

3 Use the skewer to make holes in the foam, then insert marigold stems so that the flowers create a patch of vibrant colour on the ring.

Positioning some short marigold stems horizontally – with the flowers nestling closely against the inner and outer rims of the ring – will do a good cover-up job.

Rose bed

4 Create neighbouring patches of roses in contrasting colours (you will not need a skewer to make way for these much tougher stems).

As you work around the ring, insert stems at varying angles so that the flowers face in different directions, just as they would grow naturally.

Cool interlude

5 Create a 'cool' area of pineapple mint, poppy seedheads, ice-plant and delphinium buds to contrast strikingly with the vivid fiesta colours of the flowers; clusters of chives tied in knots and inserted among the herbs and seedheads will add height and visual interest. Add short sprays of lady's mantle to fill in any gaps through which the foam ring is visible, turning the arrangement around to check it from every viewpoint.

If you intend to use the wreath as a table decoration, place it on a plate or dish to prevent the damp foam from marking your furniture.

In the style of an Old Master painting, this composition brings together flowers in a wide range of tints and shades spanning more than a single season.

Dutch influence

What you need...

- Bowl
- Deep, round bowl-shaped container
- Block of florist's foam
- Sharp knife
- Florist's scissors
- Craft knife

Plant material
- Sprays of foliage
- Blue delphiniums
- Apricot roses
- Magenta dahlias
- Pink and orange Peruvian lilies

...and some tips!

- Maintenance
Remember to keep the florist's foam moist by topping it up daily with water. With such a large number of stems drawing on the moisture, the foam would otherwise quickly dry out.

- Seasonal variation
In early spring, it would be lovely to combine evergreen foliage and the bright berries from the end of the winter with tulips, daffodils, hyacinth and year-round (glasshouse) carnations and spray chrysanthemums.

Preparation

1 Soak the florist's foam in a bowl of cold water for about 20 minutes (or until it sinks). Using the sharp knife, cut a slice from one end, then stand the main block on end in the bowl and wedge it in place with the offcut. Arrange foliage stems all around the foam block, creating a narrow fan shape to define the eventual height and width. Cut some stems short and angle them forwards and backwards, at the front and back of the foam, to give depth to the arrangement. Arrange the delphinium stems among the foliage, keeping within the height and width boundaries already set.
The framework of pale green foliage and soft blue flowers makes a natural background, against which the rounded flowerheads will be viewed.

Colour distribution

2 Strip all the lower leaves from the roses and use the craft knife to remove any thorns, then position the stems within the arrangement.
In a massed display like this one, it is most effective to position some of the principal flowers facing out to the sides so that they are seen in profile.

In-filling

3 Fill in the gaps with the dahlias and Peruvian lilies. Cut some lily flowers from the main stem and recess them, on the stemlets, close against the foam, where they will help to cover it up. Turn the bowl around to check that the florist's foam is concealed from every viewpoint, and fill in any gaps if necessary.
Recessing the lily flowers in this way, so that they will be seen in shadow, gives perspective to the arrangement; the viewer is also aware of hidden depths, giving greater interest.

A shallow bowl filled with a dome of golden-yellow dahlias and roses could be the centre of attraction at any family gathering, from a golden-wedding celebration to a Thanksgiving party.

Golden bowl

What you need...

- Block of florist's foam
- Wide, shallow bowl
- Florist's clay
- Kitchen knife
- 2 plastic florist's spikes ('frogs')
- Florist's scissors
- Craft knife

Plant material
- Smoke-bush foliage (or greeny-yellow or lime-green foliage – not plain dark green leaves)
- Golden dahlias
- Rudbeckia seedheads (or teasels or yellow thistles)
- Yellow roses
- Orange Peruvian lilies

...and some tips!

- Waste not...
Do not be afraid to cut the smoke-bush stems short. You need not waste the lower leaves – put them at the back of the foam, angled backwards. They will give depth here, and no-one will see their lack of leafy tips.

- Seasonal variation
An all-green-and-white arrangement would be dramatic in a green bowl: try combining sprays of rosemary and white-flowering jasmine with white camellias and green hellebores.

Preparation

1 Soak the florist's foam in cold water for about 20 minutes (or until it sinks). Cut strips of florist's clay and stick them to the undersides of the two spikes, or 'frogs'; make sure that the bowl is thoroughly dry, then press the spikes into place. Cut the foam to fit, then press it on to the prongs. Cut smoke-bush stems to varying lengths and arrange them to make a fan shape around the foam.

The tallest stem at the centre will define the eventual height of the arrangement, and the shortest ones at the sides will determine the width.

Keeping within bounds

2 With the foliage in place, all that you have to do now is to follow the outline you have set. Position the tallest dahlia in the centre, close to the tallest foliage stem, then continue arranging the golden flowers around the bowl.

Stand away from the arrangement as it takes shape, and check that you are keeping to the rounded dome shape. This is not a decoration that will tolerate any wayward stems!

Light touch

3 Arrange groups of the spiky orange rudbeckia seedheads amongst the dahlias, with some stems angled forward to create width and perspective. *Notice how these beautiful orange flower centres (which remain on the stem once the petals have fallen) catch the light in myriad ways – they are a real bonus in this arrangement.*

Roses all the way

4 It is now time to arrange the roses. Strip off all the lower leaves and use the craft knife to remove any thorns, then position the roses between the dahlias, still working within the overall outline. Cut the Peruvian lily flowers from the main stems and position them among the principal flowers, close against the florist's foam, where they will conceal it very effectively.

Even the most beautiful blooms sometimes have discoloured petals, but don't let any blemishes spoil your arrangement – gently pull off any damaged outer petals and the flowers will be perfect again.

Finishing touch

5 Turn the bowl around slowly so that you can assess it from every aspect. *If you spot any unsightly gaps, fill them in with short sprays of smoke-bush leaves or any left-over lilies.*

Techniques

Flower holders

Try to think laterally as you choose the containers that will do most to flatter your choice of flowers and foliage, as you are likely to find 'just the thing' in the least expected places. Jugs and baskets, baking pans and casseroles, glass tanks and drinking glasses, teapots and flower pots, fruit and even vegetables – all can play a role in creating the perfect partnership between container and plant materials.

When choosing a suitable container for a flower display, you do not necessarily have to be restricted by practical considerations. A container need not even be moisture-proof to display fresh flowers efficiently – in this case, you will simply have to fit it with a water-holding inner liner.

Plastic margarine tubs and yoghurt pots are ideal for this purpose, but they are unsightly. Whenever a liner of this kind would show through the container – in an open-weave basket, for example – you can fill the gap between the two with a natural material such as moss or ivy leaves, or with a colour-co-ordinated material such as crumpled tissue paper or even a piece of silk.

Secret ingredient *(right)*
This closely woven wicker basket becomes a practical fresh-flower container, having been fitted with a water-retaining holder. Check that a liner like this one is not visible from any angle and, if necessary, tuck a few extra leaves or seedhead stems around the rim of the outer container.

Practical consideration *(above)*

A baking pan with a hole in the middle has two practical advantages in flower-arranging terms: the central funnel limits the area to be filled with stems, and also makes it easier to place the first stems so that they form a supportive 'mesh'. A short tumbler or beaker placed in the centre of an ordinary dish would fulfil the same functions.

Pre-arranged *(below)*

You can arrange flowers in a wide-necked container such as this kitchen jug in two ways. Either position the stems around the outside of the container first, crossing them over to form a network to support the central stems; or, as here, arrange the flowers in your hand before lowering them into the container.

High profile

Any vase with a narrow neck – such as the classic urn shape – is a real time-saver in flower arranging. You will find it quick and easy to position a few stems with confidence in a container of this kind, knowing that they have no room to move!

Complementary containers
(opposite page, top left)

Always think about the suitability of a container for the flowers you plan to put in it. For instance, the depth of pattern on this Greek-style urn would be distracting in juxtaposition to small, delicate blooms. Big, bold sunflowers, whose centres are a match for any deeply etched and sand-brushed swirls, make a much better choice.

Dual purpose *(above)*

Aluminium flower buckets, which are sufficiently deep to give flowers and foliage the long, cool drink that they need initially, also make the grade as containers at the display stage. Their clean lines and grainy texture will complement mixed-flower groups or all-of-a-kind displays, from the palest peonies to the darkest dahlias.

One for the pot
(opposite page, top right)

New teapots in clear, bright colours, or patterned ones with the romance of age (often to be found as boot-sale bargains), make interesting containers. Here, the bright yellow of the teapot is echoed in the colour of the lily, then contrasted with the mauve shades of the verbena posy.

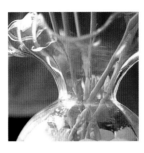

Below the water line *(above)*

Add a handful of kumquats to a glass container before arranging your chosen flower stems, and you will create a new visual dimension as well as an element to steady the stems. You could make use of this idea but vary the effect by substituting summer-green peapods or small okra, or autumn-brown walnuts or chestnuts, for the kumquats.

Sharp choice *(below)*

Orange shells make delightful holders for small nosegays of flowers, and you can ring the colour and aroma changes by using grapefruit, lime and lemon shells. Either scoop out a little of the flesh and press your chosen flower stems into what remains, or hollow the shells completely; in the latter case, you could then fit larger fruit shells with small blocks of pre-soaked florist's foam.

Clear option

The irregularly striped skin of a watermelon, in contrasting tones of green, is a perfect foil for both bright and pastel-coloured plant materials. At times and in places where watermelons are plentiful and inexpensive, you might like to press flower stems directly into this sunset-coloured fruit; a more economical option is to scoop out the flesh and to fill the shell with an inner container or with a chunk of pre-soaked florist's foam.

Salad days *(above)*

Chunks of fresh cucumber make surprisingly attractive and versatile flower-holders: the two ends provide gradually tapered 'vases', while the sections cut from the centre are straight and sturdy. Experiment with different ways of displaying these adaptable holders. One nice idea is to stand each one on a stout glass or china candlestick – or on a wooden candlestick, provided that you protect the surface beneath from moisture.

Stem treatments

Plant materials need care to accustom them to vase life. The way you harvest the materials – and even the temperature and time of day at which you do so – will affect their longevity.

If possible, gather flowers and foliage either early in the morning or in the evening – not in the middle of the day. Never snap off stems as this could damage the severed stem and the plant, but cut stems with a sharp blade or with florist's scissors. Cut at an angle to expose the largest area of plant tissue to the new moisture source (the water or soaked florist's foam in your arrangement). Make sure that all cutting, splitting and scraping tools are clean and sharp.

To condition most thin-stemmed flowers – such as snapdragons – strip off the lower leaves and place the stems in cool water. Thick stems – such as dahlias and sunflowers – need splitting at the ends so that they can absorb water; woody stems must be scraped at the ends to remove the outer tissue. Stems such as poppy and spurge, which 'bleed' readily, need a further process: hold the ends over a flame until blackened, repeating this if you need to re-cut the stems.

Thirsty work (*right*)

As soon as possible after cutting the stems of flowers, foliage, bracts and berries, place them in a deep container of cool water (ideally, take a bucket with you as you gather plant materials in the garden). Then treat all the stems in the appropriate ways and put them in water again, in a cool place and away from strong light.

Stripping leaves
(opposite page, top left)

Strip all the lower leaves from flower stems before splitting the stem ends and standing them in water for several hours. Hold each stem – this one is a lily – firmly in one hand and run your other hand down the stem, stripping off all the leaves in a single movement.

One at a time
(opposite page, top right)

Removing large leaves from a stem such as hydrangea is quite simple. Hold the stem with the flowerhead facing you and, with your thumb against the stem, push each leaf sharply downwards to snap it off.

Alternative choice *(above)*

Do not discard the hydrangea leaves that you have stripped away from the main stems, as these can come in very useful for other purposes. To keep them fresh, cut off the nodules at the end of the stemlets and put them straight into cool water. These large, pointed-oval leaves, with their prominently marked vein structure, are useful for providing visual weight when positioned close to the rim of a container or, alternatively, for adding extra depth and perspective at the back of an arrangement.

Tender care

Tender stems with supple leaves need handling with special care. Pick off leaves of this kind one by one, being extremely careful not to snap off the flowers, as you do so, which can easily happen. For a small composition, separate the flowers from the main stem and arrange each individually.

Paring woody stems *(above)*

Scraping the woody tissue from stems cut from shrubs and other woody plants is vital to prolong vase life: hold a craft knife parallel to the stem, then scrape off the outer tissue all around the stem for about 5 cm (2 in).

Splitting thick stems *(above)*

After scraping the outer tissue from woody stems, and always before arranging thick-stemmed flowers such as dahlias, sunflowers and chrysanthemums, use a sharp craft knife to split the stem for about 5 cm (2 in). This is a further way of ensuring that the stems will be able to take up water readily and so will survive for as long as possible once in a vase.

Boiling-water treatment *(above)*

Immersing stem ends in boiling water prolongs life by removing air bubbles and killing bacteria; protect flower-heads from the steam with a cloth.

A prickly operation *(below)*

Stripping thorns from rose stems is an 'optional extra' to make them more comfortable to handle, and will be essential if you plan to compose a hand-tied bunch, posy or bouquet.

More to the point

You must condition woody stems just as carefully as other stems. Cutting the ends at a sharp angle is best when you are using florist's foam, as the pointed stems will pierce the holding material more readily and so are less likely to break it up.

Winter berries

Bright clusters of berries – such as rowan and hawthorn – add an interesting textural contrast to flowers and foliage of all kinds. To prepare the berries, pare and split the stem ends, dip them in boiling water and then leave them in cool water; they should then stay fresh for several days.

On the slant *(below)*

To make sure that a free-standing bunch will be secure without support, you will need to cut the stems level but not straight across. Cut each one separately, at an angle, so that they will readily take up water when you eventually place the bunch in water.

Revival tactics

Foliage and flowers that have wilted in the sun, or have been out of water for a long time, can be revived by re-cutting the stem ends under water. Partly fill a bowl with water and, using florist's scissors, cut the stems just below the surface. As always, make each cut at a sharp angle.

Total immersion *(above)*

Another revival technique, which you can use for robust and compact flowers such as roses, carnations and ice-plant, is to plunge the flowerheads upside-down in a container of cool water for a minute or so. Shake the flowers gently to dry them off, and then stand the stems in cool water before arranging them.

Stem supports

As many of the designs in the book show, you do not need to use any holding material to create a variety of natural-looking floral decorations. However, there are times when some kind of stem-holding device will give you even greater freedom to compose arrangements that are structured yet informal.

In some designs, it is possible to arrange the stems of the flowers and foliage that form part of the design crosswise, to act as a support system for other, perhaps heavier stems at the centre. In other cases, trails of evergreen foliage such as ivy, or translucent leaves like hop or vine, are wound around the inside of a container to form a network to hold the arranged stems (this is very pretty in glass containers).

Other supports range from a simple framework of adhesive tape or a tied triangle of cinnamon sticks to ready-made stem-holders such as florist's foam; metal pin-holders will also steady the heaviest stems.

Lattice-work *(right)*

You can fit any bowl or dish – however deep or shallow – with a criss-crossing mesh of adhesive tape that will hold long stems upright or, if you cut the stems short, will support a patchwork of flowerheads. Measure and cut the strips of adhesive tape to reach from side to side of the bowl or dish. Starting at one edge, pull each strip taut, take the ends over the rim and stick them firmly in place. Continue sticking parallel strips across the bowl to the other side, then complete the mesh by sticking parallel lines of tape at right-angles to the first. The smaller the gap between the strips, the longer the stems they will support.

Edge to edge

With the lattice-work of adhesive tape in place (see page 134), you can create a variety of effects with short-stemmed flowers. Position them edge to edge to conceal the holding structure, in concentric rings or stripes of large or small flowerheads, and in toning or contrasting colours. If you pour water carefully between the holes of the mesh and do not allow the tape to get wet, you will be able to re-use the structure again and again.

Heavy metal (above)

Pin-holders are extremely useful devices: they are available from florists in a good range of shapes and sizes, and will take a firm grip on woody stems or on top-heavy plant materials. Made with thick, heavy metal bases and with sharp, closely spaced pins, holders such as the one shown here should last a lifetime.

A firm grip

Unless a pin-holder fits tightly into the base of the container that you intend to use for an arrangement, you will need to fix it in place with a strip of florist's clay pressed on to the underside (another option is to use modelling clay, although this is not waterproof and so will often be unsuitable). Secured in this way, a narrow pin-holder such as the one shown above will provide very firm support.

A perfect triangle (page 135)

Three cinnamon sticks will contribute both stem guidance and aroma when you are arranging individual stems or flower clusters in containers such as drinking glasses or beakers. To make these unconventional holders, bind three equal lengths of cinnamon quill, bamboo or twig to make a triangle. Natural-coloured raffia, coarse string or fine cord all make suitable ties.

Geometric pressure

You will be able to adjust the size of the aperture – and therefore the effectiveness of the triangular stem-holder – by sliding the ties along the sticks to narrow or widen the gap as required. Flowers in strong, bright colours look especially good with these woody holders.

Using a foam wreath (above)

With a pre-formed foam wreath base you can compose floral rings with all the charm of traditional welcome wreaths, and with the advantage of a built-in moisture source. In this way, fresh flowers arranged as table or wall wreaths will last as long as they would do in any other floral design. Most rings are made of two types of synthetic foam bonded together: a top, absorbent layer that holds the stems and a lower, non-absorbent base. If you want to make the ring narrower and less clumsy, use a sharp knife to cut away a slice from the base.

A good fit (above)

When using some containers – such as square or rectangular ones – it may be possible to wedge a block of florist's foam into them perfectly, with no need for anchoring. In a container such as this round bowl, however, the foam may need to be held steady with strips of florist's clay. The clay – which is extra-tacky – can be pressed on to the base of a purpose-made foam holder; this type of plastic prong is also known as a 'frog'.

Secure hold

With the florist's clay in place, the plastic prong is pressed on to the base of the container, and then a cylinder or block of florist's foam can be pressed down on to it. When using florist's clay, you must ensure that both surfaces – the plastic prong and the container – are thoroughly dry, or the clay will not stick (subsequent moisture will not dislodge it).

Effective cover-up

All types of florist's foam are practical but unsightly, and floral rings are no exception. Cutting a slice from the base of the ring (see above left) will help, by giving you a smaller area of foam to conceal. When you begin your arrangement, start by covering all surfaces of the ring with short sprays of foliage; these will not only act as a covering material, but will form a natural background for the flowers.

The right extension

Cutting the block of florist's foam so that it extends above the top of the container will allow you to angle some of the stems horizontally in line with the rim, and to slope others downwards. Once the arrangement is finished, you will need to check it from every viewpoint to be sure that the foam is not visible.

Vertical precision (below)

Using florist's foam will give you the freedom to arrange a restricted number of stems even in a wide-necked container. With the sides of the foam block camouflaged by flowers and foliage, the design will also need some short-stemmed materials positioned so that they obscure its upper surface.

Shaping up

Hand-tied bunches, posies, nosegays – call them what you will, they have a charm that has been popular for many years. In Victorian times posies were exchanged as expressions of love, and today hand-tied bunches – with their criss-crossing stems – are favourites with amateur flower arrangers and florists alike.

Whatever style of posy you choose to make, it is more than ever important to give the flowers a good drink of water and to condition the stems (see pages 132–3), as they are likely to be out of water for some time.

Victorian posies were surrounded by a ring of leaves, to protect and frame the flowers. Ivy, lady's mantle, scented geranium and violet are among the many leaves that will make a pretty final touch for a nosegay.

Most posies and hand-tied bunches are composed to form a gently rounded dome shape. To achieve this gentle slope from the centre to the sides, each successive layer or ring of flowerheads is placed just below the previous one, which avoids any risk of overcrowding or crushing the flowers.

Opening out *(right)*

The focal point of a flower arrangement, or the central flower around which you arrange a formal posy, should be perfect. If your chosen bloom – such as this lime-green 'Tokyo' chrysanthemum – is not yet fully developed, give nature a helping hand by gently easing out the petals all around the flower to create a more rounded shape.

Practical and pretty (above)

Here, a tiny posy has been composed for display together with larger flowers in a teapot. The posy is tied with natural-coloured raffia to hold the stems in position, before it is added to the arrangement. Raffia is a very useful material for flower arranging: it is pleasing to the eye, and so can be left visible if required; it is also practical, because it has a soft and pliable texture that will not easily cut through flower stems, even if it is tied fairly tightly.

Showing off

(opposite page, top left)

You can display this kind of posy, which has the charm and grace of a childhood composition, in many ways. For example, you could arrange several posies of similar or varying colours in a basket with a water-holding container fitted inside, or display them in a group, placing each posy in its own wineglass.

Natural ties

(opposite page, top right)

Nasturtium stems are among the most supple – and vulnerable – of all plant materials, and would almost certainly be cut through by a tie made of string or cord. Here the stems are bound with vine tendrils, which hold them gently and seem to be at one with the flowers.

Dye-casting

To some flower arrangers, the burnt-umber-coloured stamens of the lily are a strikingly attractive feature; to others they are a nuisance factor. If you wish to avoid the chance of colouring the petals, your clothes or furnishings with their almost immovable yellow dye, hold the flowers upside-down and snip off the stamens with scissors.

A flat-backed posy (above)

Before putting together a flat-backed posy that will be displayed without a moisture source – hanging on a wall or a bedpost, perhaps – you must take special care to condition the flowers properly. Having done this, arrange the flowers in your hand, using the longest stem in the centre and making each successive layer slightly shorter.

At cross purposes (above)

A modern hand-tied bunch is composed of a multitude of stems arranged to cross about halfway along their length. Begin with two stems crossing over each other to make an 'X' shape. Give them a quarter-turn

in your hand, add two more crossing stems and continue in this manner until you have incorporated all the plant material.

Full circle (below)

When you wish to grace an arrangement with gently curving hop stems, or other stems with a similarly wayward habit, exaggerate the natural curves by twisting the stems into a wide circle. Leave them for a few seconds before unwinding them and they should spring into pleasing arcs.

Gentle curves (below)

The long, slender leaves of bear grass or pampas grass, both of which are long-lasting in water, make an effective contrast of form and shape in arrangements of all kinds. To increase their natural curves, wind the leaves around your hand (or around a household item such as a preserve jar or tumbler), and wait for a few seconds before releasing them. Always handle these leaves carefully, or wear gloves – they have very sharp edges.

Modern interpretation (below)

A posy may consist of a single flower type, or of plant materials with widely differing forms, colours and characteristics. A wrapping of Cellophane (with or without tissue paper beneath) will help to protect the flowers and to draw attention to their vibrant colours.

A clear message

You must keep the water that is needed to nourish cut stems clean, clear and cool. Murky water, which contains bacteria, will not only shorten the vase life of plant materials but, in a glass container, will detract from the appearance of the arrangement.

Nourishment

The vase life of cut stems will be determined by their conditioning and by their aftercare once arranged. Moisture is the principal requirement, with flower food – designed to replace the plants' own nutrients – an optional extra.

Make sure that cut stems in any arrangement have an on-going water supply. Top up the water level, and make sure that it is always clean. If it looks cloudy or has an unpleasant smell, it needs changing completely.

Pre-soak florist's foam in water for about 20 minutes (or until it sinks); a brick-sized block will absorb about 1.7 litres (3 pints) of water in that time. Even this will not be enough to support a multitude of flower and foliage stems over several days, so you must keep the foam permanently moist.

Check that all containers and any other decorative elements that come into contact with cut stems are scrupulously clean and cannot contaminate the water.

Spray your arrangements with a fine mist of cool water from a plant sprayer once a day; you will need to do this twice or even more frequently in particularly hot and humid conditions.

The finishing touch (right)

Wrapping a posy or hand-tied bunch in Cellophane not only protects the flowers and foliage, but also adds a glamorous sheen to the composition. If you intend to display the flowers in their wrapping, carefully cut away the Cellophane at the base of the posy so that the stems will be readily able take up water.

Stage management

(page 140, top left)

Keep your flowers in water at every stage: as soon as you have cut the stems, after you have conditioned them (see pages 132–3) and while you are creating the arrangement. Here, nasturtium flowers have been left in a container of cool water before being used to make posies.

Individual needs

(page 140, top right)

Use water-holding phials like this one when you wish to arrange individual flowers or small clusters of stems in non-moisture-proof containers, or when you want to give the impression that flowers are simply tucked in among fruit or vegetables in a bowl. These plastic phials provide stems with an individual moisture source that you can easily conceal among the other decorative materials in a group; they are available from florists.

Store-cupboard option *(page 141)*

Using proprietary flower food is not the only way to prolong vase life: you can stir 1 teaspoon of caster sugar into each 600 ml (1 pint) of water to provide cut stems with nutrients. To prevent bacterial growth, you can also add 5 ml (1 teaspoon) of regular-strength household bleach to the water (do not use this solution in arrangements that could come within the reach of young children).

Cool, clear water *(above)*

Spraying cut flowers, foliage and other plant materials with a fine mist of cool water will help to keep them fresh. Use a purpose-made spray mister, as shown (these are available from florists, garden centres, DIY stores and other specialist outlets), or a laundry sprinkler. To top up the water level in a container – especially one that has a narrow aperture – you will need to use either a funnel or a watering can that has a long, thin spout.

Looking cool *(above)*

Drops of water lingering on petals and leaves after spraying have a refreshingly cool appearance, but make sure that they cannot drizzle on to furniture surfaces. Leave the arrangement on the draining board of a sink until the water has evaporated, or stand it on a moisture-proof dish or tray.

Drying out *(below)*

You can use seedheads to dramatic effect in arrangements of fresh flowers and foliage, and poppy, love-in-a-mist and rudbeckia seedheads (shown here) will need no further nourishment. Leave the seedheads on the plants until they have almost dried out, then hang them in bunches in a cool, dry place. Brush the stem ends with clear, waterproof varnish so that they will not develop mould when you arrange them in water or pre-soaked florist's foam.

Flower food *(below)*

Adding a commercially prepared flower food – designed to provide the plants with nutrients – to the water before you soak a block of florist's foam or arrange flowers in a container can help to prolong the life of cut stems. Follow the recommended proportions specified on the sachet or packet, and add more food to the water when you top up the container or change the water completely.

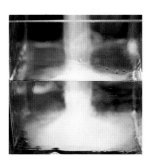

Index

THE GREAT BIG
BARBECUE
COOKBOOK

THE GREAT BIG
BARBECUE
COOKBOOK

*Over 200 sizzling recipes for barbecues, picnics
and perfect outdoor entertaining*

CONSULTANT EDITOR: CHRISTINE FRANCE

Sebastian Kelly

Paperback edition published by Sebastian Kelly
2 Rectory Road, Oxford OX4 1BW

Select Editions imprint specially produced for Selectabook Ltd

Produced by Anness Publishing Limited
Hermes House, 88–89 Blackfriars Road
London SE1 8HA

A CIP catalogue record for this book is available from the British Library

ISBN 1-84081-115-3

Publisher: Joanna Lorenz
Project Editor: Sarah Ainley
Copy Editor: Beverley Jollands
Designer: Nigel Partridge
Cover Design: Simon Balley
Illustrations: Madeleine David and Lucinda Ganderton
Photographers: Karl Adamson, William Adams-Lingwood, Edward Allwright,
Steve Baxter, James Duncan, John Freeman, Michelle Garrett, Amanda Heywood,
Don Last, Michael Michaels, Patrick McLeavey, Debbie Patterson and Juliet Piddington
Recipes: Carla Capalbo, Jacqueline Clark, Carole Clements, Roz Denny, Nicola Diggins,
Tessa Evelegh, Joanna Farrow, Christine France, Silvana Franco, Soheila Kimberley,
Ruby Le Bois, Sue Maggs, Katherine Richmond, Steven Wheeler and Elizabeth Wolf-Cohen

Also published as *The Ultimate Barbecue Cookbook*

For all recipes, quantities are given in both metric and imperial measures,
and, where appropriate, measures are also given in standard cups and spoons.
Follow one set, but not a mixture, because they are not interchangeable.

Printed and bound in China

© Anness Publishing Limited 1998, 1999
1 3 5 7 9 10 8 6 4 2

CONTENTS

∘ ∘ ∘

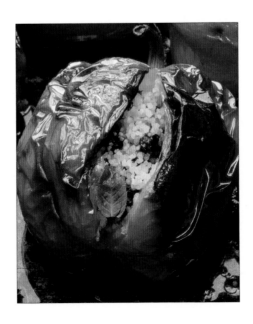

Introduction

—◆—

However simple, there's something about the char-grilled flavour of barbecued food that makes it taste extra special. Maybe it owes part of its appeal to the fresh air that sharpens the appetite and makes that tantalizing aroma so totally irresistible.

There's nothing new about cooking over charcoal; in fact, it's a method of cooking that has been used in most civilizations throughout history. The basic method has changed little over the centuries, but many modern barbecues are very sophisticated, making the job easier, cleaner and more controllable. Whether you're cooking over a simple pile of sticks or on a top-of-the-range barbecue, outdoor cooking is fun, easy and inexpensive.

There are disputes over the origin of the word barbecue, but one explanation is that it comes from *barbacoa*, an American-Spanish word used by the Arawak tribe of the Caribbean, as the name for the wooden frame that held their food over an open fire as it cooked. The Arawaks were cannibals, so the food we cook today is rather different from their offerings!

Whatever your tastes, this collection of recipes offers new, unusual ideas for your barbecue as well as some traditional favourites. There's something for every occasion, from family meals to entertaining: spicy, fruity and exotic grills using fish, meat and poultry; easy sauces and marinades to turn basic ingredients into something new and special; and luscious, indulgent desserts. For vegetarians, there's a whole chapter of innovative ideas that everyone will enjoy.

Best of all, not only does a barbecue set the cook free from the kitchen but, for once, everyone else will actually want to help with the cooking.

CHOOSING A BARBECUE

• • •

There is a huge choice of ready-made barbecues on the market, and it's important to choose one that suits your needs. First decide how many people you want to cook for and where you are likely to use the barbecue. For instance, do you usually have barbecues just for the family, or are you likely to have barbecue parties for lots of friends? Once you've decided on your basic requirements, you will be able to choose between the different types more easily.

Hibachi Barbecues

These small cast-iron barbecues originated in Japan – the word *hibachi* translates literally as 'firebox'. They are inexpensive, easy to use and easily transportable. Lightweight versions are now made in steel or aluminium.

ABOVE: Hibachi barbecue

Disposable Barbecues

These will last for about an hour and are a convenient idea for picnic-style barbecues or for cooking just a few small pieces of food.

Portable Barbecues

These are usually quite light and fold away to fit into a car boot so you can take them on picnics. Some are even small enough to fit into a rucksack.

Brazier Barbecues

These open barbecues are suitable for use on a patio or in the garden. Most have legs or wheels and it's a good idea to check that the height suits you. The grill area of a brazier barbecue varies in size and the barbecue may be round or rectangular. It's useful to choose one that has a shelf attached to the side. Other extras may include an electric, battery-powered or clockwork spit: choose one on which you can adjust the height of the spit. Many brazier barbecues have a hood, which is useful as a windbreak and gives a place to mount the spit.

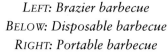

LEFT: Brazier barbecue
BELOW: Disposable barbecue
RIGHT: Portable barbecue

ordinary house bricks, but it's best to line the inside with firebricks, which will withstand the heat better. Use a metal shelf for the fuel and a grid at whatever height you choose. Packs are available containing all you need to build a barbecue.

ABOVE: Improvised barbecue

ABOVE: Gas barbecue

Kettle-grill Barbecues

These have a large, hinged lid which can be used as a windbreak; when closed, the lid allows you to use the barbecue rather like an oven. Even large joints of meat or whole turkeys cook successfully, as the heat reflected within the dome helps to brown the meat evenly. The heat is easily controlled by the use of efficient air vents. This type of barbecue can also be used for home-smoking foods.

Gas Barbecues

The main advantage of these is their convenience – the heat is instant and easily controllable. The disadvantage is that they tend to be quite expensive.

Permanent Barbecues

These are a good idea if you often have barbecues at home. They can be built simply and cheaply. Choose a sheltered site that is a little way from the house, but with easy access to the kitchen. Permanent barbecues can be built with

Improvised Barbecues

Barbecue cooking adds to the fun of eating outdoors on picnics and camping trips but transporting the barbecue for the rest of the day can make the idea more of a chore than a treat. Basic barbecues can be built at almost no cost and can be dismantled after use as quickly as they were put together. A pile of stones topped with chicken wire and fuelled with driftwood or kindling makes a very efficient barbecue. Or take a large biscuit tin with you and punch a few holes in it; fill it with charcoal and place a grid on top. With just a little planning, you can turn your trip into a truly memorable event.

ABOVE: Permanent barbecue

TYPES OF FUEL

· · ·

If you have a gas or electric barbecue, you will not need to buy extra fuel, but other barbecues require either charcoal or wood. Choose good-quality fuel from sustainable sources, and always store it in a dry place.

Lumpwood Charcoal
Lumpwood charcoal is usually made from softwood, and comes in lumps of varying size. It is easier to ignite than briquettes, but tends to burn up faster.

Charcoal Briquettes
Briquettes are a cost-effective choice of fuel as they burn for a long time with the minimum of smell and smoke. They can take a long time to ignite, however.

ABOVE: *Charcoal briquettes*

Self-igniting Charcoal
This is simply lumpwood charcoal or briquettes, treated with a flammable substance that catches light very easily. It's important to wait until the ignition agent has burnt off before cooking food, or the smell may taint the food.

Coconut-shell Charcoal
This makes a good fuel for small barbecues. It's best used on a fire grate with small holes, as the small pieces tend to fall through the gaps.

Wood
Hardwoods such as oak and olive are best for barbecues, as they burn slowly with a pleasant aroma. Softwoods tend to burn too fast and give off sparks and smoke, making them unsuitable for most barbecues. Wood fires need constant attention to achieve an even, steady heat.

CONTROLLING THE HEAT
There are three basic ways to control the heat of the barbecue during cooking.

1 Adjust the height of the grill rack. Raise it for slow cooking, or use the bottom level for searing foods. For a medium heat, the rack should be about 10cm/4in from the fire.

2 Push the burning coals apart for a lower heat; pile them closer together to increase the heat of the fire.

3 Most barbecues have air vents to allow air into the fire. Open them to make the fire hotter, or close them to lower the temperature.

Woodchips and Herbs
These are designed to be added to the fire to impart a pleasant aroma to the food. They can be soaked to make them last longer. Scatter woodchips and herbs straight on to the coals during cooking, or place them on a metal tray under the grill rack. Packs of hickory or oak chips are easily available, or you can simply scatter twigs of juniper, rosemary, thyme, sage or fennel over the fire.

LIGHTING THE FIRE
Follow these basic instructions for lighting the fire unless you are using self-igniting charcoal, in which case you should follow the manu-facturer's instructions.

1 Spread a layer of foil over the base of the barbecue, to reflect the heat and make cleaning easier.

2 Spread a layer of wood, charcoal or briquettes on the fire grate about 5cm/2in deep. Pile the fuel in a small pyramid in the centre.

3 Push one or two firelighters into the pyramid or pour over about 45ml/3 tbsp liquid firelighter and leave for 1 minute. Light with a long match or taper and leave to burn for 15 minutes. Spread the coals evenly and leave for 30–45 minutes, until they are covered with a film of grey ash, before cooking.

BELOW: *Lumpwood*

BELOW: *Coconut shell*

SAFETY TIPS

Barbecuing is a perfectly safe method of cooking if it's done sensibly – use these simple guidelines as a basic checklist to safeguard against accidents. If you have never organized a barbecue before, keep your first few attempts as simple as possible, with just one or two types of food. When you have mastered the technique of cooking on a barbecue you can start to become more ambitious. Soon you will progress from burgers for two to meals for large parties of family and friends.

☆ Make sure the barbecue is sited on a firm surface and is stable and level before lighting the fire. Once the barbecue is lit, do not move it.

☆ Keep the barbecue sheltered from the wind, and keep it well away from trees and shrubs.

☆ Always follow the manufacturer's instructions for your barbecue, as there are some barbecues that can use only one type of fuel.

☆ Don't try to hasten the fire – some fuels may take quite a time to build up heat. Never pour flammable liquid on to the barbecue.

☆ Keep children and pets away from the fire and make sure the cooking is always supervised by adults.

☆ Keep perishable foods cold until you're ready to cook – especially in hot weather. If you take them outdoors, place them in a cool bag until needed.

☆ Make sure meats such as burgers, sausages and poultry are thoroughly cooked – there should be no trace of pink in the juices. Pierce a thick part of flesh as a test: the juices should run clear.

RIGHT: Poultry can be pre-cooked in the oven or microwave, before being finished off on the barbecue.

ABOVE: Light the fire with a long match or taper, and leave it to burn for about 15 minutes.

☆ Wash your hands after handling raw meat and before touching other foods. Don't use the same utensils for raw ingredients and cooked food.

☆ You may prefer to pre-cook poultry in the microwave or oven and then transfer it to the barbecue to finish off cooking and to attain the flavour of barbecued food. Don't allow meat to cool down before transferring it to the barbecue; poultry should never be reheated once it has cooled.

☆ In case the fire should get out of control, have a bucket of sand and a water spray on hand to douse the flames.

☆ Keep a first-aid kit handy. If someone burns themselves, hold the burn under cold running water.

☆ Trim excess fat from meat and don't use too much oil in marinades. Fat can cause dangerous flare-ups if too much is allowed to drip on to the fuel.

☆ Use long-handled barbecue tools, such as forks, tongs and brushes, for turning and basting food; keep some oven gloves to hand, preferably the extra-long type, to protect your hands.

☆ Always keep the raw foods to be cooked away from foods that are ready to eat, to prevent cross-contamination.

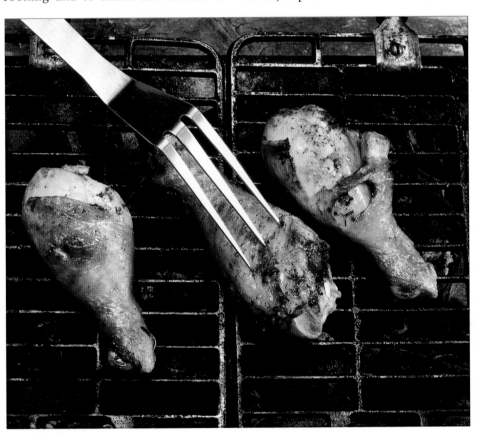

BASIC TIMING GUIDE

∘ ∘ ∘

It is almost impossible to give precise timing guides for barbecue cooking as there are so many factors to consider. The heat will depend on the type and size of barbecue, the type of fuel used, the height of the grill above the fire and, of course, the weather. Cooking times will also be affected by the thickness and type of food, the quality of the meat, and whereabouts on the grill it is placed.

Bearing this in mind, the chart below provides only a rough guide to timing. Food should always be tested to make sure it is thoroughly cooked. The times given here are total cooking times, allowing for the food to be turned. Most foods need turning only once but smaller items, such as kebabs and sausages, need to be turned more frequently to ensure even cooking. Foods wrapped in foil cook more slowly and will need longer on the barbecue.

TYPE OF FOOD	WEIGHT/ THICKNESS	HEAT	TOTAL COOKING TIME
BEEF			
steaks	2.5cm/1in	hot	rare: 5 minutes
			medium: 8 minutes
			well done: 12 minutes
burgers	2cm/¾ in	hot	6–8 minutes
kebabs	2.5cm/1in	hot	5–8 minutes
joints	1.5kg/3½ lb	spit	2–3 hours
LAMB			
leg steaks	2cm/¾ in	medium	10–15 minutes
chops	2.5cm/1in	medium	10–15 minutes
kebabs	2.5cm/1in	medium	6–15 minutes
butterfly leg	7.5cm/3in	low	rare: 40–45 minutes
			well done: 1 hour
rolled shoulder	1.5kg/3½ lb	spit	1¼–1½ hours
PORK			
chops	2.5cm/1in	medium	15–18 minutes
kebabs	2.5cm/1in	medium	12–15 minutes
spare ribs		medium	30–40 minutes
sausages	thick	medium	8–10 minutes
joints	1.5kg/3½ lb	spit	2–3 hours

TYPE OF FOOD	WEIGHT/ THICKNESS	HEAT	TOTAL COOKING TIME
CHICKEN			
whole	1.5kg/3½ lb	spit	1–1¼ hours
quarters		medium	30–35 minutes
boneless breasts		medium	10–15 minutes
drumsticks		medium	25–30 minutes
kebabs		medium	6–10 minutes
poussin, whole	450g/1lb	spit	25–30 minutes
poussin, spatchcocked	450g/1lb	medium	25–30 minutes
DUCKLING			
whole	2.25kg/5lb	spit	1–1½ hours
half		medium	35–45 minutes
breasts, boneless		medium	15–20 minutes
FISH			
large, whole	2.25–4.5kg/ 5–10lb	low/ medium	allow 10 minutes per 2.5cm/1in thickness
small, whole	500–900g/ 1¼–2lb	hot/ medium	12–20 minutes
sardines		hot/ medium	4–6 minutes
steaks or fillets	2.5cm/1in	medium	6–10 minutes
kebabs	2.5cm/1in	medium	5–8 minutes
large prawns in shell		medium	6–8 minutes
large prawns, shelled		medium	4–6 minutes
scallops/mussels in shell		medium	until open
scallops/mussels, shelled, skewered		medium	5–8 minutes
half lobster		low/ medium	15–20 minutes

MARINATING

∘ ∘ ∘

Marinades are used to add flavour and to moisten or tenderize foods, particularly meat. Marinades can be either savoury or sweet and are as varied as you want to make them: spicy, fruity, fragrant or exotic. Certain classic combinations always work well with certain foods. Usually, it is best to choose oily marinades for dry foods, such as lean meat or white fish, and wine- or vinegar-based marinades for rich foods with a higher fat content. Most marinades don't contain salt, which can draw out the juices from meat. It's better to add salt just before, or after, cooking.

1 Place the food for marinating in a wide, non-metallic dish or bowl, preferably a dish that is large enough to allow the food to lie in a single layer.

2 Mix together the ingredients for the marinade according to the recipe. The marinade can usually be prepared in advance and stored in a jar with a screw-top lid until needed.

3 Pour the marinade over the food and turn the food to coat it evenly.

4 Cover the dish or bowl with clear film and chill in the fridge for anything from 30 minutes up to several hours or overnight, depending on the recipe. Turn the food over occasionally and spoon the marinade over it to ensure it is well coated.

5 Remove the food with a slotted spoon, or lift it out with tongs, and drain off and reserve the marinade. If necessary, allow the food to come to room temperature before cooking.

6 Use the marinade for basting or brushing the food during cooking.

Cook's Tip
The amount of marinade you will need depends on the amount of food. As a rough guide, about 150ml/¼ pint/⅔ cup is enough for about 500g/1¼ lb of food.

BASIC BARBECUE MARINADE
This can be used for meat or fish.

1 garlic clove, crushed
45ml/3 tbsp sunflower or olive oil
45ml/3 tbsp dry sherry
15ml/1 tbsp Worcestershire sauce
15ml/1 tbsp dark soy sauce
freshly ground black pepper

RED WINE MARINADE
This is good with red meats and game.

150ml/¼ pint/⅔ cup dry red wine
15ml/1 tbsp olive oil
15ml/1 tbsp red wine vinegar
2 garlic cloves, crushed
2 dried bay leaves, crumbled
freshly ground black pepper

BELOW: *Marinating foods before cooking adds to the flavour and ensures the food is kept tender and moist.*

Starters and Snacks

As everyone knows, there is nothing like the aroma of char-grilling food

to whet the appetite. To keep your guests happy while they are waiting

for the main event, begin your barbecue feast with exciting appetizers

that are quick to cook and fun to eat. Here is a collection of

flavoursome and colourful dishes that are guaranteed to disappear

from the grill rack as soon as they're cool enough to snatch away.

There are lots of creative recipes for finger foods to be nibbled with

drinks – from crisp potato skins to spicy spare ribs – with plenty of

interesting dips and sauces to dunk them in, as well as delicious

suggestions for elegant starters for more formal meals.

ROASTED GARLIC TOASTS

Barbecuing garlic in its skin produces a soft, aromatic purée with a sweet, nutty flavour.
Spread on crisp toast to make a delicious starter or accompaniment to meat or vegetable dishes.

INGREDIENTS

2 whole garlic heads
extra virgin olive oil
fresh rosemary sprigs
ciabatta loaf or thick baguette
chopped fresh rosemary
salt and freshly ground black
pepper

SERVES 4

1 Slice the tops from the heads of garlic, using a sharp kitchen knife.

2 Brush the garlic heads with extra virgin olive oil and add a few sprigs of fresh rosemary, before wrapping in kitchen foil. Cook the foil parcels on a medium-hot barbecue for about 25–30 minutes, turning occasionally, until the garlic is soft.

3 Slice the bread and brush each slice generously with olive oil. Toast the slices on the barbecue until crisp and golden, turning once.

4 Squeeze the garlic cloves from their skins on to the toasts. Sprinkle with the chopped fresh rosemary and olive oil, and add salt and black pepper to taste.

ROASTED PEPPER ANTIPASTO

Jars of Italian mixed peppers in olive oil are a common sight in supermarkets, yet none can compete with this freshly made version, perfect as a starter or served with salami and cold meats.

INGREDIENTS

3 red peppers
2 yellow or orange peppers
2 green peppers
50g/2oz/$\frac{1}{2}$ cup sun-dried tomatoes
in oil, drained
1 garlic clove
30ml/2 tbsp balsamic vinegar
75ml/5 tbsp olive oil
few drops of chilli sauce
4 canned artichoke hearts, drained
and sliced
salt and freshly ground black
pepper
fresh basil leaves, to garnish

SERVES 6

1 Cook the whole peppers on a medium-hot barbecue, turning frequently, for about 10–15 minutes until they begin to char. Cover the peppers with a clean dish towel and leave to cool for 5 minutes.

2 Use a sharp kitchen knife to slice the sun-dried tomatoes into thin strips. Thinly slice the garlic clove.

3 Beat together the balsamic vinegar, olive oil and chilli sauce in a small bowl, then season with a little salt and freshly ground black pepper.

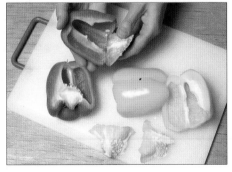

4 Stalk and slice the peppers. Mix with the sliced artichokes, sun-dried tomatoes and garlic. Pour over the dressing and scatter with basil leaves.

HERB-STUFFED MINI VEGETABLES

These little hors d'oeuvres are ideal for parties as they can be prepared in advance, and simply assembled and cooked at the last minute.

INGREDIENTS

30 mini vegetables: courgettes,
patty pan squashes and large
button mushrooms
30ml/2 tbsp olive oil
fresh basil or parsley, to garnish

FOR THE STUFFING
30ml/2 tbsp olive oil
1 onion, finely chopped
1 garlic clove, finely chopped
115g/4oz button mushrooms,
finely chopped
1 courgette, finely chopped
1 red pepper, finely chopped
65g/2½ oz/⅓ cup orzo pasta or
long grain rice
90ml/6 tbsp/⅓ cup passata
2.5ml/½ tsp dried thyme
120ml/4fl oz/½ cup chicken stock
5–10ml/1–2 tsp chopped fresh basil
or parsley
50g/2oz mozzarella or fontina
cheese, coarsely grated
salt and freshly ground black
pepper

MAKES 30

1 For the stuffing, heat the oil over a medium heat in a pan. Add the onion and cook for 2 minutes until tender. Stir in the garlic, mushrooms, courgette and red pepper. Season and cook for 2 minutes until the vegetables soften.

2 Stir in the pasta or rice, the passata, thyme and stock and bring to the boil, stirring. Reduce the heat and simmer for 10–12 minutes until reduced and thickened. Remove from the heat and cool slightly. Stir in the basil or parsley and the cheese.

3 Drop the courgettes and squashes into boiling water and cook for 3 minutes. Drain and refresh under cold running water. Trim the bottoms so they are flat, trim a small slice off the tops and scoop out the centres with a spoon or melon baller. Remove the stems from the mushrooms. Brush all the vegetables with olive oil.

4 Using a teaspoon, fill the vegetables with the stuffing and arrange on a rack. Grill over a medium-hot barbecue or grill for 10–15 minutes until the filling is hot and bubbling. Garnish with the fresh basil or parsley. The vegetables can be served either warm or cool.

POLPETTES WITH MOZZARELLA AND TOMATO

· · ·

These Italian-style meatballs are made with beef and topped with creamy melted mozzarella and savoury anchovies.

INGREDIENTS

½ slice white bread, crusts removed
45ml/3 tbsp milk
675g/1½ lb minced beef
1 egg, beaten
50g/2oz/⅔ cup dry breadcrumbs
olive oil for brushing
2 beefsteak or other large tomatoes, sliced
15ml/1 tbsp chopped fresh oregano
1 mozzarella cheese, cut into 6 slices
6 drained, canned anchovy fillets, cut in half lengthways
salt and freshly ground black pepper

SERVES 6

1 Put the bread and milk into a small saucepan and heat very gently, until the bread absorbs all the milk. Mash it to a pulp and set aside to cool.

2 Put the minced beef into a bowl with the bread mixture and the egg and season with plenty of salt and freshly ground black pepper. Mix well, then shape the mixture into six patties, using your hands. Sprinkle the breadcrumbs on to a plate and dredge the patties, coating them thoroughly.

3 Brush the polpettes with olive oil and cook them on a hot barbecue for 2–3 minutes on one side, until brown. Turn them over.

4 Without removing the polpettes from the barbecue, lay a slice of tomato on top of each polpette, sprinkle with chopped oregano and season with salt and pepper. Place a mozzarella slice on top and arrange two strips of anchovy in a cross over the cheese.

5 Cook for a further 4–5 minutes until the polpettes are cooked through and the mozzarella has melted.

STUFFED KIBBEH

Kibbeh is a tasty Middle Eastern speciality of minced lamb and bulgar wheat, which can be eaten raw or shaped into patties and cooked on the barbecue.

INGREDIENTS

450g/1lb lean lamb
45ml/3 tbsp olive oil
avocado slices and fresh coriander sprigs, to serve

FOR THE KIBBEH
225g/8oz/1⅓ cups bulgur wheat
1 red chilli, seeded and roughly chopped
1 onion, roughly chopped
salt and freshly ground black pepper

FOR THE STUFFING
1 onion, finely chopped
50g/2oz/⅔ cup pine nuts
30ml/2 tbsp olive oil
7.5ml/1½ tsp ground allspice
60ml/4 tbsp chopped fresh coriander

SERVES 4–6

1 Roughly cut the lamb into chunks, using a heavy kitchen knife. Process the chunks in a blender or food processor until finely minced. Divide the minced meat into two equal portions and set aside until needed.

2 To make the kibbeh, soak the bulgur wheat for 15 minutes in cold water. Drain well, then process in the blender or food processor with the chopped chilli and onion, half the meat and plenty of salt and pepper.

3 To make the stuffing, fry the onion and pine nuts in the olive oil for 5 minutes. Add the allspice and remaining minced meat and fry gently, breaking up the meat with a wooden spoon, until browned. Stir in the coriander and a little seasoning.

4 Turn the kibbeh mixture out on to a clean work surface and use your hands to shape the mixture into a cake. Divide the cake into 12 wedges.

5 Flatten one wedge in the palm of your hand and spoon a little stuffing into the centre. Bring the edges of the kibbeh over the stuffing to enclose it. Make into a firm egg-shaped mould between the palms of your hands, ensuring that the filling is completely encased. Repeat with the other kibbeh.

6 To barbecue the kibbeh, lightly brush with olive oil and cook on a medium barbecue for 10–15 minutes, turning carefully, until evenly browned and cooked through. To fry the kibbeh, heat oil to a depth of 5cm/2in in a large pan until a few kibbeh crumbs sizzle on the surface. Lower half the kibbeh into the oil and fry for about 5 minutes until golden. Drain on kitchen paper and keep hot while frying the remainder. Serve hot with avocado slices and fresh coriander sprigs.

HERB POLENTA

Golden polenta with fresh summer herbs makes an appetizing starter or light snack, served with barbecued tomatoes.

INGREDIENTS

750ml/1¼ pints/3 cups stock or
water
5ml/1 tsp salt
175g/6oz/1 cup polenta
25g/1oz/2 tbsp butter
75ml/5 tbsp mixed chopped fresh
parsley, chives and basil, plus extra
to garnish
olive oil for brushing
4 large plum or beef tomatoes,
halved
salt and freshly ground black
pepper

SERVES 4

3 Remove from the heat and stir in the butter, chopped herbs and pepper.

4 Lightly grease a wide tin or dish and tip the polenta into it, spreading it evenly. Leave until cool and set.

1 Prepare the polenta in advance: place the stock or water in a saucepan, with the salt, and bring to the boil. Reduce the heat and stir in the polenta.

2 Stir constantly over a moderate heat for 5 minutes, until the polenta begins to thicken and come away from the sides of the saucepan.

5 Turn out the polenta and cut into squares or stamp out rounds with a large biscuit cutter. Brush with olive oil. Lightly brush the tomatoes with oil and sprinkle with salt and pepper. Cook the tomatoes and polenta on a medium-hot barbecue for about 5 minutes, turning once. Serve garnished with fresh herbs.

Cook's Tip

Try using fresh basil or fresh chives alone, for a distinctive flavour.

BRIE PARCELS WITH ALMONDS

∘ ∘ ∘

*Creamy French Brie makes a sophisticated starter or light meal, wrapped in
vine leaves and served hot with chunks of crusty bread.*

2 Cut the Brie into four chunks and place each chunk on a vine leaf.

3 Mix together the chives, ground almonds, peppercorns and olive oil, and place a spoonful on top of each piece of cheese. Sprinkle with flaked almonds.

4 Fold the vine leaves over tightly to enclose the cheese completely. Brush the parcels with olive oil and cook on a hot barbecue for about 3–4 minutes, until the cheese is hot and melting. Serve immediately.

INGREDIENTS

4 large vine leaves, preserved in
brine
200g/7oz piece Brie cheese
30ml/2 tbsp chopped fresh chives
30ml/2 tbsp ground almonds
5ml/1 tsp crushed black
peppercorns
15ml/1 tbsp olive oil
flaked almonds

SERVES 4

1 Rinse the vine leaves thoroughly under cold running water and dry them well. Spread the leaves out on a clean work surface or chopping board.

TOFU STEAKS

o o o

*Vegetarians and meat-eaters alike will enjoy these barbecued tofu steaks. The combination of
ingredients in the marinade gives the steaks a distinctly Japanese flavour.*

INGREDIENTS

1 packet fresh tofu (10 × 8 × 3cm/
4 × 3¼ × 1¼ in), 300g/11oz
drained weight
2 spring onions, thinly sliced,
to garnish
mixed salad leaves, to garnish

FOR THE MARINADE
45ml/3 tbsp sake
30ml/2 tbsp soy sauce
5ml/1 tsp sesame oil
1 garlic clove, crushed
15ml/1 tbsp grated fresh root
ginger
1 spring onion, finely chopped

SERVES 4

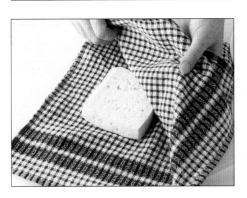

1 Wrap the tofu in a clean dish towel
and place it on a chopping board. Put a
large plate on top and leave the tofu for
30 minutes to remove any excess water.

2 Slice the tofu horizontally into
three pieces, then cut the slices into
quarters. Set aside. Mix the ingredients
for the marinade in a large bowl. Add
the tofu to the bowl in a single layer
and allow to marinate for 30 minutes.
Drain the tofu steaks and reserve the
marinade to use for basting.

3 Cook the steaks on the barbecue
for 3 minutes on each side, basting
regularly with the marinade, or fry
them for 3 minutes in a large pan.

4 Arrange three tofu steaks on each
plate. Any remaining marinade can be
heated in a pan and then poured over
the steaks. Sprinkle with the spring
onions and garnish with mixed salad
leaves. Serve immediately.

Cook's Tip
Tofu is easily obtainable
from supermarkets and health
food stores, and is an ideal
alternative to meat.

GRILLED ASPARAGUS WITH SALT-CURED HAM

∘ ∘ ∘

*Barbecued asparagus has a wonderfully intense flavour that stands up well to the wrapping
of crisp, salty ham. Serve this traditional tapas dish with drinks before a meal.*

INGREDIENTS

6 slices of serrano ham
12 asparagus spears
15ml/1 tbsp olive oil
*sea salt and coarsely ground black
pepper*

SERVES 4

1 Halve each slice of ham lengthways
and wrap one half around each of the
asparagus spears.

2 Brush the ham and asparagus
lightly with olive oil and sprinkle with
salt and pepper. Cook on a medium
barbecue for about 4 minutes, turning
frequently, until the asparagus is tender
but still firm. Serve at once.

Cook's Tip

If you can't find serrano ham,
try using Italian prosciutto or
Portuguese presunto.

POTATO SKINS WITH CAJUN DIP

*As an alternative to deep-frying, barbecuing potato skins crisps them up in no time and gives
them a wonderful char-grilled flavour. This spicy dip makes the perfect partner.*

INGREDIENTS

4 large baking potatoes
olive oil for brushing
250ml/8fl oz/1 cup natural yogurt
2 garlic cloves, crushed
10ml/2 tsp tomato paste
5ml/1 tsp green chilli paste or
1 small green chilli, chopped
2.5ml/½ tsp celery salt
*salt and freshly ground black
pepper*

SERVES 4

1 Bake or microwave the potatoes
until tender. Cut them in half and
scoop out the flesh, leaving a thin
layer of potato on the skins. The
scooped out potato can be reserved in
the fridge or freezer for another meal.

2 Cut each potato shell in half again
and lightly brush the skins with olive
oil. Cook on a medium-hot barbecue
for 4–5 minutes, or until crisp.

3 Mix together the remaining
ingredients in a bowl to make the dip.
Serve the potato skins with the Cajun
dip on the side.

Cook's Tip
If you don't have any
chilli paste or fresh chillies, add
one or two drops of hot pepper
sauce to the dip instead.

SPICY CHICKEN WINGS

° ° °

*These deliciously sticky bites will appeal to adults and children alike, although
younger eaters might prefer a little less chilli.*

INGREDIENTS

8 plump chicken wings
*2 large garlic cloves, cut
into slivers*
15ml/1 tbsp olive oil
15ml/1 tbsp paprika
5ml/1 tsp chilli powder
5ml/1 tsp dried oregano
*salt and freshly ground black
pepper*
lime wedges, to serve

SERVES 4

1 Using a small sharp kitchen knife, make one or two cuts in the skin of each chicken wing and slide a sliver of garlic under the skin. Brush the wings generously with the olive oil.

2 In a large bowl, stir together the paprika, chilli powder and oregano and season with plenty of salt and pepper. Add the chicken wings and toss together until very lightly coated in the mixture.

3 Cook the chicken wings on a medium barbecue for 15 minutes until they are cooked through, with a blackened, crispy skin. Serve with fresh lime wedges to squeeze over.

CHICKEN WINGS TERIYAKI STYLE

° ° °

This oriental glaze is very simple to prepare and adds a unique flavour to the meat. The glaze can be used with any cut of chicken or with fish.

INGREDIENTS

1 garlic clove, crushed
45ml/3 tbsp soy sauce
30ml/2 tbsp dry sherry
10ml/2 tsp clear honey
10ml/2 tsp grated fresh root ginger
5ml/1 tsp sesame oil
12 chicken wings
15ml/1 tbsp sesame seeds, toasted

SERVES 4

1 Place the garlic, soy sauce, sherry, honey, grated ginger and sesame oil in a large bowl and beat with a fork, to mix the ingredients together evenly.

2 Add the chicken wings and toss thoroughly, to coat in the marinade. Cover the bowl with clear film and chill for about 30 minutes, or longer.

3 Cook the chicken wings on a fairly hot barbecue for about 20–25 minutes, turning occasionally and basting with the remaining marinade.

4 Sprinkle the chicken wings with sesame seeds. Serve the wings on their own as a starter or side dish, or with a crisp green salad.

SKEWERED LAMB WITH RED ONION SALSA

A simple salsa makes a refreshing accompaniment to this summery dish – make sure you use a mild-flavoured red onion that is fresh and crisp, and a tomato that is ripe and full of flavour.

INGREDIENTS

225g/8oz lean lamb, cubed
2.5ml/½ tsp ground cumin
5ml/1 tsp ground paprika
15ml/1 tbsp olive oil
salt and freshly ground black pepper

FOR THE SALSA
1 red onion, very thinly sliced
1 large tomato, seeded and chopped
15ml/1 tbsp red wine vinegar
3–4 fresh basil or mint leaves, roughly torn
small mint leaves, to garnish

SERVES 4

1 Place the lamb in a large bowl with the cumin, paprika and olive oil and season with plenty of salt and freshly ground black pepper. Toss well. Cover the bowl with clear film and leave in a cool place for several hours, or in the fridge overnight, so that the lamb fully absorbs the spicy flavours.

2 Spear the lamb cubes on four small skewers. If using wooden skewers, soak them first in cold water for at least 30 minutes to prevent them burning when placed on the barbecue.

3 To make the salsa, put the sliced onion, tomato, red wine vinegar and torn fresh basil or mint leaves in a small bowl and stir together until thoroughly blended. Season to taste with salt and garnish with mint.

4 Cook the skewered lamb on a hot barbecue, or under a hot grill, for about 5–10 minutes, turning the skewers frequently, until the lamb is well browned but still slightly pink in the centre. Serve hot, with the salsa.

SPICY MEATBALLS

These meatballs are delicious served piping hot with chilli sauce. Keep the sauce on the side so that everyone can add as much heat as they like.

2 Add the minced beef, shallots, garlic, breadcrumbs, beaten egg and parsley, with plenty of salt and pepper. Mix well, then use your hands to shape the mixture into 18 small balls.

3 Brush the meatballs with olive oil and cook on a medium barbecue, or fry them in a large pan, for about 10–15 minutes, turning regularly until evenly browned and cooked through.

INGREDIENTS

115g/4oz fresh spicy sausages
115g/4oz minced beef
2 shallots, finely chopped
2 garlic cloves, finely chopped
75g/3oz/1½ cups fresh white
breadcrumbs
1 egg, beaten
30ml/2 tbsp chopped fresh parsley,
plus extra to garnish
15ml/1 tbsp olive oil
salt and freshly ground black
pepper
Tabasco or other hot chilli sauce,
to serve

SERVES 6

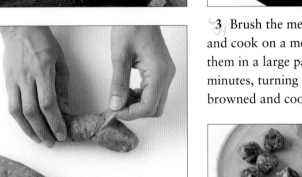

1 Use your hands to remove the skins from the spicy sausages, placing the sausagemeat in a mixing bowl and breaking it up with a fork.

4 Transfer the meatballs to a warm dish and sprinkle with chopped fresh parsley. Serve with chilli sauce.

FIVE-SPICE RIB-STICKERS
. . .

Choose the meatiest spare ribs you can find, to make these a real success, and
remember to keep a supply of paper napkins within easy reach.

2 Mix together all the remaining ingredients, except the spring onions, and pour over the ribs. Toss well to coat evenly. Cover the bowl and leave to marinate in the fridge overnight.

3 Cook the ribs on a medium-hot barbecue, turning frequently, for about 30–40 minutes. Brush occasionally with the remaining marinade.

INGREDIENTS
1kg/2¼lb Chinese-style pork
spare ribs
10ml/2 tsp Chinese five-spice
powder
2 garlic cloves, crushed
15ml/1 tbsp grated fresh
root ginger
2.5ml/½ tsp chilli sauce
60ml/4 tbsp dark soy sauce
45ml/3 tbsp dark muscovado sugar
15ml/1 tbsp sunflower oil
4 spring onions

SERVES 4

1 If the spare ribs are still attached to each other, cut between them to separate them (or you could ask your butcher to do this when you buy them). Place the spare ribs in a large bowl.

4 While the ribs are cooking, finely slice the spring onions. Scatter them over the ribs and serve immediately.

SALMON WITH SPICY PESTO

*This is a great way to bone salmon steaks to give a solid piece of fish. The pesto uses
sunflower kernels and chilli as its flavouring, rather than the classic basil and pine nuts.*

INGREDIENTS

4 salmon steaks, about
225g/8oz each
30ml/2 tbsp sunflower oil
finely grated rind and juice
of 1 lime
salt and freshly ground
black pepper

FOR THE PESTO
6 mild fresh red chillies
2 garlic cloves
30ml/2 tbsp sunflower or
pumpkin seeds
juice and finely grated rind
of 1 lime
75ml/5 tbsp olive oil

SERVES 4

1 Insert a very sharp knife close to
the top of the bone. Working closely
to the bone, cut your way to the end
of the steak to release one side. Repeat
with the other side. Pull out any extra
visible bones with a pair of tweezers.

2 Sprinkle salt on the work surface
and take hold of the end of the salmon
piece, skin-side down. Insert the knife
between the skin and the flesh and,
working away from you, remove the
skin, keeping the knife as close to it as
possible. Repeat for each piece of fish.

3 Curl each piece of fish into a
round, with the thinner end wrapped
around the fatter end. Secure the shape
tightly with a length of string.

4 Rub the sunflower oil into the
boneless fish rounds. Put the salmon
into a large bowl or dish and add the
lime juice and rind and the salt and
pepper. Allow the salmon to marinate
in the fridge for up to 2 hours.

5 For the pesto, de-seed the chillies
and place with the garlic cloves,
sunflower or pumpkin seeds, lime juice,
rind and seasoning in a food processor.
Process until well mixed. Pour the olive
oil gradually over the moving blades
until the sauce has thickened and
emulsified. Drain the salmon from its
marinade. Cook the fish steaks on a
medium barbecue for 5 minutes each
side and serve with the spicy pesto.

GRILLED KING PRAWNS WITH ROMESCO SAUCE

° ° °

This sauce comes from the Catalan region of Spain and is served with fish and seafood.
Its main ingredients are sweet pepper, tomatoes, garlic and almonds.

INGREDIENTS
24 uncooked king prawns
30–45ml/2–3 tbsp olive oil
flat leaf parsley, to garnish
lemon wedges, to serve

FOR THE SAUCE
2 well-flavoured tomatoes
60ml/4 tbsp olive oil
1 onion, chopped
4 garlic cloves, chopped
1 canned pimiento, chopped
2.5ml/1/2 tsp dried chilli flakes or
powder
75ml/5 tbsp fish stock
30ml/2 tbsp white wine
10 blanched almonds
15ml/1 tbsp red wine vinegar
salt

SERVES 4

1 To make the sauce, immerse the tomatoes in boiling water for about 30 seconds, then refresh them under cold running water. Peel away the skins and roughly chop the flesh.

2 Heat 30ml/2 tbsp of the oil. Add the onion and three of the garlic cloves and cook until soft. Add the pimiento, tomatoes, chilli, fish stock and wine. Cover and simmer for 30 minutes.

3 Toast the almonds under the grill until golden. Transfer to a blender or food processor and grind coarsely. Add the remaining 30ml/2 tbsp of oil, the vinegar and the last garlic clove and process until evenly combined. Add the tomato and pimiento sauce and process until smooth. Season with salt.

4 Remove the heads from the prawns, leaving them otherwise unshelled and, with a sharp knife, slit each one down the back and remove the dark vein. Rinse and pat dry on kitchen paper. Toss the prawns in olive oil, then spread them out on the barbecue and cook over a medium heat for about 2–3 minutes on each side, until pink. Serve at once, garnished with parsley and accompanied by lemon wedges and the romesco sauce.

GRILLED MUSSELS WITH PARSLEY AND PARMESAN

*Mussels release an irresistible aroma as they cook on the barbecue: don't be surprised
if they are devoured the moment they are ready.*

INGREDIENTS

450g/1lb fresh mussels
45ml/3 tbsp water
15ml/1 tbsp melted butter
15ml/1 tbsp olive oil
45ml/3 tbsp freshly grated
Parmesan cheese
30ml/2 tbsp chopped fresh parsley
2 garlic cloves, finely chopped
2.5ml/¹/₂ tsp coarsely ground black
pepper

SERVES 4

2 Place the mussels with the water in a large saucepan. Cover with the lid and steam for 5 minutes, or until all of the mussels have opened.

4 In a large bowl, mix together the melted butter, olive oil, grated Parmesan cheese, chopped parsley, garlic and ground black pepper.

1 Scrub the mussels, scraping off any barnacles and pulling out the beards. Tap any closed mussels sharply with a knife and discard any that fail to open.

3 Drain the mussels, discarding any that remain closed. Snap the top shell off each, leaving the mussel still attached to the bottom shell.

5 Using a spoon, place a small amount of the cheese mixture on top of each mussel.

6 Cook the mussels in a saucepan on a medium barbecue for 2–3 minutes or until the mussels are sizzling hot. Serve immediately, with crusty French bread.

QUICK SEAFOOD PIZZA

∘ ∘ ∘

Make four mini pizzas or one large one with the same quantities of ingredients.
If you are short of time, use a pizza-base mix instead of making the dough.

INGREDIENTS

FOR THE PIZZA BASE
5ml/1 tsp easy-blend yeast
450g/1lb/4 cups strong bread flour
15ml/1tbsp sugar
5ml/1tsp sea salt
300ml/½ pint/1¼ cups
lukewarm water
30ml/2tbsp extra virgin olive oil

FOR THE FISH TOPPING
15ml/1 tbsp olive oil
1 onion, finely chopped
800g/1¾ lb canned or fresh plum
tomatoes, chopped
salt and freshly ground black
pepper
15ml/1 tbsp chopped fresh thyme
100g/4oz cherry tomatoes, halved
12 fresh anchovy fillets, or 1 can
anchovy fillets, drained
8 fresh, peeled prawns
a few sprigs of fresh thyme,
to garnish

SERVES 4

1 Stir the easy-blend yeast into the flour in a large bowl. Add the sugar and sea salt and mix together well.

2 Add the water and olive oil to the bowl, and stir to make a firm dough.

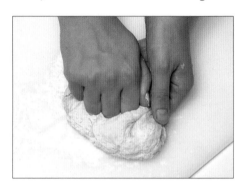

3 Knead the dough for about 10 minutes. Cover and leave in a warm place until it has doubled in size.

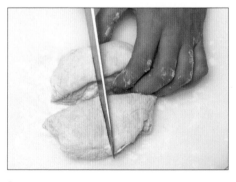

4 Knock back the dough and knead for 5 minutes, then cut the dough into four. Shape each of the four pieces of dough into 13m/5in circles.

5 Fry the onions until soft. Add the canned tomatoes, seasoning and thyme and simmer for 15 minutes. Brush the pizza bases with olive oil and cook on a medium-hot barbecue, oiled side down, for about 6–8 minutes, until firm and golden underneath. Oil the uncooked side and turn the pizzas over.

6 Cut the cherry tomatoes in half. Assemble each of the pizzas with a spoonful of the sauce, a couple of anchovy fillets and prawns and the cherry tomatoes. Return the pizzas to the barbecue and cook for a further 8–10 minutes until golden and crispy. Scatter a few fresh sprigs of thyme on top of the pizzas to serve.

Variation
Add your favourite seafood, such as fresh or canned mussels, to the topping.

CIABATTA WITH MOZZARELLA AND ONIONS
. . .

Ciabatta bread is readily available and is even more delicious when made with spinach,
sun-dried tomatoes or olives: you can find these variations in most supermarkets.

INGREDIENTS
1 ciabatta loaf
60ml/4 tbsp red pesto
2 small onions
olive oil, for brushing
225g/8oz mozzarella cheese, sliced
8 black olives, halved and stoned

MAKES 4

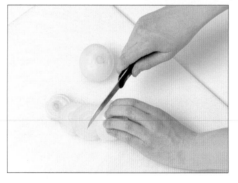

1 Cut the bread in half horizontally and toast the cut sides lightly on the barbecue. Spread with the red pesto.

2 Peel the onions and cut them horizontally into slices. Brush with oil and cook on a hot barbecue for 4–5 minutes until the edges are caramelized.

3 Arrange the cheese slices on the bread. Add the onion slices and scatter some olives over. Cut in half. Return to the barbecue or grill to melt the cheese.

CROSTINI WITH TOMATO AND ANCHOVY

Crostini are little rounds of bread cut from a baguette and crisply toasted, then covered with a topping such as this savoury mixture of tomato and anchovy.

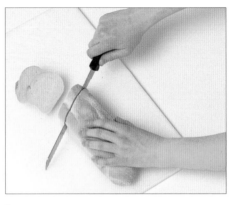

2 Cut the bread diagonally into 8 slices about 1cm/½in thick and brush with the remaining oil. Toast on the barbecue until golden, turning once.

3 Spoon a little tomato mixture on to each slice of bread. Place an anchovy fillet on each one and dot with the halved olives. Serve the crostini garnished with a sprig of fresh basil.

INGREDIENTS

60ml/4 tbsp olive oil
2 garlic cloves
4 tomatoes, peeled and chopped
15ml/1 tbsp chopped fresh basil
15ml/1 tbsp tomato paste
1 small baguette (large enough to give 8 slices)
8 canned anchovy fillets
12 black olives, halved and stoned
salt and freshly ground black pepper
fresh basil, to garnish

MAKES 8

1 Heat half the olive oil in a frying pan and fry the whole garlic cloves with the chopped tomatoes for about 4 minutes. Stir in the chopped basil, tomato paste and season with plenty of salt and freshly ground black pepper.

Variation

CROSTINI WITH ONION AND OLIVE
Fry 2 large onions, sliced, in 30ml/2 tbsp olive oil until golden. Stir in 8 chopped anchovy fillets, 12 halved, stoned black olives, some seasoning, and 5ml/1 tsp dried thyme. Spread the bread with 15ml/1 tbsp black olive paste and cover with the onion mixture.

MEAT DISHES

———✦———

Succulent grilled cuts of meat are often the starting-point when planning

a meal cooked on the barbecue, and char-grilling gives meat a unique

flavour. A perfect steak or lamb chop, simply seasoned and brushed with

oil before grilling, is utterly delicious. Even ordinary sausages and

burgers for an impromptu family supper can be turned into a treat on

the barbecue. But with a little forethought you can add variety and

originality to your cooking by marinating the meat for a few hours

before you cook it. The simplest marinade will work wonders:

improving the texture and juiciness of the meat as well as adding

the flavours of herbs and spices. The recipes in this chapter draw on

cuisines from all over the world to offer an exciting range of dishes

that are all easy to prepare and delicious.

MIXED GRILL SKEWERS WITH HORSERADISH SAUCE

. . .

This hearty selection of meats, cooked on a skewer and drizzled with horseradish sauce, makes a popular main course. Keep all the pieces of meat about the same thickness so they cook evenly.

INGREDIENTS

4 small lamb noisettes, each about 2.5cm/1in thick
4 lamb's kidneys
4 streaky bacon rashers
8 cherry tomatoes
8 chipolata sausages
12–16 bay leaves
salt and freshly ground black pepper

FOR THE HORSERADISH SAUCE
30ml/2 tbsp horseradish relish
45ml/3 tbsp melted butter

SERVES 4

1 Trim any excess fat from the lamb noisettes with a sharp knife. Halve the kidneys and remove the cores, using kitchen scissors.

2 Cut each bacon rasher in half and wrap around the tomatoes or kidneys.

3 Thread the lamb noissettes, bacon-wrapped kidneys and cherry tomatoes, chipolatas and bay leaves on to four long metal skewers. Set aside while you prepare the sauce.

4 Mix the horseradish relish with the melted butter in a small bowl and stir until thoroughly mixed.

5 Brush a little of the horseradish sauce over the meat and sprinkle with salt and freshly ground black pepper.

6 Cook the skewers on a medium barbecue for 12 minutes, turning occasionally, until the meat is golden brown and thoroughly cooked. Serve hot, drizzled with the remaining sauce.

SAUSAGES WITH PRUNES AND BACON

Sausages are a perennial barbecue favourite and this is a delicious way to ring the changes.
Serve with crusty French bread or warmed ciabatta.

2 Spread the cut surface with the mustard and then place three prunes in each sausage, pressing them in firmly.

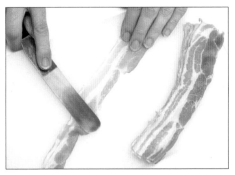

3 Stretch the bacon rashers out thinly, using the back of a palette knife.

INGREDIENTS

8 large, meaty sausages, such as Toulouse or other good-quality pork sausages
30ml/2 tbsp Dijon mustard, plus extra to serve
24 ready-to-eat prunes
8 smoked streaky bacon rashers

SERVES 4

1 Use a sharp knife to cut a long slit down the length of each sausage, about three-quarters of the way through.

4 Wrap one bacon rasher tightly around each of the sausages, to hold them in shape. Cook over a hot barbecue for 15–18 minutes, turning occasionally, until evenly browned and thoroughly cooked. Serve at once, with lots of fresh crusty bread and the additional mustard.

SHISH KEBAB

Many different kinds of kebab are eaten throughout the Middle East, and they are almost always cooked over an open wood or charcoal fire.

INGREDIENTS
450g/1lb boned leg of lamb, cubed
1 large green pepper, seeded and cut into squares
1 large yellow pepper, seeded and cut into squares
8 baby onions, halved
225g/8oz button mushrooms
4 tomatoes, halved
15ml/1 tbsp melted butter
bulgur wheat, to serve

FOR THE MARINADE
45ml/3 tbsp olive oil
juice of 1 lemon
2 garlic cloves, crushed
1 large onion, grated
15ml/1 tbsp fresh oregano
salt and freshly ground black pepper

SERVES 4

1 First make the marinade: blend together the olive oil, lemon juice, crushed garlic, onion, fresh oregano and seasoning. Place the meat in a shallow dish and pour over the marinade. Cover with clear film and leave to marinate for several hours, or overnight, in the fridge.

2 Thread the lamb on to metal skewers, alternating with pieces of pepper, onions and mushrooms. Thread the tomatoes on to separate skewers.

3 Cook the kebabs and tomatoes on a hot barbecue for 10 minutes, turning occasionally and basting with butter. Serve with bulgur wheat.

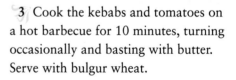

47

BACON KOFTA KEBABS AND SALAD

° ° °

*Kofta kebabs can be made with any type of minced meat, but bacon is very successful,
if you have a food processor.*

INGREDIENTS

250g/9oz lean streaky bacon
rashers, roughly chopped
1 small onion, roughly chopped
1 celery stick, roughly chopped
75ml/5 tbsp fresh wholemeal
breadcrumbs
45ml/3 tbsp chopped fresh thyme
30ml/2 tbsp Worcestershire sauce
1 egg, beaten
salt and freshly ground black
pepper
olive oil, for brushing

FOR THE SALAD
115g/4oz/³/4 cup bulgur wheat
60ml/4 tbsp toasted sunflower
seeds
15ml/1 tbsp olive oil
salt and freshly ground black
pepper
handful celery leaves, chopped

SERVES 4

1 Place the bacon, onion, celery and breadcrumbs in a food processor and process until chopped. Add the thyme, Worcestershire sauce and seasoning. Bind to a firm mixture with the egg.

2 Divide the mixture into eight equal portions and use your hands to shape them around eight bamboo skewers.

3 For the salad, place the bulgur wheat in a bowl and pour over boiling water to cover. Leave to stand for 30 minutes, until the grains are tender.

4 Drain well, then stir in the sunflower seeds, olive oil, salt and pepper. Stir in the celery leaves.

5 Cook the kofta skewers over a medium-hot barbecue for 8–10 minutes, turning occasionally, until golden brown. Serve with the salad.

PEPPERED STEAKS IN BEER AND GARLIC

· · ·

The robust flavours of this dish will satisfy the heartiest appetites.
Serve the steaks with jacket potatoes and a crisp mixed salad.

2 Remove the steaks from the dish and reserve the marinade. Sprinkle the peppercorns over the steaks and press them into the surface.

3 Cook the steaks on a hot barbecue, basting them occasionally with the reserved marinade during cooking. (Take care when basting, as the alcohol will tend to flare up: spoon or brush on just a small amount at a time.)

INGREDIENTS

4 beef sirloin or rump steaks,
about 175g/6oz each
2 garlic cloves, crushed
120ml/4fl oz/½ cup brown
ale or stout
30ml/2 tbsp dark muscovado sugar
30ml/2 tbsp Worcestershire sauce
15ml/1 tbsp corn oil
15ml/1 tbsp crushed black
peppercorns

SERVES 4

1 Place the steaks in a dish and add the garlic, ale or stout, sugar, Worcestershire sauce and oil. Turn to coat evenly, then leave to marinate in the fridge for 2–3 hours or overnight.

4 Turn the steaks once during cooking, and cook them for about 3–6 minutes on each side, depending on how rare you like them.

SIRLOIN STEAKS WITH BLOODY MARY SAUCE

*This cocktail of ingredients is just as delicious as the drink that inspired it, and as the alcohol
evaporates in cooking you need not worry about a hangover.*

INGREDIENTS

*4 sirloin steaks, about
225g/8oz each*

FOR THE MARINADE
*30ml/2 tbsp dark soy sauce
60ml/4 tbsp balsamic vinegar
30ml/2 tbsp olive oil*

FOR THE BLOODY MARY SAUCE
*1kg/2¼lb very ripe tomatoes,
peeled and chopped
tomato purée, if required
50g/2oz/½ cup chopped onions
2 spring onions
5ml/1 tsp chopped fresh coriander
5ml/1 tsp ground cumin
5ml/1 tsp salt
15ml/1 tbsp fresh lime juice
120ml/4fl oz/½ cup beef
consommé
60ml/4 tbsp vodka
15ml/1 tbsp Worcestershire sauce*

SERVES 4

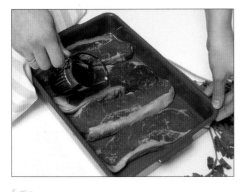

1 Lay the steaks in a shallow dish.
Mix the marinade ingredients together,
pour over the steaks and leave to
marinate in the fridge for at least
2 hours, turning once or twice.

2 Place all the sauce ingredients in
a food processor and blend to a fairly
smooth texture. If the tomatoes are
not quite ripe, add a little tomato
purée. Put in a saucepan, bring to the
boil and simmer for about 5 minutes.

3 Remove the steaks from the dish
and discard the marinade. Cook the
steaks on a medium-hot barbecue
for about 3–6 minutes each side,
depending on how rare you like them,
turning once during cooking. Serve the
steaks with the Bloody Mary sauce.

BEEF RIB WITH ONION SAUCE

. . .

Rib of beef is a classic large roasting joint, but just one rib, barbecued on the bone then carved into succulent slices, makes a perfect dish for two. Serve with a mellow red onion sauce.

INGREDIENTS

*1 beef rib on the bone, about
1kg/2¼lb and about 4cm/1½ in
thick, well trimmed of fat
5ml/1 tsp "steak pepper" or lightly
crushed black peppercorns
15ml/1 tbsp coarse sea salt,
crushed
30–45ml/2–3 tbsp olive oil*

FOR THE RED ONION SAUCE
*40g/1½ oz butter
1 large red onion or 8–10 shallots,
sliced
250ml/8fl oz/1 cup fruity red wine
250ml/8fl oz/1 cup beef or chicken
stock
15–30ml/1–2 tbsp redcurrant jelly
or seedless raspberry preserve
1.5ml/¼ tsp dried thyme
salt and freshly ground black
pepper*

SERVES 2

1 Wipe the beef with damp kitchen paper. Mix the "steak pepper" or crushed peppercorns with the crushed salt and press on to both sides of the meat. Leave the meat to stand, loosely covered, for 30 minutes.

2 To make the sauce, melt the butter over a medium heat. Add the onion or shallots and cook for 3 minutes until softened. Add the wine, stock, jelly or preserve and thyme and bring to the boil. Reduce the heat and simmer for 30–35 minutes until the liquid has evaporated and the sauce has thickened. Season and keep warm.

3 Brush the meat with olive oil and cook on a hot barbecue, or in a pan over a high heat, for 5–8 minutes each side, depending on how rare you like it. Transfer the beef to a board, cover loosely and leave to stand for about 10 minutes. Using a knife, loosen the meat from the rib bone, then carve into thick slices. Serve with the red onion sauce.

STILTON BURGERS

∘ ∘ ∘

A variation on the traditional burger, this tasty recipe contains a delicious surprise:
a creamy filling of lightly melted Stilton cheese.

INGREDIENTS

450g/1lb/4 cups minced beef
1 onion, chopped
1 celery stick, chopped
5ml/1 tsp dried mixed herbs
5ml/1 tsp prepared mustard
50g/2oz/¹/₂ cup crumbled Stilton
cheese
4 burger buns
salt and freshly ground black
pepper

SERVES 4

1 Mix the minced beef with the chopped onion, celery, mixed herbs and mustard. Season well with salt and pepper, and bring together with your hands to form a firm mixture.

2 Divide the mixture into eight equal portions. Shape four portions into rounds and flatten each one slightly. Place a little of the crumbled cheese in the centre of each round.

3 Shape and flatten the remaining four portions and place on top. Use your hands to mould the rounds together, encasing the crumbled cheese, and shaping them into four burgers.

4 Cook on a medium barbecue for about 10 minutes or until cooked through, turning once. Split the burger buns and place a burger inside each. Serve with salad and mustard pickle.

THAI BEEF SALAD

° ° °

A hearty salad of beef and crunchy vegetables, laced with a tangy chilli and lime dressing.
The barbecued meat gives a truly delicious flavour to the salad.

INGREDIENTS

2 sirloin steaks, about
225g/8oz each
1 red onion, finely sliced
1/2 cucumber, finely sliced into
matchsticks
1 stalk lemon grass, finely chopped
30ml/2 tbsp chopped spring onions
juice of 2 limes
15–30ml/1–2 tbsp Thai fish sauce
2–4 red chillies, finely sliced, to
garnish
fresh coriander, Chinese mustard
cress and mint leaves, to garnish

SERVES 4

1 Barbecue or pan-fry the beef steaks until they are medium-rare. Allow the steaks to rest for 10–15 minutes.

2 When the steaks have cooled slightly, slice them thinly, using a heavy knife, and put the slices into a large bowl.

3 Add the sliced onion, cucumber matchsticks and chopped lemon grass.

4 Add the spring onions. Toss and season with lime juice and Thai fish sauce. Serve at room temperature or chilled, garnished with the chillies, coriander, mustard cress and mint.

NEW ORLEANS STEAK SALAD

o o o

The New Orleans "Poor Boy" started life in the Italian Creole community, as a sandwich filled
with leftover scraps. This salad, made with tender beef steak, is a variation on the sandwich.

INGREDIENTS

4 sirloin or rump steaks,
about 175g/6oz each
1 escarole lettuce
1 bunch watercress
4 tomatoes, quartered
4 large gherkins, sliced
4 spring onions, sliced
4 canned artichoke hearts, halved
175g/6oz button mushrooms,
sliced
12 green olives
120ml/4fl oz French dressing
salt and freshly ground black
pepper

SERVES 4

1 Season the steaks with plenty of black pepper and cook on a hot barbecue, or under a hot grill, for 4–6 minutes, turning once, until medium-rare. Cover and leave the steaks to rest in a warm place.

2 Combine the salad leaves with all the ingredients except the steak, and toss with the French dressing.

3 Divide the salad between 4 plates. Slice each steak diagonally and arrange the slices over the salad. Season with salt and fresh black pepper and serve.

SPICED BEEF SATAY

o o o

*Tender strips of steak threaded on skewers and spiced with the characteristic flavours
of Indonesia are popular with everyone.*

INGREDIENTS
*450g/1lb rump steak, cut in
1cm/1/2 in strips
5ml/1 tsp coriander seeds, dry-fried
and ground
2.5ml/1/2 tsp cumin seeds, dry-fried
and ground
5ml/1 tsp tamarind pulp
1 small onion
2 garlic cloves
15ml/1 tbsp brown sugar
15ml/1 tbsp dark soy sauce
salt*

TO SERVE
*cucumber chunks
lemon or lime wedges
Sambal Kecap*

MAKES 18 SKEWERS

1 Mix the meat and spices in a large
non-metallic bowl. Soak the tamarind
pulp in 75ml/3fl oz/1/3 cup water.

2 Strain the tamarind and reserve the
juice. Put the onion, garlic, tamarind
juice, sugar and soy sauce in a food
processor and blend well.

3 Pour the marinade over the meat
and spices in the bowl and toss well
together. Leave for at least 1 hour.

4 Meanwhile, soak some bamboo
skewers in water to prevent them
from burning while cooking. Thread
5 or 6 pieces of meat on to each skewer
and sprinkle with salt. Cook on a
medium-hot barbecue, turning the
skewers frequently and basting with
the marinade, until the meat is tender.

5 Serve with cucumber chunks
and wedges of lemon or lime for
squeezing over the meat. Sambal Kecap
makes a traditional accompaniment.

SAMBAL KECAP
Mix 1 fresh red chilli,
seeded and finely chopped,
2 crushed garlic cloves and
60ml/4 tbsp dark soy sauce with
20ml/4 tsp lemon juice and
30ml/2 tbsp hot water in a bowl.
Leave to stand for 30 minutes
before serving.

VEGETABLE-STUFFED BEEF ROLLS

· · ·

These Japanese-style beef rolls are very popular for al fresco meals. You could roll up many other vegetables in the sliced beef. Pork is also very good cooked this way.

INGREDIENTS

50g/2oz carrot
50g/2oz green pepper, seeded
bunch of spring onions
400g/14oz beef topside,
thinly sliced
plain flour, for dusting
15ml/1 tbsp olive oil
fresh parsley sprigs, to garnish

FOR THE SAUCE
30ml/2 tbsp sugar
45ml/3 tbsp soy sauce
45ml/3 tbsp mirin

SERVES 4

1 Use a sharp knife to shred the carrot and green pepper into 4–5cm/ 1½–2in lengths. Wash and peel the outer skins from the spring onions, then halve them lengthways. Shred the spring onions diagonally into 4–5cm/1½–2in lengths.

2 The beef slices should be no more than 2mm/1/12 in thick, and about 15cm/6in square. Lay a slice of beef on a chopping board and top with strips of the carrot, green pepper and spring onion. Roll up quite tightly and dust lightly with flour. Repeat with the remaining beef and vegetables.

3 Secure the beef rolls with cocktail sticks, soaked in water to prevent them from burning, and cook on a medium barbecue or in a pan over a medium heat, for 10–15 minutes, turning frequently, until golden brown and thoroughly cooked.

4 Blend the ingredients for the sauce in a small pan and cook to dissolve the sugar and form a glaze. Halve the cooked rolls, cutting at a slant, and stand them on a plate with the sloping cut ends facing upwards. Dress with the sauce and garnish with fresh parsley.

LAMB STEAKS MARINATED IN MINT AND SHERRY

° ° °

*The marinade in this recipe is extremely quick to prepare, and is the key
to its success: the sherry imparts a wonderful tang to the meat.*

INGREDIENTS

6 large lamb steaks or
12 smaller chops

FOR THE MARINADE
30ml/2 tbsp chopped fresh mint
leaves
15ml/1 tbsp black peppercorns
1 medium onion, chopped
120ml/4fl oz/½ cup sherry
60ml/4 tbsp extra virgin olive oil
2 garlic cloves

SERVES 6

1 Blend the mint leaves and
peppercorns in a food processor until
finely chopped. Add the onion and
process again until smooth. Add the
rest of the marinade ingredients and
process until completely mixed. The
marinade should be a thick consistency.

2 Add the marinade to the steaks or
chops and cover with clear film. Leave
in the fridge to marinate overnight.

3 Cook the steaks on a medium
barbecue for 10–15 minutes, basting
occasionally with the marinade.

SKEWERED LAMB WITH CORIANDER YOGURT

These Turkish kebabs are traditionally made with lamb, but lean beef or pork work equally well.
You can alternate pieces of pepper, lemon or onions with the meat for extra flavour and colour.

INGREDIENTS
900g/2lb lean boneless lamb
1 large onion, grated
3 bay leaves
5 thyme or rosemary sprigs
grated rind and juice of 1 lemon
2.5ml/¹/₂ tsp caster sugar
75ml/3fl oz/¹/₃ cup olive oil
salt and freshly ground black
pepper
sprigs of fresh rosemary, to garnish
barbecued lemon wedges, to serve

FOR THE CORIANDER YOGURT
150ml/¹/₄ pint/²/₃ cup thick natural
yogurt
15ml/1 tbsp chopped fresh mint
15ml/1 tbsp chopped fresh
coriander
10ml/2 tsp grated onion

SERVES 4

1 To make the coriander yogurt, mix together the natural yogurt, chopped fresh mint, chopped fresh coriander and grated onion. Transfer the yogurt to a serving bowl.

2 To make the kebabs, cut the lamb into 2.5cm/1in cubes and put in a bowl. Mix together the onion, herbs, lemon rind and juice, sugar and oil, then season to taste.

3 Pour the marinade over the meat in the bowl and stir to ensure the meat is thoroughly covered. Cover with clear film and leave to marinate in the fridge for several hours or overnight.

4 Drain the meat and thread on to metal skewers. Cook on a hot barbecue for about 10 minutes. Garnish with rosemary and barbecued lemon wedges and serve with the coriander yogurt.

LAMB BURGERS WITH REDCURRANT CHUTNEY

° ° °

These rather special burgers take a little extra time to prepare but are well worth it.
The redcurrant chutney is the perfect complement to the minty lamb taste.

INGREDIENTS

500g/1¼ lb minced lean lamb
1 small onion, finely chopped
30ml/2 tbsp finely chopped
fresh mint
30ml/2 tbsp finely chopped
fresh parsley
115g/4oz mozzarella cheese
30ml/2 tbsp oil, for basting
salt and freshly ground black
pepper

FOR THE REDCURRANT CHUTNEY
115g/4oz/1½ cups fresh or frozen
redcurrants
10ml/2 tsp clear honey
5ml/1 tsp balsamic vinegar
30ml/2 tbsp finely chopped mint

SERVES 4

1 In a large bowl, mix together the minced lamb, chopped onion, mint and parsley until evenly combined. Season well with plenty of salt and freshly ground black pepper.

Cook's Tip

If time is short, or if fresh redcurrants are not available, serve the burgers with ready-made redcurrant sauce.

2 Roughly divide the meat mixture into eight equal pieces and use your hands to press each of the pieces into flat rounds.

3 Cut the mozzarella cheese into four chunks. Place one chunk of cheese on half the lamb rounds. Top each with another round of meat mixture.

4 Press each of the two rounds of meat together firmly, making four flattish burger shapes. Use your fingers to blend the edges and seal in the cheese completely.

5 Place all the ingredients for the chutney in a bowl and mash them together with a fork. Season well with salt and freshly ground black pepper.

6 Brush the lamb burgers with olive oil and cook them over a moderately hot barbecue for about 15 minutes, turning once, until golden brown. Serve with the redcurrant chutney.

BARBECUED LAMB WITH POTATO SLICES

° ° ○

A traditional mixture of fresh herbs adds a summery flavour to this simple lamb dish.
A leg of lamb is easier to cook evenly on the barbecue if it's boned out, or "butterflied" first.

INGREDIENTS

1 leg of lamb, about 1.75kg/4½ lb
1 garlic clove, thinly sliced
handful of fresh flat-leaf parsley
handful of fresh sage
handful of fresh rosemary
handful of fresh thyme
90ml/6 tbsp dry sherry
60ml/4 tbsp walnut oil
500g/1¼ lb medium-size potatoes
salt and freshly ground
black pepper

SERVES 4

2 Use a sharp kitchen knife to scrape away the meat from the bone on both sides, until the bone is completely exposed. Carefully remove the bone and cut away any sinews and excess fat from the meat.

4 Place the meat in a bowl and pour over the sherry and walnut oil. Chop half the remaining herbs and scatter over the meat. Cover the bowl with a clean dish towel and leave to marinate in the fridge for 30 minutes.

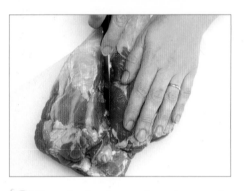

1 Place the lamb on a board, smooth side downwards, so that you can see where the bone lies. Using a sharp heavy knife, make a long cut through the flesh down to the bone.

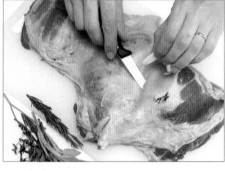

3 Cut through the thickest part of the meat so that you can open it out as flat as possible. Make several cuts in the lamb with a sharp kitchen knife, and push slivers of garlic and sprigs of fresh herbs into the cuts.

5 Remove the lamb from the marinade and season. Cook on a medium-hot barbecue for 30–35 minutes, turning occasionally and basting with the reserved marinade.

Cook's Tip

If you have a spit-roasting attachment, the lamb can be rolled and tied with herbs inside, and spit roasted for 1–1½ hours. A spit makes it much easier to cook larger pieces of lamb.

6 Scrub the potatoes, then cut them in thick slices. Brush with the marinade and place around the lamb. Cook for about 15 minutes, until golden brown.

LAMB WITH LAVENDER BALSAMIC MARINADE

Lavender is an unusual flavour to use with meat, but its heady, summery scent works well with barbecued lamb. If you prefer, rosemary can take its place.

2 Sprinkle the chopped fresh lavender over the lamb in the bowl.

3 Beat together the vinegar, olive oil and lemon juice and pour them over the lamb. Season well with salt and pepper and then turn to coat evenly.

4 Scatter a few lavender sprigs over the grill or on the coals of a medium-hot barbecue. Cook the lamb for about 15–20 minutes, turning once and basting with any remaining marinade, until golden brown on the outside and still slightly pink in the centre.

INGREDIENTS
4 racks of lamb, with 3–4 cutlets each
1 shallot, finely chopped
45ml/3 tbsp chopped fresh lavender
15ml/1 tbsp balsamic vinegar
30ml/2 tbsp olive oil
15ml/1 tbsp lemon juice
salt and freshly ground black pepper
handful of lavender sprigs

SERVES 4

1 Place the racks of lamb in a large mixing bowl or wide dish and sprinkle over the chopped shallot.

Lamb with Mint and Lemon

Use this simple and traditional marinade to make the most of fine quality lamb leg steaks.
Lemon and fresh mint combine extremely well with the flavour of barbecued lamb.

INGREDIENTS

4 lamb steaks, about
225g/8oz each
fresh mint leaves, to garnish

FOR THE MARINADE
grated rind and juice of ½ lemon
1 garlic clove, crushed
1 spring onion, finely chopped
5ml/1 tsp finely chopped fresh mint
30ml/2 tbsp extra virgin olive oil
salt and freshly ground black
pepper

SERVES 4

1 Mix all the marinade ingredients and season to taste. Place the lamb steaks in a shallow dish and add the marinade. Cover with clear film and leave to marinate in the fridge for several hours or overnight.

2 Drain the lamb and cook on a medium-hot barbecue for about 10–15 minutes until just cooked, basting with the marinade occasionally and turning once. Garnish the lamb steaks with the fresh mint leaves.

STUFFED AUBERGINES WITH LAMB

*Minced lamb and aubergines go together beautifully. This is an attractive dish,
using different coloured peppers in the lightly spiced stuffing mixture.*

INGREDIENTS

2 medium aubergines
30ml/2 tbsp vegetable oil
1 medium onion, sliced
5ml/1 tsp grated fresh root ginger
5ml/1 tsp chilli powder
1 garlic clove, crushed
1.5ml/¼ tsp turmeric
5ml/1 tsp salt
5ml/1 tsp ground coriander
1 medium tomato, chopped
350g/12oz minced lean lamb
1 medium green pepper, roughly
chopped
1 medium orange pepper, roughly
chopped
30ml/2 tbsp chopped fresh
coriander

FOR THE GARNISH
½ onion, sliced
2 cherry tomatoes, quartered
fresh coriander sprigs

SERVES 4

1 Cut the aubergines in half
lengthways with a heavy knife. Scoop
out most of the flesh and reserve it for
another dish. Brush the shells with a
little vegetable oil.

2 In a medium saucepan, heat 15ml/
1 tbsp oil and fry the sliced onion until
golden brown. Stir in the grated ginger,
chilli powder, garlic, turmeric, salt and
ground coriander. Add the chopped
tomato, lower the heat and cook for
about 5 minutes, stirring continuously.

3 Add the minced lamb to the
saucepan and continue to cook over
a medium heat for about 7–10 minutes.
Stir in the chopped fresh peppers and
the fresh coriander.

4 Spoon the lamb mixture into the
aubergine shells and brush the edges
of the shells with the remaining oil.
Cook on a medium barbecue for 15–20
minutes until cooked through. Garnish
with sliced onion, cherry tomatoes and
coriander, and serve with rice, if liked.

VEAL CHOPS WITH BASIL BUTTER

∘ ∘ ∘

Veal chops from the loin are an expensive cut and are best cooked quickly and simply.
The flavour of basil goes well with veal, but other herbs can be used instead if you prefer.

INGREDIENTS

25g/1oz/2 tbsp butter, softened
15ml/1 tbsp Dijon mustard
15ml/1 tbsp chopped fresh basil
olive oil, for brushing
2 veal loin chops, 2.5cm/1in thick,
about 225g/8oz each
salt and freshly ground black
pepper
fresh basil sprigs, to garnish

SERVES 2

1 To make the basil butter, cream the softened butter with the Dijon mustard and chopped fresh basil in a large mixing bowl, then season with plenty of freshly ground black pepper.

2 Brush both sides of each chop with olive oil and season with a little salt.

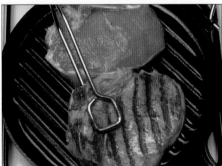

3 Cook the chops on a hot barbecue for 7–10 minutes, basting with oil and turning once, until done to your liking. (Medium-rare meat will still be slightly soft when pressed, medium meat will be springy and well-done firm.) Top each chop with half the basil butter and serve at once, garnished with basil.

PORK AND PINEAPPLE SATAY

. . .

This variation on the classic satay has added pineapple, but keeps the traditional coconut and peanut sauce.

INGREDIENTS

500g/1¼ lb pork fillet
1 small onion, chopped
1 garlic clove, chopped
60ml/4 tbsp soy sauce
finely grated rind of ½ lemon
5ml/1 tsp ground cumin
5ml/1 tsp ground coriander
5ml/1 tsp ground turmeric
5ml/1 tsp dark muscovado sugar
225g/8oz can pineapple chunks, or
1 small fresh pineapple, peeled and
diced
salt and freshly ground black
pepper

FOR THE SATAY SAUCE
175ml/6fl oz/¾ cup coconut milk
115g/4oz/6 tbsp crunchy peanut
butter
1 garlic clove, crushed
10ml/2 tsp soy sauce
5ml/1 tsp dark muscovado sugar

SERVES 4

1 Using a sharp kitchen knife, trim any fat from the pork fillet and cut it in 2.5cm/1in cubes. Place the meat in a large mixing bowl and set aside.

2 Place the onion, garlic, soy sauce, lemon rind, spices and sugar in a blender or food processor. Add two pieces of pineapple and process until the mixture is almost smooth.

3 Add the paste to the pork, tossing well to coat evenly. Thread the pieces of pork on to bamboo skewers, with the remaining pineapple pieces.

4 To make the sauce, pour the coconut milk into a small saucepan and stir in the peanut butter. Stir in the remaining sauce ingredients and heat gently over the barbecue, stirring until smooth and hot. Cover and keep warm on the edge of the barbecue.

5 Cook the pork and pineapple skewers on a medium-hot barbecue for 10–12 minutes, turning occasionally, until golden brown and thoroughly cooked. Serve with the satay sauce.

Cook's Tip

If you cannot buy coconut milk, use creamed coconut in a block. Dissolve a 50g/2oz piece in 150ml/¼ pint/⅔ cup boiling water and use as above.

LEMON GRASS PORK CHOPS WITH MUSHROOMS

○ ○ ○

Thai flavourings are used to make an aromatic marinade and a spicy sauce. The sauce can be put together in a pan on the barbecue while the chops and mushrooms are cooking.

INGREDIENTS

4 pork chops, about 225g/8oz each
4 large field mushrooms
45ml/3 tbsp vegetable oil
4 red chillies, seeded and finely sliced
45ml/3 tbsp Thai fish sauce
90ml/6 tbsp lime juice
4 shallots, chopped
5ml/1 tsp roasted ground rice
30ml/2 tbsp spring onions, chopped
fresh coriander leaves, to garnish
4 spring onions, shredded, to garnish

FOR THE MARINADE

2 garlic cloves, chopped
15ml/1 tbsp sugar
15ml/1 tbsp Thai fish sauce
30ml/2 tbsp soy sauce
15ml/1 tbsp sesame oil
15ml/1 tbsp whisky or dry sherry
2 stalks lemon grass, finely chopped
2 spring onions, chopped

SERVES 4

3 Place the mushrooms and marinated pork chops on a rack and brush with 15ml/1 tbsp vegetable oil. Cook the pork chops on a medium-hot barbecue for 10–15 minutes and the mushrooms for about 2 minutes, turning once. Brush both with the marinade while cooking.

4 Meanwhile, heat the remaining oil in a small frying pan, then remove from the heat and mix in the remaining ingredients. Put the pork chops and mushrooms on a serving plate and spoon over the sauce. Garnish with the fresh coriander leaves and shredded spring onions.

1 To make the marinade, mix all the ingredients together . Arrange the pork chops in a shallow dish. Pour over the marinade and leave for 1–2 hours.

FARMHOUSE PIZZA

∘ ∘ ∘

Pizza is not a dish usually associated with barbecue cooking, but in fact the open fire gives the base a wonderfully crisp texture. Shape the dough to fit the grill rack of your barbecue.

INGREDIENTS

90ml/6 tbsp olive oil
225g/8oz button mushrooms,
sliced
300g/11oz packet pizza-base mix
300ml/½ pint/1¼ cups tomato
sauce
300g/11oz mozzarella cheese,
thinly sliced
115g/4oz wafer-thin smoked
ham slices
6 bottled artichoke hearts in oil,
drained and sliced
50g/2oz can anchovy fillets,
drained and halved lengthways
10 stoned black olives, halved
30ml/2 tbsp chopped fresh oregano
45ml/3 tbsp freshly grated
Parmesan cheese
freshly ground black pepper

SERVES 8

1 Heat 30ml/2 tbsp oil in a pan, add the mushrooms and fry until all the juices have evaporated. Leave to cool.

2 Make up the pizza dough according to the directions on the packet. Roll it out on a floured surface to a 30 × 25cm/12 × 10in rectangle. Brush with oil and place, oiled side down, on a medium-hot barbecue. Cook for 6 minutes until firm.

3 Brush the uncooked side of the dough with oil and turn over. Spread over the tomato sauce and arrange the sliced mozzarella on top. Scrunch up the smoked ham and arrange on top with the artichoke hearts, anchovies and cooked mushrooms.

4 Dot with the halved olives, then sprinkle over the fresh oregano and Parmesan. Drizzle over the remaining olive oil and season with black pepper. Return to the barbecue and cook for a further 8–10 minutes, or until the dough is golden brown and crisp.

71

Poultry
And Game

—◁◈▷—

Chicken cooked on a barbecue is unfailingly popular with both adults

and children, and it can be as simple or sophisticated as you choose:

it is very versatile and takes on a whole range of flavours with great

success. Buy breast fillets to make delicious kebabs and salads with a

minimum of preparation, or cook drumsticks and thighs with robust

spicy coatings. Whole birds can be roasted very effectively on a spit,

or they can be flattened out by removing the backbone and cooked on

the grill rack. It is vital to make sure chicken is always very thoroughly

cooked – it needs a medium heat to cook it through without charring

the outside. Don't forget other types of poultry, particularly duck,

which stays beautifully juicy and moist when cooked on a barbecue.

CHICKEN WITH PINEAPPLE

° ° °

The pineapple juice in this Indian recipe is used to tenderize the meat, but it also gives the chicken a deliciously tangy sweetness.

INGREDIENTS

225g/8oz can pineapple chunks in juice
5ml/1 tsp ground cumin
5ml/1 tsp ground coriander
1 garlic clove, crushed
5ml/1 tsp chilli powder
5ml/1 tsp salt
30ml/2 tbsp natural low-fat yogurt
15ml/1 tbsp chopped fresh coriander
few drops orange food colouring (optional)
275g/10oz/2 cups chicken breast and thigh meat, skinned and boned
½ red pepper
½ yellow or green pepper
1 large onion
6 cherry tomatoes
15ml/1 tbsp vegetable oil

SERVES 6

1 Drain the canned pineapple into a bowl. Reserve twelve large chunks of pineapple. Squeeze the juice from the remaining chunks into the bowl, then discard the chunks. You should be left with about 120ml/4fl oz/½ cup pineapple juice.

2 In a large bowl, blend together the cumin, ground coriander, garlic, chilli powder, salt, yogurt, fresh coriander and food colouring, if using. Pour in the pineapple juice and mix together.

3 Cut the chicken into cubes, add to the yogurt and spice mixture and leave to marinate for about 1–1½ hours. Cut the peppers and onion into chunks.

4 Arrange the chicken pieces, vegetables and reserved pineapple chunks alternately on 6 skewers.

5 Brush the kebabs with oil and cook on a medium barbecue for about 10 minutes, turning regularly and basting the chicken pieces regularly with the marinade, until cooked through. Serve with salad or plain boiled rice.

CITRUS KEBABS

○ ○ ○

Serve these succulent barbecued chicken kebabs on a bed of lettuce leaves, garnished with sprigs of fresh mint and orange and lemon slices.

INGREDIENTS

4 chicken breasts, skinned and boned
fresh mint sprigs, to garnish
orange, lemon or lime slices, to garnish

FOR THE MARINADE
finely grated rind and juice of ½ orange
finely grated rind and juice of ½ lemon or lime
30ml/2 tbsp olive oil
30ml/2 tbsp clear honey
30ml/2 tbsp chopped fresh mint
1.5ml/¼ tsp ground cumin
salt and freshly ground black pepper

SERVES 4

1 Use a heavy knife to cut the chicken into 2.5cm/1in cubes.

2 Mix the marinade ingredients together in a large mixing bowl, add the chicken and cover with clear film. Leave to marinate for at least 2 hours, or overnight in the fridge.

3 Thread the chicken on to metal skewers and cook on a medium barbecue for 10 minutes, basting with the marinade and turning frequently. Garnish with mint and citrus slices.

SWEET AND SOUR KEBABS
∘ ∘ ∘

*This marinade contains sugar and will burn very easily, so cook the kebabs slowly
and turn them often. Serve these kebabs with Harlequin Rice.*

INGREDIENTS

*2 chicken breasts, skinned and
boned*
*8 pickling onions or 2 medium
onions*
4 rindless streaky bacon rashers
3 firm bananas
1 red pepper, diced

FOR THE MARINADE
30ml/2 tbsp soft brown sugar
15ml/1 tbsp Worcestershire sauce
30ml/2 tbsp lemon juice
*salt and freshly ground black
pepper*

FOR THE HARLEQUIN RICE
30ml/2 tbsp olive oil
1 small red pepper, diced
*225g/8oz/generous 1 cup cooked
rice*
115g/4oz/1 cup cooked peas

SERVES 4

1 Mix together the marinade ingredients. Cut each chicken breast into four pieces, add to the marinade, cover and leave for at least 4 hours, or preferably overnight in the fridge.

2 Peel the pickling onions, blanch them in boiling water for 5 minutes and drain. If using medium onions, quarter them after blanching.

3 Cut each rasher of bacon in half with a sharp knife. Peel the bananas and cut each one into three pieces. Wrap half a bacon rasher around each of the banana pieces.

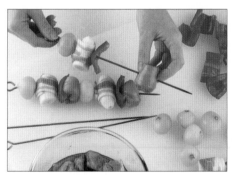

4 Thread the bacon and bananas on to metal skewers with the chicken pieces, onions and pepper pieces. Brush generously with the marinade.

5 Cook on a low barbecue for about 15 minutes, turning and basting frequently with the marinade.

6 Meanwhile, heat the oil in a frying pan and stir-fry the diced pepper briefly. Add the rice and peas and stir until heated through. Serve the Harlequin Rice with the kebabs.

BLACKENED CAJUN CHICKEN AND CORN

° ° °

This is a classic American Deep-South method of cooking in a spiced coating, which can be used
for poultry, meat or fish. The coating should begin to char and blacken slightly at the edges.

INGREDIENTS

8 chicken joints (drumsticks,
thighs or wings)
2 whole corn cobs
10ml/2 tsp garlic salt
10ml/2 tsp ground black pepper
7.5ml/1½ tsp ground cumin
7.5ml/1½ tsp paprika
5ml/1 tsp cayenne pepper
45ml/3 tbsp melted butter
chopped parsley, to garnish

SERVES 4

1 Trim any excess fat from the
chicken, but leave the skin in place.
Slash the thickest parts with a knife,
to allow the flavours to penetrate the
meat as much as possible.

2 Pull the husks and silks off the
corn cobs, then rinse them under cold
running water and pat them dry with
kitchen paper. Cut the cobs into thick
slices, using a heavy kitchen knife.

3 Mix together all the spices. Brush
the chicken and corn with the melted
butter and sprinkle the spices over
them. Toss well to coat evenly.

4 Cook the chicken pieces on a
medium-hot barbecue for about 25
minutes, turning occasionally. Add
the corn after 15 minutes, and grill,
turning often, until golden brown.
Serve garnished with chopped parsley.

CHICKEN WITH HERB AND RICOTTA STUFFING

These little chicken drumsticks are full of flavour and the stuffing and bacon help to keep them moist and tender.

INGREDIENTS

60ml/4 tbsp ricotta cheese
1 garlic clove, crushed
45ml/3 tbsp mixed chopped fresh herbs, such as chives, flat-leaf parsley and mint
30ml/2 tbsp fresh brown breadcrumbs
8 chicken drumsticks
8 smoked streaky bacon rashers
5ml/1 tsp whole-grain mustard
15ml/1 tbsp sunflower oil
salt and freshly ground black pepper

SERVES 4

1 Mix together the ricotta, garlic, herbs and breadcrumbs. Season well with plenty of salt and pepper.

2 Carefully loosen the skin from each drumstick and spoon a little of the herb stuffing under each, smoothing the skin back over firmly.

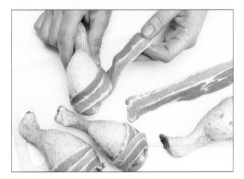

3 Wrap a bacon rasher tightly around the wide end of each drumstick, to hold the skin in place over the stuffing during the cooking time.

4 Mix together the mustard and oil and brush them over the chicken. Cook on a medium-hot barbecue for about 25 minutes, turning occasionally.

BABY CHICKENS WITH LIME AND CHILLI

· · ·

Poussins are small birds which are ideal for one to two portions. The best way to prepare them is spatchcocked – flattened out – to ensure more even cooking.

INGREDIENTS

4 poussins or Cornish hens, about
450g/1lb each
45ml/3 tbsp butter
30ml/2 tbsp sun-dried tomato
paste
finely grated rind of 1 lime
10ml/2 tsp chilli sauce
juice of ½ lime
lime wedges, to serve
fresh flat leaf parsley sprigs,
to garnish

SERVES 4

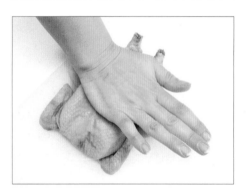

1 Place each poussin on a chopping board, breast-side upwards, and press down firmly with your hand, to break the breastbone.

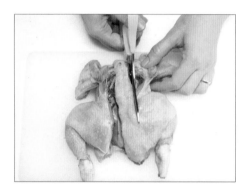

2 Turn the poussin over and, with poultry shears or strong kitchen scissors, cut down either side of the backbone. Remove it and discard.

3 Turn the poussin breast-side up and flatten it gently. Lift the breast skin carefully and gently ease your fingertips underneath, to loosen it from the flesh.

4 Mix together the butter, sun-dried tomato paste, lime rind and chilli sauce in a small bowl. Spread about three-quarters of the mixture under the skin of the poussins, smoothing it evenly over the surface of the flesh.

5 To hold the poussins flat during cooking, thread two bamboo skewers through each bird, crossing at the centre. Each skewer should pass through a drumstick and then out through a wing on the other side.

6 Mix the reserved paste with the lime juice and brush it over the skin of the poussins. Cook on a medium-hot barbecue, turning occasionally, for 25–30 minutes, or until there is no trace of pink in the juices when the flesh is pierced. Garnish with lime wedges and fresh flat leaf parsley.

CHICKEN COOKED IN SPICES AND COCONUT

∘ ∘ ∘

This chicken dish can be prepared in advance until you are ready to light the barbecue.
Serve the chicken with naan bread.

INGREDIENTS

200g/7oz block creamed coconut
300ml/½ pint/1¼ cups boiling
water
3 garlic cloves, chopped
2 spring onions, chopped
1 fresh green chilli, chopped
5cm/2in piece fresh root ginger,
chopped
5ml/1 tsp fennel seeds
2.5ml/½ tsp black peppercorns
seeds from 4 cardamom pods
30ml/2 tbsp ground coriander
5ml/1 tsp ground cumin
5ml/1 tsp ground star anise
5ml/1 tsp ground nutmeg
2.5ml/½ tsp ground cloves
2.5ml/½ tsp ground turmeric
4 large chicken breasts, skinned
and boned
onion rings and fresh coriander
sprigs, to garnish

SERVES 4

2 Make several diagonal cuts across the chicken breasts. Arrange in a layer in a shallow dish. Spoon over half the coconut mixture and toss well to coat the chicken breasts evenly. Cover the dish and leave to marinate for at least 30 minutes, or overnight in the fridge.

3 Cook the chicken on a medium barbecue for about 12–15 minutes, turning once, until well browned and thoroughly cooked. Heat the remaining coconut mixture gently until boiling. Serve with the chicken, garnished with onion rings and sprigs of coriander.

1 Break up the coconut and put it in a jug. Pour the boiling water over and leave to dissolve. Place the chopped garlic, spring onions, chilli, ginger and all of the spices in a blender or food processor. Pour in the coconut mixture and blend to a smooth paste.

GRILLED CASHEW NUT CHICKEN

° ° °

This dish comes from the beautiful Indonesian island of Bali, where nuts are widely used as a base for sauces and marinades. Serve it with a green salad and a hot chilli dipping sauce.

INGREDIENTS

4 chicken legs
radishes, sliced, to garnish
½ cucumber, sliced, to garnish
Chinese leaves, to serve

FOR THE MARINADE
50g/2oz raw cashew or macadamia nuts
2 shallots, or 1 small onion, finely chopped
2 garlic cloves, crushed
2 small red chillies, chopped
5cm/2in piece lemon grass
15ml/1 tbsp tamarind sauce
30ml/2 tbsp dark soy sauce
15ml/1 tbsp Thai fish sauce
10ml/2 tsp sugar
2.5ml/½ tsp salt
15ml/1 tbsp rice or white wine vinegar

SERVES 4

1 Using a sharp kitchen knife, slash the chicken legs several times through to the bone. Chop off the knuckle end and discard.

2 To make the marinade, place the cashew or macadamia nuts in a food processor or pestle and mortar and grind until fine.

3 Add the chopped shallots or onion, garlic, chillies and lemon grass and blend. Add the remaining marinade ingredients and blend again.

4 Spread the marinade over the chicken and leave for up to 8 hours in the fridge. Cook the chicken on a medium barbecue for 25 minutes, basting and turning occasionally. Garnish with radishes and cucumber and serve on a bed of Chinese leaves.

HOT AND SOUR CHICKEN SALAD

° ° °

This chicken salad from Vietnam is equally delicious made with prawns.
Allow 450g/1lb fresh prawn tails to serve four people.

INGREDIENTS

2 chicken breasts, skinned and boned
115g/4oz bean sprouts
1 head Chinese leaves, shredded
2 medium carrots, cut into matchsticks
1 red onion, thinly sliced
2 large gherkins, sliced

FOR THE MARINADE
1 small red chilli, seeded and finely chopped
1cm/1/2in piece fresh root ginger, chopped
1 garlic clove, crushed
15ml/1 tbsp crunchy peanut butter
30ml/2 tbsp chopped fresh coriander
5ml/1 tsp sugar
2.5ml/1/2 tsp salt
15ml/1 tbsp rice or white wine vinegar
60ml/4 tbsp vegetable oil
10ml/2 tsp Thai fish sauce

SERVES 4–6

1 Slice the chicken breasts thinly and place in a shallow bowl. Grind the chilli, ginger and garlic in a food processor or pestle and mortar, then add the peanut butter, chopped fresh coriander, sugar and salt.

2 Add the rice or white wine vinegar, 30ml/2 tbsp of the oil and the fish sauce to the ingredients in the food processor. Combine well. Cover the chicken with the spice mixture and let marinate for at least 2–3 hours.

3 Cook the chicken on a medium-hot barbecue or in a frying pan on the hob for about 5 minutes, basting often and turning once. Arrange the salad ingredients on a serving dish and top with the cooked chicken.

CHICKEN SALAD WITH LAVENDER AND HERBS
○ ○ ○

The delightful scent of lavender has a natural affinity with sweet garlic, orange and other wild herbs. The addition of fried polenta makes this salad both filling and delicious.

INGREDIENTS

4 boneless chicken breasts
900ml/1½ pints/3¾ cups light chicken stock
175g/6oz/1 cup fine polenta or cornmeal
50g/2oz butter, plus extra for greasing
450g/1lb young spinach
175g/6oz lamb's lettuce
8 sprigs fresh lavender
8 small tomatoes, halved
salt and freshly ground black pepper

FOR THE MARINADE
6 fresh lavender flowers
10ml/2 tsp finely grated orange zest
2 garlic cloves, crushed
10ml/2 tsp clear honey
30ml/2 tbsp olive oil
10ml/2 tsp chopped fresh thyme
10ml/2 tsp chopped fresh marjoram
salt

SERVES 4

1 To make the marinade, strip the lavender flowers from the stems and combine with the orange zest, garlic, honey and salt. Add the oil and herbs. Slash the chicken deeply, spread the mixture over the chicken and leave to marinate in the fridge for 20 minutes.

2 To make the polenta, bring the chicken stock to the boil in a heavy saucepan. Add the cornmeal in a steady stream, stirring all the time until thick. Turn the cooked polenta out on to a shallow buttered tray and leave to cool.

3 Cook the chicken on a medium barbecue or under the grill for about 15 minutes, basting with the marinade and turning once, until cooked through.

4 Cut the polenta into 2.5cm/1in cubes using a wet knife. Heat the butter in a large frying pan and fry the polenta until golden.

5 Divide the salad leaves between four dinner plates. Slice each chicken breast and arrange over the salad. Arrange the polenta among the salad, decorate with sprigs of lavender and tomato halves, season with salt and freshly ground black pepper and serve.

CHICKEN SALAD WITH CORIANDER DRESSING

° ° °

Serve this salad warm to make the most of the wonderful flavour of barbecued chicken basted with a marinade of coriander, sesame and mustard.

INGREDIENTS

4 medium chicken breasts, skinned
and boned
225g/8oz mangetout
2 heads decorative lettuce such as
lollo rosso or feuille de chêne
3 carrots, cut into matchsticks
175g/6oz button mushrooms,
sliced
6 bacon rashers, fried and chopped

FOR THE CORIANDER DRESSING
120ml/4fl oz/½ cup lemon juice
30ml/2 tbsp wholegrain mustard
250ml/8fl oz/1 cup olive oil
65ml/2½ fl oz/⅓ cup sesame oil
5ml/1 tsp coriander seeds, crushed
15ml/1 tbsp chopped fresh
coriander, to garnish

SERVES 6

1 Mix all the dressing ingredients in a bowl. Place the chicken breasts in a dish and pour over half the dressing. Marinate overnight in the fridge. Refrigerate the remaining dressing.

2 Cook the mangetout for 2 minutes in boiling water, then refresh in cold water. Tear the lettuces into small pieces and mix all the other salad ingredients and the bacon together. Arrange the salad on individual dishes.

3 Cook the chicken breasts on a medium barbecue for 10–15 minutes, basting with the marinade and turning once, until cooked through. Slice them on the diagonal into thin pieces. Divide between the bowls of salad and add some of the dressing to each dish. Combine quickly and scatter some fresh coriander over each bowl.

MARYLAND SALAD

Barbecue-grilled chicken, sweetcorn, bacon, banana and watercress combine here in a sensational main course salad. Serve with buttered jacket potatoes.

INGREDIENTS

4 boneless chicken breasts
olive oil, for brushing
225g/8oz rindless unsmoked bacon
4 whole corn cobs
45ml/3 tbsp melted butter
4 ripe bananas, peeled and halved
4 tomatoes, halved
1 escarole or butterhead lettuce
1 bunch watercress
salt and freshly ground black pepper

FOR THE DRESSING
75ml/5 tbsp groundnut oil
15ml/1 tbsp white wine vinegar
10ml/2 tsp maple syrup
10ml/2 tsp mild mustard

SERVES 4

3 Combine the dressing ingredients with 15ml/1 tbsp water in a screw-top jar and shake well to mix. Wash and spin the lettuce leaves, then toss the salad in the dressing.

4 Distribute the dressed leaves between four large plates. Slice the chicken and arrange over the leaves with the bacon, banana, sweetcorn and tomatoes. Season well and serve.

1 Season the chicken breasts, brush with oil and cook on a medium barbecue or under the grill for 15–20 minutes, turning once. Barbecue the bacon for 8–10 minutes or until crisp.

2 Bring a large pan of water to the boil and cook the corn cobs for 20 minutes, until tender. For extra flavour, brush with butter and brown on the barbecue. Barbecue the bananas and tomatoes for 6–8 minutes: brush these with butter too if you wish.

THAI GRILLED CHICKEN

*Thai grilled chicken is especially delicious when cooked on the barbecue.
Serve it on a bed of crisp salad with lime wedges to offset its richness.*

INGREDIENTS

900g/2lb chicken drumsticks or
thighs
salt and freshly ground
black pepper
crisp lettuce leaves, to serve
1/2 cucumber, cut into strips,
to garnish
4 spring onions, trimmed,
to garnish
2 limes, quartered, to garnish

FOR THE MARINADE
5ml/1 tsp black peppercorns
2.5ml/1/2 tsp caraway or cumin
seeds
20ml/4 tsp sugar
10ml/2 tsp paprika
2cm/3/4in piece fresh root ginger,
chopped
3 garlic cloves, crushed
15g/1/2oz coriander, white root or
stem, finely chopped
45ml/3 tbsp vegetable oil

SERVES 4–6

1 Chop through the narrow end
of each drumstick with a heavy knife.
Score the chicken pieces deeply to
allow the marinade to penetrate and
arrange in a shallow bowl.

2 Grind the peppercorns, caraway
or cumin seeds and sugar in a pestle
and mortar or a food processor. Add
the paprika, ginger, garlic, coriander
and oil and grind to a paste.

3 Spread the marinade over the
chicken and leave to marinate in the
fridge for 6 hours. Cook the chicken
on a medium barbecue for about 20
minutes, basting with the marinade and
turning once. Season, arrange on a bed
of lettuce and garnish before serving.

MEDITERRANEAN TURKEY SKEWERS

These attractive kebabs can be assembled in advance and left to marinate until you are ready to cook them. Barbecuing intensifies the Mediterranean flavours of the vegetables.

INGREDIENTS

2 medium courgettes
1 long thin aubergine
300g/11oz boneless turkey, cut into 5cm/2in cubes
12–16 pickling onions
1 red or yellow pepper, cut into 5cm/2in squares

FOR THE MARINADE
90ml/6 tbsp olive oil
45ml/3 tbsp fresh lemon juice
1 garlic clove, finely chopped
30ml/2 tbsp chopped fresh basil
salt and freshly ground black pepper

SERVES 4

3 Prepare the skewers by alternating the turkey, onions and pepper pieces. Lay the prepared skewers on a platter and sprinkle with the flavoured oil. Leave to marinate for 30 minutes.

4 Cook on a medium barbecue or under a grill for about 10 minutes, or until the turkey is cooked and the vegetables are tender, turning the skewers occasionally.

1 To make the marinade, mix the olive oil with the lemon juice, garlic and chopped fresh basil. Season well with plenty of salt and black pepper.

2 Slice the courgettes and aubergine lengthways into strips 5mm/¼ in thick. Cut them crossways about two-thirds down their length. Discard the shorter lengths. Wrap half the turkey pieces with the courgette slices and the other half with the aubergine slices.

QUAIL WITH A FIVE-SPICE MARINADE

Blending and grinding your own five-spice powder for this Vietnamese dish will give the freshest-tasting results. If you are short of time, buy a ready-mixed blend from the supermarket.

INGREDIENTS

6 quails, cleaned
2 spring onions, roughly chopped, to garnish
mandarin orange or satsuma, to garnish
banana leaves, to serve

FOR THE MARINADE
2 pieces star anise
10ml/2 tsp ground cinnamon
10ml/2 tsp fennel seeds
10ml/2 tsp Sichuan pepper
a pinch ground cloves
1 small onion, finely chopped
1 garlic clove, crushed
60ml/4 tbsp clear honey
30ml/2 tbsp dark soy sauce

SERVES 4–6

1 Remove the backbones from the quails by cutting down either side with a pair of strong kitchen scissors.

2 Flatten the birds with the palm of your hand and secure each bird using two bamboo skewers.

3 To make the marinade, place the five spices in a pestle and mortar or spice mill and grind into a fine powder. Add the chopped onion, garlic, clear honey and soy sauce, and combine until thoroughly mixed.

4 Arrange the quails on a flat dish and pour over the marinade. Cover with clear film and leave in the fridge for 8 hours or overnight for the flavours to mingle.

5 Cook the quails on a medium barbecue for 15–20 minutes until golden brown, basting occasionally with the marinade and turning once.

6 To garnish, remove the outer zest from the mandarin orange or satsuma, using a vegetable peeler. Shred the zest finely and combine with the chopped spring onions. Arrange the quails on a bed of banana leaves and garnish with the orange zest and spring onions.

Cook's Tip
If you prefer, or if quails are not available, you could use other poultry such as poussins as a substitute.

PHEASANTS WITH SAGE AND LEMON

Pheasant is quick to cook and makes a really special summer meal.
This recipe can also be used for guinea fowl.

INGREDIENTS

2 pheasants, about 450g/1lb each
1 lemon
60ml/4 tbsp chopped fresh sage
3 shallots
5ml/1 tsp Dijon mustard
15ml/1 tbsp brandy or dry sherry
150ml/5fl oz/⅔ cup crème fraîche
salt and freshly ground black
pepper
lemon wedges and sage sprigs, to
garnish

SERVES 4

2 Finely grate the rind from half the lemon and slice the rest thinly. Mix together the lemon rind and half the chopped sage in a small bowl.

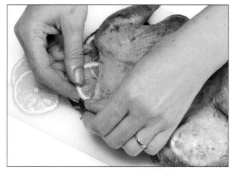

3 Loosen the skin on the breasts and legs of the pheasants and push a little of the sage mixture under each. Tuck the lemon slices under the skin, smoothing the skin back firmly.

5 Meanwhile, cook the shallots on the barbecue for about 10–12 minutes, turning occasionally, until the skin is blackened and the inside very soft. Peel off the skins, chop the flesh roughly and mash it with the Dijon mustard and brandy or sherry.

6 Stir in the crème fraîche and add the reserved chopped sage. Season with plenty of salt and freshly ground black pepper. Serve the dressing with the pheasants, garnished with lemon wedges and sprigs of fresh sage.

1 Place the pheasants, breast-side upwards, on a chopping board and cut them in half lengthways, using poultry shears or a sharp kitchen knife.

4 Place the half-pheasants on a medium-hot barbecue and cook for about 25–30 minutes, turning once.

Cook's Tip
Try to choose pheasants with undamaged skins, so that the flavourings stay in place during cooking.

SPICED DUCK WITH PEARS

⚬ ⚬ ⚬

This delicious casserole can be cooked on the barbecue or stove. The browned pears are added towards the end of cooking, along with a pine nut and garlic paste to flavour and thicken.

INGREDIENTS

*6 duck portions, either breast or
leg pieces
15ml/1 tbsp olive oil
1 large onion, thinly sliced
1 cinnamon stick, halved
2 thyme sprigs
475ml/16fl oz/2 cups duck or
chicken stock*

TO FINISH

*3 firm ripe pears, peeled and cored
30ml/2 tbsp olive oil
2 garlic cloves, sliced
25g/1oz ⅓ cup pine nuts
2.5ml/½ tsp saffron strands
25g/1oz/2 tbsp raisins
salt and freshly ground black
pepper
thyme sprigs or parsley, to garnish*

SERVES 6

1 Fry the duck portions in olive oil for 5 minutes, until golden, or brush the portions with oil and cook them on a hot barbecue for 8–10 minutes, until golden. Transfer the duck to a large flameproof dish. If frying, drain off all but 15ml/1 tbsp of fat left in the pan.

2 Fry the onion in the frying pan for 5 minutes until golden. Add the cinnamon stick, thyme and stock and bring to the boil. Pour over the duck in the dish and cook slowly on a low barbecue for about 1¼ hours.

3 Halve the pears, brush with oil and barbecue until brown, or fry the pears in the oil on the hob. Pound the garlic, pine nuts and saffron with a pestle and mortar, to make a thick, smooth paste.

4 Add the paste, raisins and pears to the flameproof dish. Cook for 15 minutes until the pears are tender.

5 Season to taste and garnish with the fresh herbs. Serve with mashed potatoes and a green vegetable, if liked.

Cook's Tip

A good stock is essential for this dish. Buy a large duck (plus two extra duck breasts if you want portions to be generous) and joint it yourself, using the giblets and carcass for stock. If you buy duck portions, use a well-flavoured chicken stock.

APRICOT DUCK WITH BEAN SPROUT SALAD

Duck is rich in fat, so it stays beautifully moist when cooked on a barbecue,
while any excess fat drains away.

INGREDIENTS
4 plump duck breasts, with skin
1 small red onion, thinly sliced
115g/4oz/³/4 cup ready-to-eat dried
apricots
15ml/1 tbsp clear honey
5ml/1 tsp sesame oil
10ml/2 tsp ground star anise
salt and freshly ground black
pepper

FOR THE SALAD
¹/2 head Chinese leaves, finely
shredded
150g/5oz/2 cups bean sprouts
2 spring onions, shredded
15ml/1 tbsp light soy sauce
15ml/1 tbsp groundnut oil
5ml/1 tsp sesame oil
5ml/1 tsp clear honey

SERVES 4

1 Place the duck breasts, skin-side down, on a chopping board or clean work surface and cut a long slit down one side with a sharp kitchen knife, cutting not quite through, to form a large pocket.

2 Tuck the slices of onion and the apricots inside the pocket and press the breast firmly back into shape. Secure with metal skewers.

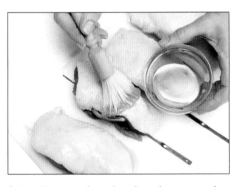

3 Mix together the clear honey and sesame oil and brush generously over the duck, particularly the skin. Sprinkle over the star anise and season with plenty of salt and fresh black pepper.

4 To make the salad, mix together the shredded Chinese leaves, bean sprouts and shredded spring onions in a large bowl.

5 Shake together all the salad dressing ingredients in a screw-topped jar. Season to taste with salt and pepper. Toss into the salad.

6 Cook the duck over a medium-hot barbecue for 12–15 minutes, turning once, until golden brown. The duck should be slightly pink in the centre.

Cook's Tip
If you prefer not to eat the bean sprouts raw, they can be blanched by plunging them into boiling water for 1 minute. Drain and refresh in cold water.

DUCK BREASTS WITH RED PEPPER JELLY GLAZE

∘ ∘ ∘

Sweet potatoes have pinkish skins and flesh varying from creamy white to deep orange.
Choose a long cylindrical tuber to make neat round slices for this Cajun dish.

INGREDIENTS

2 duck breasts
1 sweet potato, about 400g/14oz
30ml/2 tbsp red pepper jelly
15ml/1 tbsp sherry vinegar
50g/2oz/4 tbsp butter, melted
coarse sea salt and freshly ground
black pepper

SERVES 2

4 Meanwhile, warm the red pepper jelly and sherry vinegar together in a bowl set over a saucepan of hot water, stirring to mix them as the jelly melts. Brush the skin of the duck with this jelly glaze and return to the barbecue, skin-side down, for a further 2–3 minutes to caramelize it.

5 Brush the sweet potato slices with melted butter and sprinkle with coarse sea salt. Cook on a hot barbecue for 8–10 minutes until soft, brushing with more butter and sprinkling with salt and pepper when you turn them. Serve the duck sliced with the sweet potatoes and accompany with a green salad.

1 Slash the skin of the duck breasts diagonally at 2.5cm/1in intervals and rub plenty of salt and pepper over the skin and into the cuts.

2 Scrub the sweet potato and cut into 1cm/½in slices, discarding the ends.

3 Cook the duck breasts on a medium barbecue, skin-side down, for 5 minutes. Turn and cook for a further 8–10 minutes, according to how pink you like your duck.

DUCK BREASTS WITH RED PLUMS
∘ ∘ ∘

The rich fruity sauce for this dish combines brandy and red plums with double cream and coriander. The sauce can be made in a pan on the barbecue while the duck is cooking.

INGREDIENTS
*4 duck breasts, about 175g/6oz
each, skinned
10ml/2 tsp crushed cinnamon stick
50g/2oz/¼ cup butter
15ml/1 tbsp plum brandy or
Cognac
250ml/8fl oz/1 cup chicken stock
250ml/8fl oz/1 cup double cream
6 fresh red plums, stoned and sliced
6 sprigs fresh coriander leaves, plus
extra to garnish
salt and freshly ground black
pepper*

SERVES 4

1 Score the duck breasts and sprinkle with salt. Press the crushed cinnamon on to both sides of the duck breasts. Brush with butter and cook on a medium barbecue for 15–20 minutes, turning once, until the duck is tender.

2 To make the sauce, melt half the remaining butter in a saucepan. Add the brandy or Cognac and set it alight. When the flames have died down, add the stock and cream and allow to simmer gently until reduced and thick. Add seasoning to taste.

3 In a saucepan, melt the other half of the butter and fry the plums and coriander just enough to cook the fruit through. Slice the duck breasts and pour some sauce around each one, then garnish with the plum slices and the chopped fresh coriander.

JUNIPER-SPICED VENISON CHOPS

° ° °

*Depending on the type of venison available, the chops will vary in size,
so you will need either one or two per person.*

INGREDIENTS

4–8 venison chops
250ml/8 fl oz/1 cup red wine
2 medium red onions
6 juniper berries, crushed
1 cinnamon stick, crumbled
1 dried bay leaf, crumbled
thinly pared strip of orange rind
olive oil, for brushing
salt and freshly ground black
pepper

SERVES 4

2 Add the juniper berries, cinnamon, bay leaf and orange rind. Toss well to coat evenly and then cover the bowl and leave to marinate for at least an hour, or overnight in the fridge.

1 Place the venison chops in a large mixing bowl and pour over the red wine. Using a sharp knife, cut the red onions in half crossways and add them to the bowl.

3 Drain the venison and onions and reserve the marinade. Brush the venison and onions generously with the olive oil and sprinkle with plenty of salt and freshly ground black pepper.

4 Cook the venison and onions on a medium-hot barbecue for about 8–10 minutes on each side, turning once and basting regularly with the marinade. The venison should still be slightly pink inside even when fully cooked.

Cook's Tip

*Tender farmed venison
is now widely available from
supermarkets and good butchers
shops, but if venison is difficult
to find, beef steaks could be
used instead.*

FISH AND SEAFOOD

Cooking over charcoal adds a marvellous flavour to fish and seafood, and it's very quick and easy to prepare this way. Oily fish such as mackerel, sardines or tuna are perfectly suited to grilling and won't dry out, while char-grilling will enhance their robust flavours. Use plump prawns or firm meaty-textured fish such as monkfish or swordfish for kebabs, but marinate them first to keep them moist. More delicate fish, or those that are best cooked in their own steam, can also be barbecued very successfully: just wrap them securely in foil and cook them either on the rack or directly on the coals. You can include all kinds of flavourings in the foil parcels, too.

SPICED PRAWNS WITH VEGETABLES

° ° °

This is a light and nutritious Indian dish, excellent served either on a bed of lettuce leaves, or with plain boiled rice or chappatis.

INGREDIENTS

20 cooked king prawns, peeled
1 medium courgette, thickly sliced
1 medium onion, cut into 8 chunks
8 cherry tomatoes
8 baby corn cobs
mixed salad leaves, to serve

FOR THE MARINADE
30ml/2 tbsp chopped fresh
coriander
5ml/1 tsp salt
2 fresh green chillies, seeded if
wished
45ml/3 tbsp lemon juice
30ml/2 tbsp vegetable oil

SERVES 4

1 To make the marinade, blend the coriander, salt, chillies, lemon juice and oil together in a food processor

2 Empty the contents from the processor and transfer to a bowl.

3 Add the peeled king prawns to the mixture in the bowl and stir to make sure that all the prawns are well coated. Cover the bowl with clear film and set aside in a cool place, to marinate for about 30 minutes.

4 Arrange the vegetables and prawns alternately on four long skewers. Cook on a medium barbecue for 5 minutes, turning frequently, until cooked and browned. Serve immediately, on a bed of mixed salad leaves.

TIGER PRAWN SKEWERS WITH WALNUT PESTO

This is an unusual starter or main course, which can be prepared in advance and kept in the fridge until you're ready to cook it.

INGREDIENTS

12–16 large, raw, shell-on tiger prawns
50g/2oz/1/2 cup walnut pieces
60ml/4 tbsp chopped fresh flat-leaf parsley
60ml/4 tbsp chopped fresh basil
2 garlic cloves, chopped
45ml/3 tbsp grated fresh Parmesan cheese
30ml/2 tbsp extra virgin olive oil
30ml/2 tbsp walnut oil
salt and freshly ground black pepper

SERVES 4

3 Add half the pesto to the prawns in the bowl, toss them well, then cover and chill in the fridge for a minimum of 1 hour, or leave them overnight.

4 Thread the prawns on to skewers and cook them on a hot barbecue for 3–4 minutes, turning once. Serve with the remaining pesto and a green salad.

1 Peel the prawns, removing the head but leaving the tail. De-vein and then put the prawns in a large mixing bowl.

2 To make the pesto, place the walnuts, parsley, basil, garlic, cheese and oils in a food processor and process until finely chopped. Season.

MACKEREL KEBABS WITH SWEET PEPPER SALAD

Mackerel is an excellent fish for barbecuing because its natural oils keep it moist and tasty. This recipe combines mackerel with peppers and tomatoes in a flavoursome summer salad.

INGREDIENTS

4 medium mackerel, about
225g/8oz each, filleted
2 small red onions, cut in wedges
30ml/2 tbsp chopped fresh
marjoram
60ml/4 tbsp dry white wine
45ml/3 tbsp olive oil
juice of 1 lime

FOR THE SALAD
1 red pepper
1 yellow pepper
1 small red onion
2 large plum tomatoes
15ml/1 tbsp chopped fresh
marjoram
10ml/2 tsp balsamic vinegar
salt and freshly ground black
pepper

SERVES 4

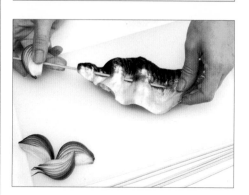

1 Thread each mackerel fillet on to a skewer, with an onion wedge on each end. Arrange the skewers in a dish.

2 Mix together the marjoram, wine, oil and lime juice and spoon over the mackerel. Cover and chill in the fridge for at least 30 minutes, turning once.

3 To make the salad, quarter and seed both peppers and halve the onion. Place the peppers and onion, skin-side down, with the whole tomatoes, on a hot barbecue and leave until the skins are blackened and charred.

4 Remove the vegetables from the barbecue and leave until they are cool enough to handle. Use a sharp knife to peel off and discard the skins.

5 Chop the vegetables roughly and put them in a bowl. Stir in the marjoram and balsamic vinegar and season to taste. Toss thoroughly.

6 Remove the kebabs from the fridge and cook on a hot barbecue for about 10–12 minutes, turning occasionally and basting with the marinade. Serve with the pepper salad.

Cook's Tip
Other oily fish can be used for this dish: try fillets or cubes of herring, rainbow trout or salmon, instead.

SWORDFISH KEBABS

Swordfish has a firm meaty texture that makes it ideal for cooking on a barbecue.
Marinade the fish first to keep it moist.

INGREDIENTS

900g/2lb swordfish steaks
45ml/3 tbsp olive oil
juice of ½ lemon
1 garlic clove, crushed
5ml/1 tsp paprika
3 tomatoes, quartered
2 onions, cut into wedges
salt and freshly ground black
pepper
salad and pitta bread, to serve

SERVES 4–6

1 Use a large kitchen knife to cut the swordfish steaks into large cubes. Arrange the cubes in a single layer in a large shallow dish.

2 Blend together the olive oil, lemon juice, garlic, paprika and seasoning in a bowl, and pour over the fish. Cover the dish loosely with clear film and leave to marinate in a cool place for up to 2 hours.

3 Thread the fish cubes on to metal skewers, alternating them with the pieces of tomato and onion wedges.

4 Cook the kebabs on a hot barbecue for about 5–10 minutes, basting frequently with the remaining marinade and turning occasionally. Serve with salad and pitta bread.

CALAMARI WITH TWO-TOMATO STUFFING

Calamari, or baby squid, are quick to cook, but do turn and baste them often and take care not to overcook them.

INGREDIENTS

500g/1¼ lb baby squid, cleaned
1 garlic clove, crushed
3 plum tomatoes, skinned and chopped
8 sun-dried tomatoes in oil, drained and chopped
60ml/4 tbsp chopped fresh basil, plus extra, to serve
60ml/4 tbsp fresh white breadcrumbs
45ml/3 tbsp olive oil
15ml/1 tbsp red wine vinegar
salt and freshly ground black pepper
lemon juice, to serve

SERVES 4

1 Remove the tentacles from the squid and roughly chop them; leave the main part of the squid whole.

2 Mix together the crushed garlic, plum tomatoes, sun-dried tomatoes, chopped fresh basil and breadcrumbs. Stir in 15ml/1 tbsp of the olive oil and the vinegar. Season well with plenty of salt and freshly ground black pepper. Soak some wooden cocktail sticks in water for 10 minutes before use, to prevent them burning on the barbecue.

3 Using a teaspoon, fill the squid with the stuffing mixture. Secure the open ends with the cocktail sticks to hold the stuffing mixture in place.

4 Brush the squid with the remaining olive oil and cook over a medium-hot barbecue for 4–5 minutes, turning often. Sprinkle with lemon juice and extra chopped fresh basil to serve.

BARBECUED SCALLOPS WITH LIME BUTTER

· · ·

Fresh scallops are quick to cook and ideal for barbecues. This recipe combines them simply with lime and fennel.

INGREDIENTS

1 head fennel
2 limes
12 large scallops, cleaned
1 egg yolk
90ml/6 tbsp melted butter
olive oil for brushing
salt and freshly ground black pepper

SERVES 4

3 Place the egg yolk and remaining lime rind and juice in a small bowl and whisk until pale and smooth.

5 Brush the fennel wedges with olive oil and cook them on a hot barbecue for 3–4 minutes, turning once.

1 Trim any feathery leaves from the fennel and reserve them. Slice the rest lengthways into thin wedges.

4 Gradually whisk in the melted butter and continue whisking until thick and smooth. Finely chop the reserved fennel leaves and stir them in, with seasoning to taste.

6 Add the scallops and cook for a further 3–4 minutes, turning once. Serve with the lime and fennel butter and the lime wedges.

2 Cut one lime into wedges. Finely grate the rind and squeeze the juice of the other lime and toss half the juice and rind on to the scallops. Season well with salt and fresh black pepper.

Cook's Tip
If the scallops are small, you may wish to thread them on to flat skewers to make turning them easier.

SARDINES WITH WARM HERB SALSA

Plain grilling is the very best way to cook fresh sardines. Served with this luscious herb salsa the only other essential item is fresh, crusty bread, to mop up the tasty juices.

INGREDIENTS

12–16 fresh sardines
oil for brushing
juice of 1 lemon

FOR THE SALSA
15ml/1 tbsp butter
4 spring onions, chopped
1 garlic clove, finely chopped
rind of 1 lemon
30ml/2 tbsp finely chopped fresh
parsley
30ml/2 tbsp finely snipped fresh
chives
30ml/2 tbsp finely chopped fresh
basil
30ml/2 tbsp green olive paste
10ml/2 tsp balsamic vinegar
salt and freshly ground black
pepper

SERVES 4

1 To clean the sardines, use a pair of small kitchen scissors to slit the fish along the belly and pull out the innards. Wipe the fish with kitchen paper and then arrange on a grill rack.

2 To make the salsa, melt the butter in a small pan and gently sauté the spring onions and garlic for about 2 minutes, shaking the pan occasionally, until softened but not browned.

3 Add the lemon rind and remaining salsa ingredients to the onions and garlic in the pan and keep warm on the edge of the barbecue, stirring occasionally. Do not allow to boil.

4 Brush the sardines lightly with oil and sprinkle with lemon juice, salt and pepper. Cook for about 2 minutes on each side, over a moderate heat. Serve with the warm salsa and crusty bread.

STUFFED SARDINES

This Middle Eastern-inspired dish doesn't take much preparation and is a meal in itself.
Just serve with a crisp green salad tossed in a fresh lemon vinaigrette to make it complete.

INGREDIENTS

10g/¼ oz fresh parsley
3–4 garlic cloves, crushed
8–12 fresh or frozen sardines, prepared
30ml/2 tbsp lemon juice
50g/2oz plain flour
2.5ml/½ tsp ground cumin
olive oil, for brushing
salt and freshly ground black pepper
naan bread and green salad, to serve

SERVES 4

1 Finely chop the parsley and mix in a small bowl with the garlic. Pat the parsley and garlic mixture all over the outsides and insides of the prepared sardines. Sprinkle the sardines with lemon juice, then place them in a dish, cover and set aside in a cool place for up to 2 hours, to absorb the flavours.

2 Place the flour on a large plate and season with the cumin, salt and pepper. Roll the sardines in the flour.

3 Brush the sardines with olive oil and cook on a medium-hot barbecue for about 3 minutes each side. Serve with naan bread and a green salad.

MONKFISH WITH PEPPERED CITRUS MARINADE

Monkfish is a firm, meaty fish that cooks well on the barbecue and keeps its shape.
Serve with a green salad.

INGREDIENTS

2 monkfish tails, about
350g/12oz each
1 lime
1 lemon
2 oranges
handful of fresh thyme sprigs
30ml/2 tbsp olive oil
15ml/1 tbsp mixed peppercorns,
roughly crushed
salt and freshly ground
black pepper

SERVES 4

2 Turn the fish and repeat on the other side, to remove the second fillet. Repeat on the second tail. (If you prefer, you can ask your fishmonger to do this for you.) Lay the four fillets out flat on a chopping board.

5 Squeeze the juice from the citrus fruits and mix it with the olive oil and more salt and pepper. Spoon over the fish. Cover with clear film and leave to marinate in the fridge for about 1 hour, turning occasionally and spooning the marinade over the fish.

1 Using a sharp kitchen knife, remove any skin from the monkfish tails. Cut carefully down one side of the backbone, sliding the knife between the bone and flesh, to remove the fillet on one side.

3 Cut two slices from each of the citrus fruits and arrange them over two of the fillets. Add a few sprigs of fresh thyme and sprinkle with plenty of salt and freshly ground black pepper. Finely grate the rind from the remaining fruit and sprinkle it over the fish.

6 Drain the monkfish, reserving the marinade, and sprinkle with the crushed peppercorns. Cook on a medium-hot barbecue for 15–20 minutes, basting with the marinade and turning occasionally, until the fish is evenly cooked.

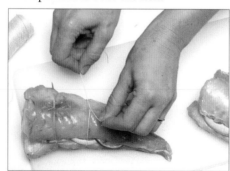

4 Lay the other two fillets on top and tie them firmly at intervals.

SMOKED MACKEREL WITH BLUEBERRIES

*Fresh blueberries burst with flavour when cooked, and their sharpness complements
the rich flesh of mackerel very well.*

INGREDIENTS

15g/½oz *plain flour*
4 *hot-smoked mackerel fillets*
50g/2oz/4 tbsp *unsalted butter*
juice of ½ *lemon*
*salt and freshly ground black
pepper*

FOR THE BLUEBERRY SAUCE
450g/1lb *blueberries*
25g/1oz/2 tbsp *caster sugar*
15g/½oz/1 tbsp *unsalted butter*
*salt and freshly ground black
pepper*

SERVES 4

1 Season the flour with salt and
freshly ground black pepper. Coat each
fish fillet in the flour, covering it well.

2 Brush the fillets with butter and
cook on a medium barbecue for a few
minutes until heated through with
a crisp coating.

3 To make the sauce, place the
blueberries, sugar, butter and salt
and pepper in a small roasting pan
and cook on the barbecue, stirring
occasionally, for about 10 minutes.
Serve immediately, drizzling the lemon
juice over the mackerel and with the
blueberries on the side.

MACKEREL WITH TOMATOES, PESTO AND ONION

° ° °

Rich oily fish like mackerel needs a sharp, fresh-tasting sauce to go with it,
and this aromatic pesto is excellent drizzled over the top.

INGREDIENTS

4 mackerel, cleaned and gutted
30ml/2 tbsp olive oil
115g/4oz onion, roughly chopped
450g/1lb tomatoes, roughly
chopped
salt and freshly ground
black pepper

FOR THE PESTO
50g/2oz pine nuts
30ml/2 tbsp fresh basil leaves
2 garlic cloves, crushed
30ml/2 tbsp freshly grated
Parmesan cheese
150ml/¼ pint/⅔ cup extra virgin
olive oil

SERVES 4

1 To make the pesto, place the pine nuts, fresh basil leaves and garlic in a food processor and blend to a rough paste. Add the Parmesan and, with the blades running, gradually add the oil.

2 Season the mackerel well with plenty of salt and freshly ground black pepper and cook on a medium-hot barbecue for about 12–15 minutes, turning once.

3 Meanwhile, heat the olive oil in a large, heavy-based saucepan and sauté the chopped onions until soft and golden brown.

4 Stir the chopped tomatoes into the contents of the saucepan and cook for 5 minutes. Serve the fish on top of the tomato mixture and top with a generous spoonful of the pesto.

CHAR-GRILLED TUNA WITH FIERY PEPPER PUREE

Tuna is an oily fish that barbecues well and is meaty enough to combine successfully with strong flavours – even hot chilli, as in this red pepper purée, which is excellent served with crusty bread.

INGREDIENTS

4 tuna steaks, about 175g/6oz each
finely grated rind and juice of 1 lime
30ml/2 tbsp olive oil
salt and freshly ground black pepper
lime wedges, to serve

FOR THE PEPPER PURÉE
2 red peppers, halved
45ml/3 tbsp olive oil, plus extra for
brushing
1 small onion
2 garlic cloves, crushed
2 red chillies
1 slice white bread without crusts,
diced
salt

SERVES 4

2 To make the pepper purée, brush the pepper halves with a little olive oil and cook them, skin-side down, on a hot barbecue, until the skin is charred and blackened. Place the onion in its skin on the barbecue and cook until browned, turning it occasionally.

3 Leave the peppers and onion until cool enough to handle, then remove the skins, using a sharp kitchen knife.

4 Place the cooked peppers and onion with the garlic, chillies, bread and olive oil in a food processor. Process until smooth. Add salt to taste.

5 Drain the tuna steaks from the marinade and cook them on a hot barbecue for 8–10 minutes, turning once, until golden brown. Serve the steaks with the pepper purée and lime wedges, with crusty bread if liked.

1 Trim any skin from the tuna and place the steaks in a single layer in a wide dish. Sprinkle over the lime rind and juice, olive oil, salt and black pepper. Cover with clear film and chill in the fridge until required.

Cook's Tip

The pepper purée can be made in advance, cooking the peppers and onion under a hot grill; keep it in the fridge until you cook the fish.

TROUT WITH BACON

The smoky, savoury flavour of crispy grilled bacon perfectly complements the delicate flesh of the trout in this simple dish.

INGREDIENTS

4 trout, cleaned and gutted
25g/1oz/1 tbsp plain flour
4 rashers smoked streaky bacon
30ml/2 tbsp olive oil
juice of ½ lemon
salt and freshly ground
black pepper

SERVES 4

1 Place the trout on a chopping board and pat dry with kitchen paper. Season the flour with the salt and freshly ground black pepper. Stretch the bacon rashers out thinly using the back of a heavy kitchen knife.

2 Roll the fish in the seasoned flour mixture and wrap tightly in the streaky bacon. Brush with olive oil and cook on a medium-hot barbecue for 10–15 minutes, turning once. Serve at once, with the lemon juice drizzled on top.

RED MULLET WITH BASIL AND CITRUS

*This Italian recipe is full of the warm, distinctive flavours of the Mediterranean.
Serve the dish with plain boiled rice and a green salad, or with lots of fresh crusty bread.*

INGREDIENTS

4 red mullet, about 225g/8oz each,
filleted
60ml/4 tbsp olive oil
10 peppercorns, crushed
2 oranges, one peeled and sliced
and one squeezed
1 lemon
15g/½ oz/1 tbsp butter
2 drained canned anchovies,
chopped
60ml/4 tbsp shredded fresh basil
salt and freshly ground black
pepper

SERVES 4

2 Halve the lemon. Remove the skin and pith from one half using a small, sharp knife, and slice the flesh thinly. Squeeze the juice from the other half.

3 Drain the fish, reserving the marinade and orange slices, and cook on a medium-hot barbecue for about 10–12 minutes, turning once and basting with the marinade.

4 Melt the butter in a saucepan with any remaining marinade. Add the chopped anchovies and cook until completely soft. Stir in the orange and lemon juice and allow to simmer on the edge of the barbecue until slightly reduced. Stir in the basil and check the seasoning. Pour over the fish and garnish with the reserved orange slices and the lemon slices.

1 Place the fish fillets in a shallow dish in a single layer. Pour over the olive oil and sprinkle with the crushed peppercorns. Lay the orange slices on top of the fish. Cover the dish with clear film, and leave to marinate in the fridge for at least 4 hours.

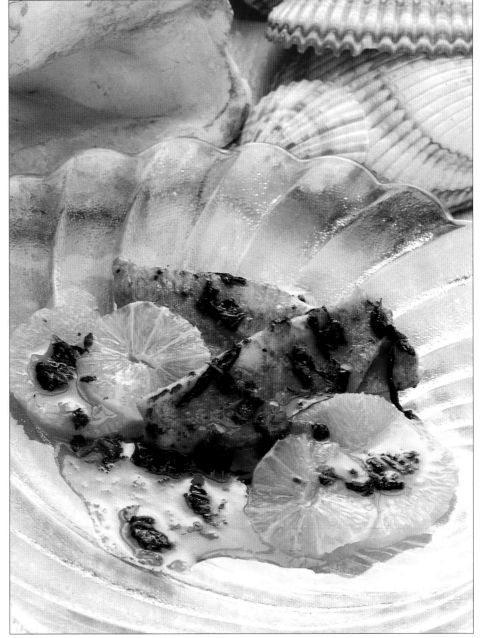

FISH PARCELS

∘ ∘ ∘

*Sea bass is good for this recipe, but you could also use small whole trout
or a white fish fillet such as cod or haddock.*

INGREDIENTS

4 pieces sea bass fillet, or 4 small
sea bass, about 450g/1lb each
olive oil for brushing
2 shallots, thinly sliced
1 garlic clove, chopped
15ml/1 tbsp capers
6 sun-dried tomatoes, finely
chopped
4 black olives, stoned and thinly
sliced
grated rind and juice of 1 lemon
5ml/1 tsp paprika
salt and freshly ground black
pepper

SERVES 4

2 Place a piece of fish in the centre
of each piece of baking foil and season
well with plenty of salt and pepper.

3 Scatter over the shallots, chopped
garlic, capers, tomatoes, sliced olives
and grated lemon rind. Sprinkle with
the lemon juice and paprika.

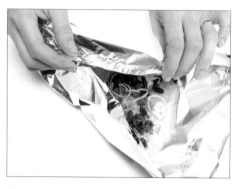

4 Fold over the baking foil to enclose
the fish loosely, sealing the edges firmly
so that none of the juices can escape
during cooking. Place the parcels on a
moderately hot barbecue and cook for
about 8–10 minutes. To serve, place
each of the parcels on a plate and
loosen the tops to open.

Cook's Tip
These parcels can also be
baked in the oven: place them
on a baking sheet and cook at
200°C/400°F/Gas 6 for
about 15–20 minutes.

1 Clean the fish if whole. Cut four
squares of double-thickness baking foil,
large enough to enclose the fish; brush
lightly with a little olive oil.

SPICED FISH BAKED THAI STYLE

○ ○ ○

Banana leaves make a perfect, natural wrapping for barbecued foods, but if they are not available you can use baking foil instead.

INGREDIENTS

*4 red snapper or mullet, about
350g/12oz each
banana leaves
1 lime
1 garlic clove, thinly sliced
2 spring onions, thinly sliced
30ml/2 tbsp Thai red
curry paste
60ml/4 tbsp coconut milk*

SERVES 4

1 Clean the fish, removing the scales, and make several deep slashes in the side of each with a sharp knife. Place each fish on a layer of banana leaves.

2 Thinly slice half the lime and tuck the slices into the slashes in the fish, with the slivers of garlic. Scatter the sliced spring onions over the fish.

3 Grate the rind and squeeze the juice from the remaining half-lime and mix with the curry paste and coconut milk. Spoon over the fish.

4 Wrap the leaves over the fish, to enclose them completely. Tie firmly with string and cook on a medium-hot barbecue for 15–20 minutes, turning occasionally. To serve, open up the parcels by cutting along the top edge with a knife and fanning out the leaves.

SEA BREAM WITH ORANGE BUTTER SAUCE

o o o

Sea bream is a revelation to anyone unfamiliar with its creamy rich flavour.
The fish has a firm white flesh that goes well with this rich butter sauce, sharpened with orange.

INGREDIENTS

2 sea bream, about 350g/12oz
each, scaled and gutted
10ml/2 tsp Dijon mustard
5ml/1 tsp fennel seeds
30ml/2 tbsp olive oil
50g/2oz watercress
175g/6oz mixed lettuce leaves,
such as curly endive or frisée

FOR THE ORANGE BUTTER SAUCE
30ml/2 tbsp frozen orange juice
concentrate
175g/6oz/3/4 cup unsalted butter,
diced
salt and cayenne pepper

SERVES 2

1 Slash the sea bream four times on either side. Combine the mustard and fennel seeds, then spread over both sides of the fish. Brush with olive oil and cook on a medium-hot barbecue for 10–12 minutes, turning once.

2 Place the orange juice concentrate in a bowl and heat over a saucepan of simmering water. Remove the pan from the heat and gradually whisk in the butter until creamy. Season well.

3 Dress the watercress and lettuce leaves with the remaining olive oil, and arrange with the fish on two plates. Spoon the sauce over the fish and serve with jacket potatoes, if liked.

HALIBUT WITH FRESH TOMATO AND BASIL SALSA

. . .

Take care when cooking this dish as halibut has a tendency to break easily, especially when the skin has been removed. Season well to bring out the flavour of the fish and the taste of the sauce.

INGREDIENTS

4 halibut fillets, about 175g/6oz each
45ml/3 tbsp olive oil

FOR THE SALSA
1 medium tomato, roughly chopped
¼ red onion, finely chopped
1 small jalapeño pepper
30ml/2 tbsp balsamic vinegar
10 large fresh basil leaves
15ml/1 tbsp olive oil
salt and freshly ground black pepper

SERVES 4

1 To make the salsa, mix together the chopped tomato, red onion, jalapeño pepper and balsamic vinegar in a bowl. Slice the fresh basil leaves finely, using a sharp kitchen knife.

2 Stir the basil and the olive oil into the tomato mixture. Season to taste. Cover the bowl with clear film and leave to marinate for at least 3 hours.

3 Rub the halibut fillets with oil and season. Cook on a medium barbecue for 8 minutes, basting with oil and turning once. Serve with the salsa.

COD FILLET WITH FRESH MIXED-HERB CRUST

*Use fresh herbs and wholemeal breadcrumbs to make a delicious crisp crust for the fish.
Season the fish well and serve with large lemon wedges.*

INGREDIENTS

*25g/1oz/2 tbsp butter
15ml/1 tbsp fresh chervil
15ml/1 tbsp fresh parsley, plus
extra sprigs to garnish
15ml/1 tbsp fresh chives
175g/6oz/3 cups breadcrumbs
4 thick pieces of cod fillet, about
225g/8oz each, skinned
15ml/1 tbsp olive oil
lemon wedges, to garnish
salt and freshly ground black
pepper*

SERVES 4

1 Melt the butter and chop all the herbs finely, using a sharp knife. Brush the cod fillets with melted butter and mix any remaining butter with the breadcrumbs, fresh herbs and plenty of salt and freshly ground black pepper.

2 Press a quarter of the mixture on to each fillet, spreading evenly, and lightly sprinkle with olive oil. Cook on a medium barbecue for about 10 minutes, turning once. Serve the fish garnished with lemon wedges and the sprigs of fresh parsley.

Grilled Snapper with Hot Mango Salsa

∘ ∘ ∘

A ripe mango provides the basis for a deliciously rich fruity salsa. The dressing needs no oil and features the tropical flavours of coriander, ginger and chilli.

INGREDIENTS

350g/12oz new potatoes
3 eggs
115g/4oz French beans, topped,
tailed and halved
4 red snapper, about 350g/12oz
each, cleaned, scaled and gutted
30ml/2 tbsp olive oil
175g/6oz mixed lettuce leaves,
such as frisée or Webb's
2 cherry tomatoes
salt and freshly ground black
pepper

FOR THE SALSA
45ml/3 tbsp chopped fresh
coriander
1 medium-sized ripe mango,
peeled, stoned and diced
1/2 red chilli, seeded and chopped
2.5cm/1in fresh root ginger, grated
juice of 2 limes
generous pinch of celery salt

SERVES 4

1 Bring the potatoes to the boil in a large saucepan of salted water and simmer for 15–20 minutes. Drain.

2 Bring a second large saucepan of salted water to the boil. Put in the eggs and boil for 4 minutes, then add the beans and cook for a further 6 minutes, so that the eggs have had a total of 10 minutes. Drain and refresh the beans. Remove the eggs from the saucepan. Cool, then shell and cut into quarters.

3 Using a sharp knife, slash each snapper three times on either side. Brush with olive oil and cook on a medium-hot barbecue for 12 minutes, basting occasionally and turning once.

4 To make the salsa, place the chopped fresh coriander in a food processor. Add the mango chunks, chilli, grated ginger, lime juice and celery salt and process until smooth.

5 Dress the lettuce leaves with olive oil and distribute them evenly between four large plates.

6 Arrange the snapper on the lettuce and season to taste. Halve the new potatoes and distribute them with the beans, tomatoes and quartered hard-boiled eggs over the salad. Serve immediately, with the salsa.

Variation
If fresh mangoes are unavailable, use canned ones, draining well. Sea bream are also good served with this hot mango salsa.

SMOKED HADDOCK WITH QUICK PARSLEY SAUCE

Make any herb sauce by this method, making sure it is thickened and seasoned well to complement the smoky flavour of the fish.

INGREDIENTS

4 smoked haddock fillets, about 225g/8oz each
75g/3oz/6 tbsp butter, softened
25g/1oz/2 tbsp plain flour
300ml/½ pint/1¼ cups milk
60ml/4 tbsp chopped fresh parsley
salt and freshly ground black pepper

SERVES 4

1 Smear the fish fillets on both sides with 50g/2oz/4 tbsp of the butter.

2 Beat the remaining butter and flour together to make a paste.

3 Cook the fish on a medium-hot barbecue for about 10 minutes, turning once. Meanwhile, to make the sauce, heat the milk in a saucepan to just below boiling point. Add the flour mixture in small spoonfuls, whisking constantly over the heat. Continue until the sauce is smooth and thick.

4 Add the seasoning and chopped fresh parsley to the saucepan and stir well. Pour the parsley sauce over the haddock fillets to serve.

SALMON WITH RED ONION MARMALADE

° ° °

Salmon barbecues well but is most successful when it is at least 2.5cm/1in thick. The red onion marmalade is rich and delicious. Puréed blackcurrants work as well as crème de cassis.

INGREDIENTS

4 salmon steaks, about 175g/6oz each
30ml/2 tbsp olive oil
salt and freshly ground black pepper

FOR THE RED ONION MARMALADE
5 medium red onions, peeled and finely sliced
50g/2oz/4 tbsp butter
175ml/6floz/¾ cup red wine vinegar
50ml/2fl oz/¼ cup crème de cassis
50ml/2fl oz/¼ cup grenadine
50ml/2fl oz/¼ cup red wine

SERVES 4

1 Use your hands to rub the olive oil into the salmon flesh and season well with plenty of salt and freshly ground black pepper.

2 Melt the butter in a large heavy-based saucepan and add the sliced onions. Sauté the onions for 5 minutes until golden brown.

3 Stir in the vinegar, crème de cassis, grenadine and wine and continue to cook for about 10 minutes until the liquid has almost entirely evaporated and the onions are glazed. Season well.

4 Brush the fish with a little more oil, and cook on a medium barbecue for about 6–8 minutes, turning once.

GRILLED SEA BASS WITH CITRUS FRUIT
o o o

*Sea bass is a beautiful fish with a soft, dense texture and a delicate flavour. In this recipe
it is complemented by citrus fruits and fruity olive oil.*

INGREDIENTS
1 small grapefruit
1 orange
1 lemon
*1 sea bass, about 1.5kg/
3–3½ lb, cleaned and
scaled*
6 fresh basil sprigs
45ml/3 tbsp olive oil
4–6 shallots, halved
60ml/4 tbsp dry white wine
15g/½ oz/1 tbsp butter
*salt and freshly ground black
pepper*
fresh dill, to garnish

SERVES 6

1 Using a vegetable peeler, remove
the rind from the grapefruit, orange
and lemon. Cut into thin julienne
strips. Peel the pith from the fruits and,
working over a bowl to catch the
juices, cut out the segments from the
grapefruit and the orange and set aside
for the garnish. Slice the lemon thickly.

2 Season the cavity of the fish with
salt and pepper and slash the flesh
three times on each side. Reserving a
few basil sprigs for the garnish, fill
the cavity with the remaining basil, the
lemon slices and half the julienne strips
of citrus rind. Brush with olive oil and
cook on a low–medium barbecue for
about 20 minutes, basting occasionally
and turning once.

3 Meanwhile, heat 15ml/1 tbsp
olive oil in a pan and cook the shallots
gently until soft. Add the wine and
30–45ml/2–3 tbsp of the fruit juice to
the pan. Bring to the boil over a high
heat, stirring. Stir in the remaining
julienne strips of rind and boil for
2–3 minutes, then whisk in the butter.

4 When the fish is cooked, transfer it
to a serving dish. Remove and discard
the cavity stuffing. Spoon the shallots
and sauce around the fish and garnish
with fresh dill sprigs, the reserved basil
and segments of grapefruit and orange.

GRILLED SEA BASS WITH FENNEL

∘ ∘ ∘

The classic combination of sea bass and fennel works particularly well when the fish is cooked over charcoal. Traditionally fennel twigs are used but this version of the recipe uses fennel seeds.

INGREDIENTS

*1 sea bass, about 1.5kg/3–3 ½ lb,
cleaned and scaled
60ml/4 tbsp olive oil
10ml/2 tsp fennel seeds
2 large fennel bulbs
60ml/4 tbsp Pernod
salt and freshly ground black
pepper*

SERVES 6

1 Make four deep slashes in each side of the fish. Brush the fish with olive oil and season well with salt and freshly ground black pepper. Sprinkle the fennel seeds in the cavity and slashes of the fish. Cook on a low barbecue for 20 minutes, basting occasionally and turning once.

2 Meanwhile, trim and slice the fennel bulbs thinly, reserving any leafy fronds to use as a garnish. Brush the slices with olive oil and barbecue for about 8–10 minutes, turning the fish occasionally, until tender. Remove the fish from the heat and keep it warm.

3 Scatter the fennel slices on a serving plate. Lay the fish on top and garnish with the reserved fennel fronds.

4 When ready for eating, heat the Pernod in a small pan on the side of the barbecue, light it and pour it, flaming, over the fish. Serve at once.

133

MEXICO BARBECUED SALMON

The sauce for this dish is vibrant with hot, sweet and sour flavours that permeate the fish before and during cooking.

INGREDIENTS

1 small red onion
1 garlic clove
6 plum tomatoes
25g/1oz/2 tbsp butter
45ml/3 tbsp tomato ketchup
30ml/2 tbsp Dijon mustard
30ml/2 tbsp dark brown sugar
15ml/1 tbsp runny honey
5ml/1 tbsp cayenne pepper
15ml/1 tbsp ancho chilli powder
15ml/1 tbsp paprika
15ml/1 tbsp Worcestershire sauce
4 salmon fillets, about 175g/6oz
each

SERVES 4

3 Melt the butter in a large, heavy-based saucepan and gently cook the onion and garlic until translucent.

4 Add the tomatoes to the saucepan and allow to simmer for 15 minutes.

5 Add the remaining ingredients, excluding the salmon, and simmer for a further 20 minutes. Pour the mixture into a food processor and blend until smooth. Leave to cool.

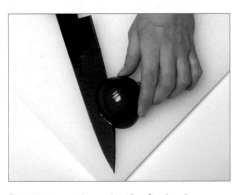

1 Using a sharp knife, finely chop the red onion and finely dice the garlic.

2 Next, dice the plum tomatoes finely and set them aside.

6 Brush the salmon with the sauce, and chill for at least 2 hours. Cook on a hot barbecue for 6 minutes, basting with the sauce and turning once.

SALMON WITH TROPICAL FRUIT SALSA

° ° °

*Fresh salmon really needs little adornment, but it does combine very well
with the exotic flavours in this colourful salsa.*

INGREDIENTS

*4 salmon steaks or fillets, about
175g/6oz each
finely grated rind and juice of
1 lime
1 small, ripe mango
1 small, ripe paw-paw
1 red chilli
45ml/3 tbsp chopped fresh
coriander
salt and freshly ground black
pepper*

SERVES 4

3 Halve the paw-paw, scoop out
the seeds with a spoon and remove the
peel. Finely chop the flesh and add it
to the mango chunks in the bowl.

5 Combine the mango, paw-paw,
chilli and coriander in a bowl and stir
in the remaining lime rind and juice.
Season to taste with plenty of salt and
freshly ground black pepper.

1 Place the salmon in a wide dish
and sprinkle over half the lime rind
and juice. Season with salt and pepper.

4 Cut the chilli in half lengthways.
Leave the seeds in to make the salsa hot
and spicy, or remove them for a milder
flavour. Finely chop the chilli.

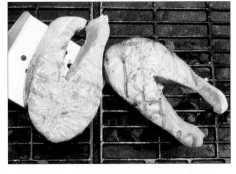

6 Cook the salmon on a medium
barbecue for about 5–8 minutes,
turning once. Serve with the fruit salsa.

2 Cut the mango in half, cutting
either side of the stone, and remove
the stone. Finely chop the mango flesh
and place the chunks in a bowl.

VEGETARIAN DISHES AND VEGETABLES

—◆—

Vegetables cooked on the barbecue acquire a richness and depth

of flavour that will add an extra dimension to your meal. There are

lots of ideas here for vegetable accompaniments to meat and fish dishes,

as well as for substantial main dishes that everyone, vegetarian or not,

will love. All vegetables can be cooked in foil parcels, but many are

ideally suited to grilling on the barbecue: jacket potatoes, peppers,

aubergines and corn on the cob are irresistible cooked over charcoal,

or you can spear a mixture of vegetables on to skewers to make

colourful and delicious kebabs. Barbecued vegetables can also be cooled

and made into fabulous salads. They certainly shouldn't be

an afterthought on your barbecue menu.

RED BEAN AND MUSHROOM BURGERS

· · · ○

Vegetarians, vegans and meat-eaters alike will enjoy these healthy, low-fat veggie burgers.
With salad, pitta bread and Greek-style yogurt, they make a substantial meal.

INGREDIENTS

15ml/1 tbsp olive oil
1 small onion, finely chopped
1 garlic clove, crushed
5ml/1 tsp ground cumin
5ml/1 tsp ground coriander
2.5ml/$\frac{1}{2}$ tsp ground turmeric
115g/4oz/1$\frac{1}{2}$ cups finely chopped
mushrooms
400g/14oz can red kidney beans
30ml/2 tbsp chopped fresh
coriander
wholemeal flour (optional)
olive oil, for brushing
salt and freshly ground black
pepper
Greek-style yogurt, to serve

SERVES 4

1 Heat the olive oil in a frying pan and fry the chopped onion and garlic over a moderate heat, stirring, until softened. Add the spices and cook for a further minute, stirring continuously.

Cook's Tip

These burgers are not quite as firm as meat burgers, and will need careful handling on the barbecue.

2 Add the chopped mushrooms and cook, stirring, until softened and dry. Remove the pan from the heat and empty the contents into a large bowl.

3 Drain the beans thoroughly, place them in a bowl and mash with a fork.

4 Stir the kidney beans into the frying pan, with the chopped fresh coriander, and mix thoroughly. Season the mixture well with plenty of salt and freshly ground black pepper.

5 Using floured hands, form the mixture into four flat burger shapes. If the mixture is too sticky to handle, mix in a little wholemeal flour.

6 Lightly brush the burgers with olive oil and cook on a hot barbecue for 8–10 minutes, turning once, until golden brown. Serve with a spoonful of yogurt and a green salad, if liked.

BARBECUED GOAT'S CHEESE PIZZA

Pizzas cooked on the barbecue have a beautifully crisp and golden base. The combination of goat's cheese and red onion in this recipe makes for a flavoursome main course dish.

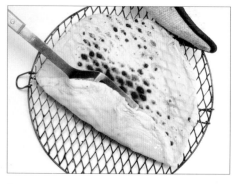

2 Brush the dough round with olive oil and place, oiled side down, on a medium barbecue. Cook for about 6–8 minutes until firm and golden underneath. Brush the uncooked side with olive oil and turn the pizza over.

3 Mix together the passata and red pesto and quickly spread over the cooked side of the pizza, to within about 1cm/½in of the edge. Arrange the onion, tomatoes and cheese on top and sprinkle with salt and pepper.

INGREDIENTS

150g/5oz packet pizza-base mix
olive oil, for brushing
150ml/¼ pint/⅔ cup passata
30ml/2 tbsp red pesto
1 small red onion, thinly sliced
8 cherry tomatoes, halved
115g/4oz firm goat's cheese, thinly sliced
handful shredded fresh basil leaves
salt and freshly ground black pepper

SERVES 4

1 Make up the pizza dough according to the directions on the packet. Roll out the dough on a lightly floured surface to a round of about 25cm/10in diameter.

4 Cook the pizza for 10 minutes more, until golden brown and crisp. Sprinkle with fresh basil and serve.

RED ONION GALETTES

∘ ∘ ∘

If non-vegetarians are to eat these pretty puff pastry tarts, you can scatter some chopped anchovies over them before barbecuing to add extra piquancy.

INGREDIENTS

60–75ml/4–5 tbsp olive oil
500g/1¼ lb red onions, sliced
1 garlic clove, crushed
30ml/2 tbsp chopped fresh mixed herbs, such as thyme, parsley and basil
225g/8oz ready-made puff pastry
15ml/1 tbsp sun-dried tomato paste
freshly ground black pepper
fresh thyme sprigs, to garnish

SERVES 4

1 Heat 30ml/2 tbsp oil in a frying pan and add the onions and garlic. Cover and cook gently for 15–20 minutes, stirring occasionally, until soft but not browned. Stir in the herbs.

2 Divide the pastry into four and roll out each piece to a 15cm/6in round. Flute the edges, prick all over with a fork and place on baking sheets.

3 Chill the rounds, on the baking sheets, in the fridge for 10 minutes. Mix 15ml/1 tbsp of the remaining olive oil with the sun-dried tomato paste and spread over the pastry rounds, to within about 1cm/½ in of the edge.

4 Spread the onion mixture over the pastry and season with pepper. Drizzle over a little oil, then place the baking sheets on a medium barbecue for 15 minutes, until the pastry is crisp. Serve hot, garnished with thyme sprigs.

TOFU SATAY

Grill cubes of tofu until crispy then serve with a Thai-style peanut sauce. Soak the satay sticks before use to prevent them burning while on the barbecue.

INGREDIENTS

2 × 200g/7oz packs smoked tofu
45ml/3 tbsp light soy sauce
10ml/2 tsp sesame oil
1 garlic clove, crushed
1 yellow and 1 red pepper, cut in squares
8–12 fresh bay leaves
sunflower oil, for brushing

FOR THE PEANUT SAUCE
2 spring onions, finely chopped
2 garlic cloves, crushed
good pinch chilli powder, or a few drops hot chilli sauce
5ml/1 tsp sugar
15ml/1 tbsp white wine vinegar
30ml/2 tbsp light soy sauce
45ml/3 tbsp crunchy peanut butter

SERVES 4–6

1 Cut the tofu into bite-sized cubes and place in a large bowl. Add the soy sauce, sesame oil and crushed garlic and mix well. Cover with clear film and marinate for at least 20 minutes.

2 Beat all the peanut sauce ingredients together in a large bowl, using a wooden spoon, until well blended. Avoid using a food processor to blend the ingredients, as the texture should be slightly chunky.

3 Drain the tofu and thread the cubes on to 8–12 satay sticks, alternating the tofu with the pepper squares and bay leaves. Larger bay leaves may need to be halved before threading.

4 Brush the satays with sunflower oil and cook on a hot barbecue or grill, turning the sticks occasionally, until the tofu and peppers are browned and crisp. Serve hot with the peanut sauce.

SWEET AND SOUR VEGETABLES WITH PANEER

∘ ∘ ∘

The Indian cheese used in this recipe, called paneer, can be bought from Asian stores, or you can use tofu in its place. Paneer has a good firm texture and cooks very well on the barbecue.

INGREDIENTS

1 green pepper, cut into squares
1 yellow pepper, cut into squares
8 cherry, or 4 medium, tomatoes
8 cauliflower florets
8 fresh or canned pineapple chunks
8 cubes paneer

FOR THE SEASONED OIL
15ml/1 tbsp soya oil
30ml/2 tbsp lemon juice
5ml/1 tsp salt
5ml/1 tsp freshly ground black pepper
15ml/1 tbsp clear honey
30ml/2 tbsp chilli sauce

SERVES 4

1 Thread the prepared vegetables, pineapple and paneer cubes on to four skewers, alternating the ingredients.

2 Mix together all the ingredients for the seasoned oil. If the mixture is a little too thick, add 15ml/1 tbsp water to loosen it. Brush the vegetables with the seasoned oil, ready for cooking.

3 Cook on a hot barbecue or grill for 10 minutes, until the vegetables begin to char slightly, turning the skewers often and basting with the seasoned oil. Serve on a bed of plain boiled rice.

VEGETABLE KEBABS WITH PEPPERCORN SAUCE

*Vegetables invariably taste good when cooked on the barbecue. You can include other
vegetables in these kebabs, depending on what is available at the time.*

INGREDIENTS

24 mushrooms
16 cherry tomatoes
16 large fresh basil leaves
2 courgettes, cut into 16 thick
slices
16 large fresh mint leaves
1 large red pepper, cut into
16 squares

TO BASTE
120ml/4fl oz/$\frac{1}{2}$ cup melted butter
1 garlic clove, crushed
15ml/1 tbsp crushed green
peppercorns
salt

FOR THE GREEN PEPPERCORN SAUCE
50g/2oz/$\frac{1}{4}$ cup butter
45ml/3 tbsp brandy
250ml/8fl oz/1 cup double cream
5ml/1 tsp crushed green
peppercorns

SERVES 4

1 Thread the vegetables on to
8 bamboo skewers that you have
soaked in water to prevent them
burning. Place the fresh basil leaves
immediately next to the tomatoes,
and wrap the mint leaves around
the courgette slices.

2 Mix the basting ingredients in a
bowl and baste the kebabs thoroughly.
Cook the skewers on a medium-hot
barbecue, turning and basting regularly
until the vegetables are just cooked –
this should take about 5–7 minutes.

3 Heat the butter for the green
peppercorn sauce in a frying pan,
then add the brandy and light it. When
the flames have died down, stir in the
cream and the peppercorns. Cook for
2 minutes, stirring all the time. Serve
the sauce with the barbecued kebabs.

CASSAVA AND VEGETABLE KEBABS

This is an attractive and delicious assortment of African vegetables, marinated in a spicy garlic sauce, then roasted over hot coals. If cassava is unavailable, use sweet potato or yam instead.

INGREDIENTS

175g/6oz cassava
1 onion, cut into wedges
1 aubergine, cut into bite-sized pieces
1 courgette, sliced
1 ripe plantain, sliced
½ red pepper and ½ green pepper, sliced
16 cherry tomatoes
rice or couscous, to serve

FOR THE MARINADE
60ml/4 tbsp lemon juice
60ml/4 tbsp olive oil
45–60ml/3–4 tbsp soy sauce
15ml/1 tbsp tomato paste
1 green chilli, seeded and finely chopped
½ onion, grated
2 garlic cloves, crushed
5ml/1 tsp mixed spice
pinch of dried thyme

SERVES 4

1 Peel the cassava and cut into bite-size pieces. Place in a large bowl, cover with boiling water and leave to blanch for about 5 minutes. Drain well.

2 Place all the prepared vegetables, including the cassava, in a large bowl and mix with your hands so that all the vegetables are evenly distributed.

3 Blend the marinade ingredients in a jug and pour over the vegetables. Cover and leave to marinate for 1–2 hours.

4 Thread the vegetables, with the cherry tomatoes, on to eight skewers and cook on a hot barbecue for about 15 minutes until tender and browned. Turn the skewers frequently and baste them occasionally with the marinade.

5 Meanwhile, pour the remaining marinade into a small saucepan and simmer for about 10 minutes to reduce. Strain the reduced marinade into a jug. Serve the kebabs on a bed of rice or couscous, with the sauce on the side.

BAKED SQUASH WITH PARMESAN

Almost all types of squash are suitable for barbecue cooking, and they are extemely easy to deal with: simply wrap them in baking foil and place them in the hot embers until they soften.

INGREDIENTS

2 acorn or butternut squashes, about 450g/1lb each
15ml/1 tbsp olive oil
50g/2oz/4 tbsp butter, melted
75g/3oz/1 cup grated Parmesan cheese
60ml/4 tbsp pine nuts, toasted
salt and freshly ground black pepper
2.5ml/½ tsp freshly grated nutmeg

SERVES 4

2 Brush the cut surfaces with oil and sprinkle with salt and black pepper.

5 Dice the flesh, then stir in the melted butter. Add the Parmesan, pine nuts, salt and pepper. Toss well to mix.

1 Cut the squashes in half and scoop out the seeds with a spoon.

3 Wrap each squash in baking foil and place in the embers of the fire. Cook for 25–30 minutes, until tender. Turn the parcels occasionally so that the squash cook evenly.

6 Spoon the mixture back into the shells. Sprinkle with nutmeg to serve.

4 Leave the squash until cool enough to handle. Unwrap the squashes from the foil parcels and scoop out the flesh, leaving the skins intact.

Cook's Tip

Spaghetti squash can also be cooked in this way. Just scoop out the spaghetti-like strands and toss with butter and Parmesan cheese.

POTATO AND CHEESE POLPETTES

*These little morsels of potato and Greek feta cheese, flavoured with dill and lemon juice, are
excellent when grilled on the barbecue, or they can be tossed in flour and fried in olive oil.*

INGREDIENTS

500g/1¼ lb potatoes
115g/4oz feta cheese
4 spring onions, chopped
45ml/3 tbsp chopped fresh dill
1 egg, beaten
15ml/1 tbsp lemon juice
30ml/2 tbsp olive oil
salt and freshly ground black
pepper

SERVES 4

1 Boil the potatoes in their skins in
salted water until soft. Drain, then peel
while still warm. Place in a bowl and
mash. Crumble the feta cheese into the
potatoes and add the spring onions,
dill, egg and lemon juice and season
with pepper and a little salt. Stir well.

2 Cover the mixture and chill until
firm. Divide the mixture into walnut-
size balls, then flatten them slightly.
Brush lightly with olive oil. Arrange
the polpettes on a grill rack and cook
on a medium barbecue, turning once,
until golden brown. Serve at once.

LOOFAH AND AUBERGINE RATATOUILLE

° ° °

Loofahs are edible gourds with spongy, creamy-white flesh. Like aubergine, their flavour is intensified by roasting. Cooking the vegetables in a pan over the barbecue will retain their juices.

INGREDIENTS

1 large or 2 medium aubergines
450g/1lb young loofahs or sponge gourds
1 large red pepper, cut into large chunks
225g/8oz cherry tomatoes
225g/8oz shallots
10ml/2 tsp ground coriander
60ml/4 tbsp olive oil
2 garlic cloves, finely chopped
a few fresh coriander sprigs
salt and freshly ground black pepper

SERVES 4

1 Cut the aubergines into thick chunks and sprinkle the pieces liberally with salt to draw out the bitter juices. Leave to drain for about 45 minutes, then rinse under cold running water and pat dry with kitchen paper.

2 Slice the loofahs into 2cm/¾in pieces. Place the aubergines, loofah and pepper pieces, together with the cherry tomatoes and shallots, in a roasting pan large enough to take all the vegetables in a single layer.

3 Sprinkle the vegetables with the ground coriander and olive oil. Scatter the chopped garlic and fresh coriander leaves on top and season to taste.

4 Cook on the barbecue for about 25 minutes, stirring the vegetables occasionally, until the loofah is golden and the peppers are beginning to char. As an alternative, you could thread the vegetables on skewers and grill them.

BAKED STUFFED COURGETTES

• • •

The tangy goat's cheese stuffing contrasts well with the very delicate flavour of the courgettes in this recipe. Wrap the courgettes and bake them in the embers of the fire.

2 Insert pieces of goat's cheese in the slits. Add a little chopped mint and sprinkle over the oil and black pepper.

3 Wrap each courgette in foil, place in the embers of the fire and bake for about 25 minutes, until tender.

INGREDIENTS

*8 small courgettes, about
450g/1lb total weight
15ml/1 tbsp olive oil, plus
extra for brushing
75–115g/3–4oz goat's cheese,
cut into thin strips
a few sprigs of fresh mint,
finely chopped, plus extra
to garnish
freshly ground black pepper*

SERVES 4

1 Cut eight pieces of baking foil large enough to encase each courgette, and lightly brush each piece with olive oil. Trim the courgettes and cut a thin slit along the length of each.

Cook's Tip

While almost any cheese can be used in this recipe, mild cheeses such as Cheddar or mozzarella, will best allow the flavour of the courgettes to be appreciated.

VEGETABLE PARCELS WITH FLOWERY BUTTER

*Nasturtium leaves and flowers are edible and have a distinctive peppery flavour.
They make a pretty addition to summer barbecue dishes.*

INGREDIENTS

200g/7oz baby carrots
250g/9oz yellow patty-pan
squashes or yellow courgettes
115g/4oz baby sweetcorn
1 onion, thinly sliced
50g/2oz/4 tbsp butter, plus extra
for greasing
finely grated rind of ½ lemon
6 young nasturtium leaves
4–8 nasturtium flowers
salt and freshly ground
black pepper

SERVES 4

1 Trim the vegetables with a sharp knife, leaving them whole unless they are very large – if necessary, cut them into even-size pieces.

2 Divide the vegetables between four double-thickness squares of buttered baking foil and season well.

3 Mix the butter with the lemon rind in a small bowl. Roughly chop the nasturtium leaves and add them to the butter. Place a generous spoonful of the butter on each pile of vegetables in the squares of baking foil.

4 Fold over the foil and seal the edges to make a neat parcel. Cook on a medium-hot barbecue for 30 minutes until the vegetables are tender. Open the parcels and top each with one or two nasturtium flowers. Serve at once.

GRILLED AUBERGINE PARCELS
∘ ∘ ∘

These little Italian bundles of tomatoes, mozzarella cheese and basil, wrapped in slices of aubergine, taste delicious cooked on the barbecue.

INGREDIENTS
2 large, long aubergines
225g/8oz mozzarella cheese
2 plum tomatoes
16 large fresh basil leaves
30ml/2 tbsp olive oil
salt and freshly ground black pepper

FOR THE DRESSING
60ml/4 tbsp olive oil
5ml/1 tsp balsamic vinegar
15ml/1 tbsp sun-dried tomato paste
15ml/1 tbsp lemon juice

FOR THE GARNISH
30ml/2 tbsp toasted pine nuts
torn fresh basil leaves

SERVES 4

3 Cut the mozzarella cheese into eight slices. Cut each tomato into eight slices, not counting the first and last slices. Take two aubergine slices and arrange in a cross. Place a slice of tomato in the centre, season, then add a basil leaf, followed by a slice of mozzarella, another basil leaf, another slice of tomato and more seasoning.

4 Fold the ends of the aubergine slices around the filling to make a neat parcel. Repeat with the rest of the assembled ingredients to make eight parcels. Chill the parcels in the fridge for about 20 minutes.

5 To make the tomato dressing, whisk together the olive oil, vinegar, sun-dried tomato paste and lemon juice. Season to taste with plenty of salt and freshly ground black pepper.

1 Remove the stalks from the aubergines and cut them lengthways into thin slices using a mandolin or long-bladed knife – aim to get 16 slices in total, each about 5mm/¼in thick, disregarding the first and last slices.

2 Bring a large saucepan of salted water to the boil and cook the aubergine slices for about 2 minutes, until just softened. Drain the slices, then pat them dry on kitchen paper.

6 Brush the parcels with olive oil and cook on a hot barbecue for about 10 minutes, turning once, until golden. Serve hot, with the dressing, sprinkled with pine nuts and basil.

STUFFED TOMATOES AND PEPPERS

○ ○ ○

Colourful peppers and tomatoes make perfect containers for meat and vegetable stuffings. The barbecued flavours in this dish are simply superb.

INGREDIENTS

2 large ripe tomatoes
1 green pepper
1 yellow or orange pepper
60ml/4 tbsp olive oil, plus extra for sprinkling
2 onions, chopped
2 garlic cloves, crushed
50g/2oz/½ cup blanched almonds, chopped
75g/3oz/scant ½ cup long grain rice, boiled and drained
30ml/2 tbsp fresh mint, roughly chopped
30ml/2 tbsp fresh parsley, roughly chopped
25g/1oz/2 tbsp sultanas
45ml/3 tbsp ground almonds
salt and freshly ground black pepper
chopped mixed fresh herbs, to garnish

SERVES 4

2 Halve the peppers, leaving the cores intact. Scoop out the seeds. Brush the peppers with 15ml/1 tbsp olive oil and cook on a medium barbecue for 15 minutes. Place the peppers and tomatoes on a grill rack and season well with salt and pepper.

3 Fry the onions in the remaining olive oil for 5 minutes. Add the crushed garlic and chopped almonds to the pan and fry for a further minute.

4 Remove the pan from the heat and stir in the rice, chopped tomatoes, mint, parsley and sultanas. Season well with salt and pepper and spoon the mixture into the tomatoes and peppers.

1 Cut the tomatoes in half and scoop out the pulp and seeds, using a teaspoon. Leave the tomatoes to drain on kitchen paper with the cut sides facing down. Roughly chop the tomato pulp and set it aside.

5 Scatter with the ground almonds and sprinkle with a little extra olive oil. Cook on a medium barbecue for about 15 minutes. Garnish with fresh herbs.

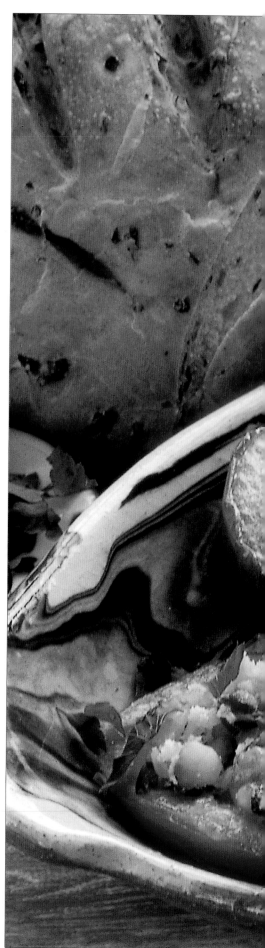

COUSCOUS STUFFED PEPPERS

Couscous makes a good basis for a stuffing, and in this recipe it is studded with raisins and flavoured with fresh mint. Charred peppers make the combination of flavours truly special.

2 To cook the couscous, bring 250ml/8fl oz/1 cup water to the boil. Add the oil and salt, then remove from the heat and add the couscous. Stir and leave to stand, covered, for 5 minutes. Stir in the onion, raisins and mint. Season well and stir in the egg yolk.

3 Use a teaspoon to fill the peppers with the couscous mixture to about three-quarters full (the couscous will swell while cooking). Wrap each pepper in a piece of oiled baking foil.

4 Cook on a medium barbecue for 20 minutes, until tender. Serve hot or cold, garnished with fresh mint leaves.

INGREDIENTS

6 peppers
25g/1oz/2 tbsp butter
1 onion, finely chopped
5ml/1 tsp olive oil
2.5ml/½ tsp salt
175g/6oz/1 cup couscous
25g/1oz/2 tbsp raisins
30ml/2 tbsp chopped fresh mint
1 egg yolk
salt and freshly ground black pepper
mint leaves, to garnish

SERVES 4

1 Carefully slit each pepper with a sharp knife and remove the core and seeds. Melt the butter in a small saucepan and add the chopped onion. Cook until soft but not browned.

SWEETCORN IN A GARLIC BUTTER CRUST
○ ○ ○

*Whether you are catering for vegetarians or serving this with meat dishes, it will disappear
in a flash. The charred garlic butter crust adds a new dimension to the corn cobs.*

INGREDIENTS

6 ripe corn cobs
225g/8oz/1 cup butter
30ml/2 tbsp olive oil
2 garlic cloves, crushed
*115g/4oz/1 cup wholemeal
breadcrumbs*
15ml/1 tbsp chopped fresh parsley
*salt and freshly ground black
pepper*

SERVES 6

1 Pull off the husks and silks and boil the corn cobs in a large saucepan of salted water until tender. Drain the corn cobs and leave to cool.

2 Melt the butter in a saucepan and add the olive oil, crushed garlic, salt and freshly ground black pepper, and stir to blend. Pour the mixture into a shallow dish. In another shallow dish blend the breadcrumbs and chopped fresh parsley. Roll the corn cobs in the melted butter mixture and then in the breadcrumbs until they are well coated.

3 Cook the corn cobs on a hot barbecue for about 10 minutes, turning frequently, until the breadcrumbs are golden brown.

STUFFED PARSLEYED ONIONS

These stuffed onions are a popular vegetarian dish served with fresh crusty bread and a crisp salad. They also make a very good accompaniment to meat dishes.

INGREDIENTS

4 large onions
60ml/4 tbsp cooked rice
20ml/4 tsp finely chopped fresh parsley, plus extra to garnish
60ml/4 tbsp strong Cheddar cheese, finely grated
30ml/2 tbsp olive oil
15ml/1 tbsp white wine
salt and freshly ground black pepper

SERVES 4

1 Cut a slice from the top of each onion and scoop out the centre to leave a fairly thick shell. Combine all the remaining ingredients in a large bowl and stir to mix, moistening with enough white wine to bind the ingredients together well.

2 Use a spoon to fill the onions, then wrap each one in a piece of oiled baking foil. Bake in the embers of the fire for 30–40 minutes, until tender, turning the parcels often so they cook evenly. Serve the onions garnished with chopped fresh parsley.

STUFFED ARTICHOKE BOTTOMS

∘ ∘ ∘

The distinctive flavour of char-grilled globe artichokes is matched in this dish by
an intensely savoury stuffing of mushrooms, cheese and walnuts.

INGREDIENTS

225g/8oz button mushrooms
15g/½ oz/1 tbsp butter
2 shallots, finely chopped
50g/2oz full- or medium-fat soft
cheese
30ml/2 tbsp chopped walnuts
45ml/3 tbsp grated Gruyère cheese
4 large or 6 small artichoke
bottoms (from cooked artichokes,
leaves and choke removed, or
cooked frozen or canned artichoke
hearts)
salt and freshly ground black
pepper
fresh parsley sprigs, to garnish

SERVES 4

1 To make the duxelles for the stuffing, put the mushrooms in a food processor or blender and pulse until finely chopped.

2 Melt the butter in a frying pan and cook the shallots over a medium heat for about 2–3 minutes until just softened. Add the mushrooms, raise the heat slightly, and cook for 5–7 minutes more, stirring frequently, until all the liquid from the mushrooms has been driven off and they are almost dry. Season with plenty of salt and freshly ground black pepper.

3 In a large bowl, combine the soft cheese and cooked mushrooms. Add the chopped walnuts and half the grated Gruyère cheese, and stir well to combine the mixture.

4 Divide the mixture among the artichoke bottoms arranged in an oiled baking tin. Sprinkle over the remaining cheese. Cook on the barbecue for 12 minutes, garnish with parsley and serve.

SPINACH WITH RAISINS AND PINE NUTS

Raisins and pine nuts are frequent partners in Spanish recipes. In this recipe they are tossed with wilted spinach and croûtons, and can be cooked quickly in a flameproof pan on the barbecue.

INGREDIENTS

50g/2oz/⅓ cup raisins
1 thick slice crusty white bread
45ml/3 tbsp olive oil
25g/1oz/⅓ cup pine nuts
500g/1¼ lb young spinach, stalks removed
2 garlic cloves, crushed
salt and freshly ground black pepper

SERVES 4

1 Put the raisins in a bowl, cover with boiling water and leave to soak for 10 minutes. Drain and set aside.

2 Cut the bread into cubes and discard the crusts. Heat 30ml/2 tbsp of the olive oil in a large frying pan and fry the bread until golden brown.

3 Heat the remaining oil and fry the pine nuts, on the barbecue or hob, until beginning to colour. Add the spinach and garlic and cook quickly, turning the spinach until it has just wilted. Toss in the raisins and season lightly with salt and pepper. Transfer to a serving dish. Scatter with croûtons and serve.

GRILLED VEGETABLE TERRINE

∘ ∘ ∘

*A colourful, layered terrine, using all the vegetables associated with the Mediterranean, makes
a successful and elegant dish for outdoor eating. Barbecuing the vegetables adds to the flavour.*

INGREDIENTS

*2 large red peppers, quartered,
cored and seeded
2 large yellow peppers, quartered,
cored and seeded
1 large aubergine, sliced lengthways
2 large courgettes, sliced
lengthways
90ml/6 tbsp olive oil
1 large red onion, thinly sliced
75g/3oz/½ cup raisins
15ml/1 tbsp tomato purée
15ml/1 tbsp red wine vinegar
400ml/14fl oz/1⅔ cups tomato
juice
15g/½oz/2 tbsp powdered gelatine
fresh basil leaves, to garnish*

FOR THE DRESSING
*90ml/6 tbsp extra virgin olive oil
30ml/2 tbsp red wine vinegar
salt and freshly ground black
pepper*

SERVES 6

1 Grill the peppers, skin-side down, on a hot barbecue or grill, until the skins are beginning to blacken. Transfer to a bowl, cover and leave to cool.

2 Brush the aubergine and courgette slices with oil and cook until tender and golden, turning occasionally.

3 Heat the remaining oil in a pan and add the onion, raisins, tomato purée and red wine vinegar. Cook until soft and syrupy. Leave to cool in the pan.

4 Pour half the tomato juice into a saucepan and sprinkle with the gelatine. Dissolve gently over a very low heat, stirring continuously.

5 Line an oiled 1.75 litre/3 pint/ 7½ cup terrine with clear film, leaving a little hanging over the sides. Place a layer of red peppers in the bottom and pour in enough of the tomato juice with gelatine to cover. Repeat with the aubergines, courgettes, yellow peppers and onion mixture, ending with another layer of red peppers and covering each layer with tomato juice and gelatine.

6 Add the remaining tomato juice to any left in the pan and pour into the terrine. Give it a sharp tap to eliminate air bubbles. Cover the terrine with clear film and chill until set.

7 To make the dressing, whisk the oil and vinegar, and season with salt and black pepper. Turn out the terrine and serve in thick slices, drizzled with the dressing. Garnish with the basil leaves.

SUMMER VEGETABLES WITH YOGURT PESTO

*Char-grilled vegetables make a meal on their own, or are delicious served as a
Mediterranean-style accompaniment to grilled meats and fish.*

INGREDIENTS

2 small aubergines
2 large courgettes
1 red pepper
1 yellow pepper
1 fennel bulb
1 red onion
olive oil, for brushing
salt and freshly ground black
pepper

FOR THE YOGURT PESTO
150ml/¼ pint/⅔ cup Greek-style
yogurt
45ml/3 tbsp pesto

SERVES 4

2 Use a sharp kitchen knife to cut the courgettes in half lengthways. Cut the peppers in half, removing the seeds but leaving the stalks in place.

3 Slice the fennel bulb and the red onion into thick wedges, using a sharp kitchen knife.

5 Arrange the vegetables on the hot barbecue, brush generously with olive oil and sprinkle with plenty of salt and freshly ground black pepper.

6 Cook the vegetables until golden brown and tender, turning occasionally. The aubergines and peppers will take 6–8 minutes to cook, the courgettes, onion and fennel 4–5 minutes. Serve the vegetables as soon as they are cooked, with the yogurt pesto.

1 Cut the aubergines into 1cm/½in slices. Sprinkle with salt and leave to drain for about 30 minutes. Rinse well in cold running water and pat dry.

4 Stir the yogurt and pesto lightly together in a bowl, to make a marbled sauce. Spoon the yogurt pesto into a serving bowl and set aside.

Cook's Tip

Baby vegetables make excellent candidates for grilling whole, so look out for baby aubergines and peppers, in particular. There's no need to salt the aubergines if they're small.

WILD RICE WITH VEGETABLES

Wild rice makes a special accompaniment to barbecued vegetables in a simple vinaigrette dressing. This recipe can be served as a side dish, but it also makes a tasty meal on its own.

INGREDIENTS

225g/8oz/1 cup wild and long
grain rice mixture
1 large aubergine, thickly sliced
1 red, 1 yellow and 1 green pepper,
quartered, cored and seeded
2 red onions, sliced
225g/8oz shiitake mushrooms
2 small courgettes, cut in half
lengthways
olive oil, for brushing
30ml/2 tbsp chopped fresh thyme

FOR THE DRESSING
90ml/6 tbsp extra virgin olive oil
30ml/2 tbsp balsamic vinegar
2 garlic cloves, crushed
salt and freshly ground black
pepper

SERVES 4

1 Put the wild and long grain rice mixture in a pan of cold salted water. Bring to the boil, then reduce the heat, cover and cook gently for about 30–40 minutes until the grains are tender (or follow the cooking instructions on the packet, if appropriate).

2 To make the dressing, mix together the olive oil, vinegar, crushed garlic and seasoning in a bowl or screw-topped jar until well blended.

3 Arrange the vegetables on a rack. Brush with olive oil and cook on a hot barbecue or grill for 8–10 minutes, until tender and well browned, turning them occasionally and basting with oil.

4 Drain the rice and toss in half the dressing. Tip into a serving dish and arrange the grilled vegetables on top. Pour over the remaining dressing and scatter over the chopped fresh thyme.

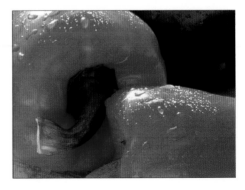

POTATO SKEWERS WITH MUSTARD DIP

∘ ∘ ∘

Potatoes cooked on the barbecue have a tasty flavour and crisp skin.
These skewers are served with a thick, garlic-rich dip.

INGREDIENTS

1kg/2¼lb small new potatoes
200g/7oz/2 cups shallots, halved
30ml/2 tbsp olive oil
15ml/1 tbsp sea salt

FOR THE MUSTARD DIP
4 garlic cloves, crushed
2 egg yolks
30ml/2 tbsp lemon juice
300ml/½ pint/1¼ cups extra
virgin olive oil
10ml/2 tsp whole-grain mustard
salt and freshly ground black
pepper

SERVES 4

1 To make the mustard dip, place the garlic, egg yolks and lemon juice in a blender or food processor and process for a few seconds until smooth.

2 With the motor running, add the oil, until the mixture forms a thick cream. Add the mustard and season.

3 Par-boil the potatoes in salted boiling water for about 5 minutes. Drain well and then thread them on to metal skewers with the shallots.

4 Brush with olive oil and sprinkle with sea salt. Cook for 10–12 minutes over a hot barbecue, turning often, until tender. Serve with the mustard dip.

POTATO WEDGES WITH GARLIC AND ROSEMARY

° ° °

*Toss the potato wedges in fragrant, garlicky olive oil with chopped fresh rosemary
before barbecuing them over the coals.*

INGREDIENTS

675g/1½ lb medium old potatoes
15ml/1 tbsp olive oil
2 garlic cloves, thinly sliced
*60ml/4 tbsp chopped fresh
rosemary*
*salt and freshly ground black
pepper*

SERVES 4

1 Cut each potato into four wedges
and par-boil in boiling salted water for
5 minutes. Drain well.

2 Toss the potatoes in the olive oil
with the garlic, rosemary and black
pepper. Arrange on a grill rack.

3 Cook the potatoes on a hot
barbecue for about 15 minutes, turning
occasionally, until the wedges are crisp
and golden brown.

SPANISH POTATOES

∘ ∘ ∘

This is an adaptation of a traditional recipe for peppery fried potatoes. Cook the potatoes in a flameproof dish on the barbecue or in a pan on the hob, and serve them with barbecued meats.

INGREDIENTS

675g/1½ lb small new potatoes
75ml/5 tbsp olive oil
2 garlic cloves, sliced
2.5ml/½ tsp crushed chillies
2.5ml/½ tsp ground cumin
10ml/2 tsp paprika
30ml/2 tbsp red or white wine
vinegar
1 red or green pepper, sliced
coarse sea salt, to serve (optional)

SERVES 4

1 Cook the potatoes in a saucepan of boiling salted water until almost tender. Drain and cut into chunks.

2 Heat the olive oil in a large frying pan or sauté pan and fry the potatoes, turning them frequently, until golden.

3 Meanwhile, crush together the garlic, chillies and cumin using a pestle and mortar. Mix with the paprika and wine vinegar to form a thick paste.

4 Add the garlic mixture to the potatoes with the sliced pepper and cook, stirring, for 2 minutes. Serve warm, or leave until cold. Scatter with coarse sea salt, if you wish, to serve.

SALADS AND ACCOMPANIMENTS

———✦———

Cool salads are a perfect foil to barbecued food, but they

should have assertive characters of their own. The recipes that

follow include some marvellous sunny, Mediterranean flavours that

taste especially good on summer days, and a selection of them would

be perfect as part of a buffet for a party. Don't forget that you can use

the barbecue to grill ingredients such as tomatoes, peppers, aubergines

and radicchio – it will give them an intense, smoky flavour that

will pervade the whole salad.

APPLE COLESLAW

° ° °

There are many variations of this traditional salad; this recipe combines the sweet flavours of apple and carrot with a hint of celery. Prepare the salad in advance and chill until needed.

INGREDIENTS

450g/1lb white cabbage
1 medium onion
2 apples, peeled and cored
175g/6oz carrots, peeled
150ml/5fl oz/²⁄₃ cup mayonnaise
5ml/1 tsp celery salt
freshly ground black pepper

SERVES 4

1 Remove the outer leaves from the white cabbage and, using a heavy knife, cut it into 5cm/2in wedges. Remove and discard the stem sections.

2 Feed the cabbage wedges and the onion through the slicing blade of a food processor. Change to a grating blade and grate the apples and carrots. If you do not have a food processor, use a vegetable slicer and a hand grater.

3 Combine the salad ingredients in a large mixing bowl. Fold in the mayonnaise and season with celery salt and freshly ground black pepper.

Cook's Tip

This recipe can be adapted easily to suit different tastes. Add 125g/4oz/¹⁄₂ cup chopped walnuts or raisins for added texture, or, for a richer, more substantial coleslaw, add 125g/4oz/¹⁄₂ cup grated Cheddar cheese.

172

TOMATO AND FETA CHEESE SALAD

° ° °

Sweet sun-ripened tomatoes are rarely more delicious than when mixed with feta cheese and olive oil. This salad can be served with any barbecued meats, fish or vegetables.

INGREDIENTS

900g/2lb tomatoes
200g/7oz feta cheese
120ml/4fl oz/½ cup olive oil
12 black olives
4 sprigs fresh basil
freshly ground black pepper

SERVES 4

3 Crumble the feta cheese over the tomatoes, sprinkle with olive oil, then sprinkle with olives and fresh basil. Season with freshly ground black pepper and serve at room temperature.

1 Remove the tough cores from the tomatoes with a small kitchen knife.

2 Slice the tomatoes thickly on a chopping board and arrange the slices in a wide-based shallow dish.

Cook's Tip

Feta cheese has a strong flavour and can be very salty. For an authentic flavour and texture, look out for Greek, Cypriot or Turkish feta.

CURLY ENDIVE SALAD WITH BACON

When they are in season, young dandelion leaves could be included in this French salad.
If you wish, sprinkle the salad with chopped hard-boiled egg.

2 Heat 15ml/1 tbsp oil in a pan over a medium heat and add the bacon. Fry until browned. Remove the bacon and drain on kitchen paper.

3 Add another 30ml/2 tbsp oil to the pan and fry the bread cubes over a medium heat, turning frequently, until browned. Remove the bread cubes with a slotted spoon and drain on kitchen paper. Discard any remaining fat.

INGREDIENTS

225g/8oz/6 cups curly endive or escarole leaves
75–90ml/5–6 tbsp extra virgin olive oil
175g/6oz piece of smoked bacon, diced
thick slice white bread, cubed
1 small garlic clove, finely chopped
15ml/1 tbsp red wine vinegar
10ml/2 tsp Dijon mustard
salt and freshly ground black pepper

SERVES 4

1 Tear the lettuce leaves into bite-size pieces and put them in a large salad bowl. Set the bowl aside.

4 Stir the garlic, vinegar and mustard into the pan with the remaining oil and warm through. Season to taste. Pour the dressing over the salad and sprinkle with the fried bacon and croûtons.

POTATO SALAD WITH SAUSAGE

The addition of garlic sausage makes this a substantial salad to serve as part of a buffet, but if it is to accompany barbecued meat or fish you can make it with potatoes alone.

INGREDIENTS

450g/1lb small waxy potatoes
30–45ml/2–3 tbsp dry white wine
2 shallots, finely chopped
15ml/1 tbsp chopped fresh parsley
15ml/1 tbsp chopped fresh tarragon
175g/6oz French garlic sausage
fresh parsley, to garnish
salt and freshly ground black pepper

FOR THE VINAIGRETTE
10ml/2 tsp Dijon mustard
15ml/1 tbsp tarragon vinegar or white wine vinegar
75ml/5 tbsp extra virgin olive oil

SERVES 4

1 Cook the potatoes in boiling salted water for 10–15 minutes, until tender. Drain them, and refresh under cold running water. Cut them into 5mm/¼ in slices, place them in a large bowl and sprinkle with the white wine and the chopped shallots.

2 To make the vinaigrette, mix the Dijon mustard and vinegar in a small bowl, then whisk in the olive oil, 15ml/1 tbsp at a time. Season well with salt and freshly ground black and pour over the potatoes.

3 Add the chopped fresh parsley and tarragon to the potatoes in the bowl and toss until well mixed.

4 Slice the garlic sausage thinly and toss with the potatoes. Season with salt and pepper to taste and serve at room temperature, garnished with parsley.

GREEN BEAN SALAD WITH EGG TOPPING

∘ ∘ ∘

When green beans are fresh and plentiful, serve them lightly cooked as a salad topped with butter-fried breadcrumbs, egg and fresh parsley.

INGREDIENTS

675g/1½ lb green beans, topped and tailed
30ml/2 tbsp extra virgin olive oil
30ml/2 tbsp butter
50g/2oz/1 cup fresh white breadcrumbs
60ml/4 tbsp chopped fresh parsley
1 egg, hard-boiled and shelled
salt

SERVES 4

1 Bring a large pan of salted water to the boil. Add the beans and cook for 6 minutes. Drain well, toss the beans in olive oil and allow to cool.

2 Heat the butter in a large frying pan, add the breadcrumbs and fry until golden. Remove the frying pan from the heat, add the chopped fresh parsley, then grate in the hard-boiled egg.

3 Place the beans in a shallow serving dish and spoon on the breadcrumb topping. If preparing the salad in advance and chilling it in the fridge until needed, allow it to come to room temperature before serving.

TABBOULEH

This classic Lebanese salad has become very popular everywhere. It makes an ideal substitute for a rice dish and is especially good with barbecued lamb.

INGREDIENTS

175g/6oz/1 cup fine bulgur wheat
juice of 1 lemon
45ml/3 tbsp olive oil
40g/1½ oz fresh parsley, finely chopped
45ml/3 tbsp fresh mint, chopped
4–5 spring onions, chopped
1 green pepper, sliced
salt and freshly ground black pepper
2 large tomatoes, diced, and black olives, to garnish

SERVES 4

1 Put the bulgur wheat in a large bowl. Add enough cold water to cover the wheat and let it stand for at least 30 minutes and up to 2 hours.

2 Drain and squeeze the wheat with your hands to remove excess water. The bulgur wheat will swell to double its original size. Spread the wheat on kitchen paper to allow to dry completely.

3 Place the bulgur wheat in a large bowl, add the lemon juice, the olive oil and a little salt and pepper. Allow to stand for 1–2 hours if possible, in order for the flavours to develop.

4 Add the chopped parsley, mint, spring onions and pepper to the wheat in the bowl and mix well. Garnish with diced tomatoes and olives and serve. The tabbouleh can be prepared in advance, covered with clear film and stored in the fridge until needed.

PEPPERS WITH TOMATOES AND ANCHOVIES

This is a Sicilian-style salad full of warm Mediterranean flavours. The salad improves if it is made and dressed an hour or two before serving.

INGREDIENTS

1 red pepper
1 yellow pepper
4 ripe plum tomatoes, sliced
2 canned anchovies, drained and chopped
4 sun-dried tomatoes in oil, drained and sliced
15ml/1 tbsp capers, drained
15ml/1 tbsp pine nuts
1 garlic clove, very finely sliced

FOR THE DRESSING
75ml/5 tbsp extra virgin olive oil
15ml/1 tbsp balsamic vinegar
5ml/1 tsp lemon juice
chopped fresh mixed herbs
salt and freshly ground black pepper

SERVES 4

1 Cut the peppers in half and remove the seeds and stalks. Cut into quarters and cook, skin side down, over a hot barbecue or grill until the skin chars. Transfer to a bowl and leave to cool. Peel the peppers and cut into strips.

2 Arrange the peppers and fresh tomatoes on a serving dish. Scatter over the anchovies, sun-dried tomatoes, capers, pine nuts and garlic.

3 To make the dressing, mix together the olive oil, vinegar, lemon juice and chopped fresh herbs and season with plenty of salt and pepper. Pour the dressing over the salad before serving.

SWEET AND SOUR ONION SALAD

This recipe for tangy, glazed onions in the Provençal style makes an unusual and flavourful accompaniment to barbecued steaks.

INGREDIENTS

450g/1lb baby onions, peeled
50ml/2fl oz/¼ cup wine vinegar
45ml/3 tbsp olive oil
40g/1½ oz/3 tbsp caster sugar
45ml/3 tbsp tomato purée
1 bay leaf
2 parsley sprigs
65g/2½ oz/½ cup raisins
salt and freshly ground black pepper

SERVES 6

1 Put all the ingredients in a pan with 300ml/½ pint/1¼ cups water. Bring to the boil and simmer gently, uncovered, for 45 minutes, or until the onions are tender and the liquid has evaporated.

2 Remove the bay leaf and parsley, from the pan and check the seasoning. Transfer the contents of the pan to a large serving dish. Serve the salad at room temperature.

SPICED AUBERGINE SALAD

Serve this Middle-Eastern influenced salad with warm pitta bread as a starter, or as an accompaniment to any number of barbecued main course dishes.

INGREDIENTS

2 small aubergines, sliced
75ml/5 tbsp olive oil
50ml/2fl oz/¼ cup red wine vinegar
2 garlic cloves, crushed
15ml/1 tbsp lemon juice
2.5ml/½ tsp ground cumin
2.5ml/½ tsp ground coriander
½ cucumber, thinly sliced
2 well-flavoured tomatoes, thinly sliced
30ml/2 tbsp natural yogurt
salt and freshly ground black pepper
chopped flat leaf parsley, to garnish

SERVES 4

1 Brush the aubergine slices lightly with some of the olive oil and cook over a hot barbecue or grill until golden and tender, turning once. Allow the slices to cool slightly, then cut them into quarters.

2 Mix the remaining olive oil with the vinegar, crushed garlic, lemon juice, cumin and ground coriander. Season with plenty of salt and pepper and mix thoroughly. Add the warm aubergines, stir well and chill for at least 2 hours. Add the cucumber and tomatoes. Transfer the salad to a serving dish and spoon the natural yogurt on top. Garnish with chopped parsley, to serve.

RADICCHIO, ARTICHOKE AND WALNUT SALAD

The distinctive, earthy taste of Jerusalem artichokes makes a lovely contrast to the sharp
freshness of radicchio and lemon. Serve warm or cold as an accompaniment to barbecued meats.

INGREDIENTS

1 large radicchio or 150g/5oz
radicchio leaves, washed
40g/1½ oz/6 tbsp walnut pieces
45ml/3 tbsp walnut oil
500g/1¼ lb Jerusalem artichokes
grated rind and juice of
1 lemon
coarse sea salt and freshly ground
black pepper
flat leaf parsley, to garnish

SERVES 4

1 If using a whole radicchio, cut it into 8–10 wedges. Place the wedges or leaves in a flameproof dish. Scatter on the walnuts, drizzle with oil and season. Grill for 2–3 minutes.

2 Peel the artichokes and cut up any large ones so that the pieces are all roughly the same size. Add to a pan of boiling salted water with half the lemon juice and cook for 5–7 minutes until tender. Drain.

3 Toss the artichokes into the salad with the remaining lemon juice and the grated rind. Season with coarse sea salt and freshly ground black pepper. Grill until just beginning to brown and then serve at once, garnished with fresh flat leaf parsley.

WARM BROAD BEAN AND FETA SALAD

*This recipe is loosely based on a typical medley of fresh-tasting salad ingredients –
broad beans, tomatoes and feta cheese. It's lovely either warm or cold.*

INGREDIENTS

900g/2lb fresh broad beans, or
350g/12oz frozen beans
60ml/4 tbsp olive oil
175g/6oz plum tomatoes, halved,
or quartered if large
4 garlic cloves, crushed
115g/4oz firm feta cheese, cut into
chunks
45ml/3 tbsp chopped fresh dill,
plus extra to garnish
12 black olives
salt and freshly ground black
pepper

SERVES 4–6

1 Shell the broad beans, then cook them in boiling, salted water until they are just tender. Drain and set aside.

2 Meanwhile, heat the olive oil in a heavy-based frying pan and add the tomatoes and garlic. Cook until the tomatoes are beginning to colour.

3 Add the feta to the frying pan and toss the ingredients together for 1 minute. Mix with the drained beans, dill, olives and salt and pepper. Serve garnished with the chopped fresh dill.

GRILLED HALLOUMI AND GRAPE SALAD

∘ ∘ ∘

In the eastern Mediterranean, halloumi cheese is often served grilled or fried for breakfast or supper. In this recipe it's tossed with sweet, juicy grapes which complement its distinctive flavour.

INGREDIENTS

150g/5oz mixed green salad leaves
75g/3oz seedless green grapes
75g/3oz seedless black grapes
250g/9oz halloumi cheese
30ml/2 tbsp olive oil
fresh young thyme leaves or dill, to garnish

FOR THE DRESSING
60ml/4 tbsp olive oil
15ml/1 tbsp lemon juice
2.5ml/½ tsp caster sugar
15ml/1 tbsp chopped fresh thyme or dill
salt and freshly ground black pepper

SERVES 4

1 To make the dressing, mix the olive oil, lemon juice and sugar together in a bowl. Season well with plenty of salt and black pepper. Stir in the chopped fresh thyme or dill and set aside.

2 Toss together the mixed green salad leaves and the green and black grapes, then transfer to a large serving plate or salad bowl.

3 Slice the halloumi cheese. Brush the slices with olive oil and cook briefly over a medium barbecue, or pan-fry on the stove, until golden, turning once.

4 Arrange the cooked cheese over the salad. Pour over the dressing and garnish with thyme or dill leaves.

183

CHORIZO IN OLIVE OIL

o ⚬ o

*Spanish chorizo sausage has a deliciously pungent taste. Frying chorizo with onions and olive oil
is one of the best ways of using it; you can also cook it on the barbecue, brushed with olive oil.*

INGREDIENTS

*75ml/5 tbsp extra virgin olive oil
350g/12oz chorizo sausage, sliced
1 large onion, thinly sliced
flat leaf parsley, roughly chopped,
to garnish*

SERVES 4

1 Heat the olive oil in a frying pan
and fry the chorizo sausage over a high
heat until beginning to colour. Remove
from the pan with a slotted spoon.

2 Add the onion slices to the pan and
fry until golden. Return the sausage
slices to the pan to heat through for
about 1 minute.

3 Tip the mixture into a shallow
serving dish and scatter with the
roughly chopped flat-leaf parsley.
Serve the chorizo on its own or as
a side dish, with warm crusty bread.

Variation

Chorizo is usually available
in large supermarkets and
delicatessens, but any other
similar spicy sausage can be
used as a substitute.

184

BROAD BEAN, MUSHROOM AND CHORIZO SALAD

This salad can be served as a first course or as part of a buffet menu. Prepare it a day in advance and store it in the fridge until needed.

INGREDIENTS

225g/8oz shelled broad beans
175g/6oz chorizo sausage
60ml/4 tbsp extra virgin olive oil
225g/8oz brown cap mushrooms,
sliced
handful of fresh chives
salt and freshly ground black
pepper

SERVES 4

1 Cook the broad beans in a large saucepan of boiling, salted water until just tender. Drain and refresh under cold running water. If the beans are large, peel away the tough outer skins.

2 Remove the skin from the chorizo sausage and cut it into small chunks. Heat the oil in a frying pan, add the chorizo and cook for 2 minutes. Empty into a bowl with the mushrooms, mix well and leave aside to cool.

3 Chop half the chives and stir the beans and chopped chives into the mushroom mixture. Season to taste. Serve the salad at room temperature, garnished with the remaining chives.

BABY AUBERGINES WITH RAISINS AND PINE NUTS

This is a recipe with an Italian influence, in a style that would have been familiar in Renaissance times. If possible, make it a day in advance, to allow the sweet and sour flavours to develop.

INGREDIENTS

12 baby aubergines, halved
250ml/8fl oz/1 cup extra virgin
olive oil
juice of 1 lemon
30ml/2 tbsp balsamic vinegar
3 cloves
25g/1oz/⅓ cup pine nuts
25g/1oz/2 tbsp raisins
15ml/1 tbsp granulated sugar
1 bay leaf
large pinch of dried chilli flakes
salt and freshly ground black
pepper

SERVES 4

1 Brush the aubergines with olive oil and grill over a hot barbecue for 10 minutes, until charred, turning once.

2 To make the dressing, combine the remaining olive oil with the lemon juice, vinegar, cloves, pine nuts, raisins, sugar and bay leaf. Add the chilli flakes and salt and pepper and mix well.

3 Place the hot aubergines in an earthenware or glass bowl, and pour over the dressing. Leave to cool, turning the aubergines once or twice. Serve the salad cold.

SQUASH A LA GRECQUE

○ ○ ○

This salad makes a wonderful side dish to almost any barbecued meal. Cook the baby squashes until they are perfectly tender, so they can fully absorb the delicious flavours of the dressing.

INGREDIENTS

175g/6oz patty-pan squashes
250ml/8fl oz/1 cup white wine
juice of 2 lemons
sprig of fresh thyme
1 bay leaf
handful of fresh chervil, roughly chopped
1.5ml/¼ tsp coriander seeds, crushed
75ml/5 tbsp olive oil
salt and freshly ground black pepper

SERVES 4

3 Reduce the liquid by boiling hard for 10 minutes. Strain it and pour it over the squashes. Leave until cool for the flavours to be absorbed. Serve cold.

1 Blanch the patty-pan squashes in boiling water for 3 minutes, drain, then refresh under cold running water.

2 Place the remaining ingredients in a pan, add 150ml/¼ pint/⅔ cup of water and let simmer. Add the squashes and cook for 10 minutes, then remove.

Salsas, Dips and Marinades

———◆———

The powerful flavours of barbecued meat and fish call for spicy,

lively accompaniments. Chunky salsas are ideal, with their

intriguing combination of cool, crisp ingredients and fiery flavours.

Tangy barbecue sauce is a more traditional alternative that children

adore. For a subtler effect, melt a pat of butter flavoured with herbs,

garlic or anchovies over a plainly grilled steak or fish. This chapter

also includes some appetizing dips to go with crisps, bread sticks

and crudités, and a selection of delicious marinades suitable for

a wide variety of meat and fish.

CHUNKY CHERRY TOMATO SALSA

Succulent cherry tomatoes and refreshing cucumber form the base of this delicious dill-seasoned salsa. Prepare up to 1 day in advance and store in the fridge until needed.

INGREDIENTS

1 ridge cucumber
5ml/1 tsp sea salt
500g/1¼ lb cherry tomatoes
grated rind and juice of 1 lemon
45ml/3 tbsp chilli oil
2.5ml/½ tsp dried chilli flakes
30ml/2 tbsp chopped fresh dill
1 garlic clove, finely chopped
salt and freshly ground black pepper

SERVES 4

1 Trim the ends off the cucumber and cut it into 2.5cm/1in lengths, then cut each piece lengthways into thin slices. Place in a colander and sprinkle with sea salt. Leave for 5 minutes.

2 Rinse the cucumber slices under cold water and dry with kitchen paper.

3 Quarter the cherry tomatoes and place in a bowl with the cucumber.

4 Whisk together the lemon rind and juice, chilli oil, chilli flakes, dill and garlic. Season, then pour over the tomato and cucumber and toss well. Marinate for 2 hours before serving.

Cook's Tip

Try flavouring the salsa with other herbs: tarragon, coriander or mint.

SALSA VERDE

There are many versions of this classic green salsa. Try this one drizzled over char-grilled squid, or with jacket potatoes.

INGREDIENTS

2–4 green chillies, halved
8 spring onions
2 garlic cloves
50g/2oz salted capers
sprig of fresh tarragon
bunch of fresh parsley
grated rind and juice of 1 lime
juice of 1 lemon
90ml/6 tbsp olive oil
about 15ml/1 tbsp green Tabasco
sauce, to taste
freshly ground black pepper

SERVES 4

1 Seed the chillies and trim the spring onions. Halve the garlic cloves. Place in a food processor and pulse briefly.

2 Use your fingers to rub the excess salt off the capers. Add them, with the tarragon and parsley, to the food processor and pulse again until the ingredients are quite finely chopped.

3 Transfer the mixture to a large bowl. Mix in the lime rind and juice, lemon juice and olive oil, stirring lightly so the citrus juice and oil do not emulsify.

4 Add green Tabasco sauce, a little at a time, and black pepper to taste. Chill the salsa in the fridge until ready to serve, but do not prepare it more than 8 hours in advance.

FIERY CITRUS SALSA

*This unusual salsa makes a fantastic marinade for shellfish and it is also
delicious drizzled over barbecued meat.*

INGREDIENTS

1 orange
1 green apple
2 fresh red chillies
1 garlic clove
8 fresh mint leaves
juice of 1 lemon
salt and freshly ground black
pepper

SERVES 4

1 Using a sharp knife, remove the peel and pith from the orange and, working over a bowl to catch the juices, cut out the segments. Squeeze any remaining juice into the bowl.

2 Use a sharp kitchen knife to peel the apple and slice it into wedges. Remove and discard the apple core.

3 Halve the chillies and remove the seeds, then place them in a blender or food processor with the orange segments and juice, apple wedges, garlic and mint.

4 Process until smooth. With the motor running, slowly pour in the lemon juice. Season to taste with salt and freshly ground black pepper and serve immediately.

BARBECUED SWEETCORN SALSA

Serve this succulent salsa with grilled gammon or pork, or with smoked meats. The char-grilled corn cob makes the salsa particularly flavoursome.

INGREDIENTS

2 corn cobs
30ml/2 tbsp melted butter
4 tomatoes
6 spring onions, finely chopped
1 garlic clove, finely chopped
30ml/2 tbsp lemon juice
30ml/2 tbsp olive oil
red Tabasco sauce, to taste
salt and freshly ground black pepper

SERVES 4

3 Skewer the tomatoes and hold over the barbecue or grill for about 2 minutes, turning, until the skin splits and wrinkles. Slip off the skins and dice the flesh. Add to the sweetcorn with the spring onions and chopped garlic.

4 Stir the lemon juice and olive oil together, adding Tabasco, salt and black pepper to taste. Pour over the salsa, stir well, cover and leave to marinate at room temperature for 1–2 hours before serving.

1 Remove the husks and silks from the corn cobs. Brush with the melted butter and gently barbecue or grill them for about 20 minutes, turning occasionally, until tender and charred.

2 To remove the kernels, stand each cob upright on a chopping board and use a large, heavy knife to slice down the length of the cob. Put the kernels in a mixing bowl.

BARBECUE SAUCE

Brush this sauce liberally over chicken drumsticks, chops or kebabs before cooking on the barbecue, or serve as a hot or cold accompaniment to hot dogs and burgers.

INGREDIENTS

30ml/2 tbsp vegetable oil
1 large onion, chopped
2 garlic cloves, crushed
400g/14oz can tomatoes
30ml/2 tbsp Worcestershire sauce
15ml/1 tbsp white wine vinegar
45ml/3 tbsp honey
5ml/1 tsp mustard powder
2.5ml/½ tsp chilli seasoning or
mild chilli powder
salt and freshly ground black
pepper

SERVES 4

3 Pour into a food processor or blender and process until smooth.

4 Press through a sieve if you prefer. Adjust the seasoning to taste.

1 Heat the vegetable oil in a large saucepan and fry the onions and garlic until soft and golden.

2 Stir in the remaining ingredients and simmer, uncovered, for about 15–20 minutes, stirring occasionally. Remove the saucepan from the heat and allow to cool slightly.

GUACAMOLE

Nachos or tortilla chips are the classic accompaniments for this classic Mexican dip, but it also tastes great served on the side with burgers or kebabs.

INGREDIENTS

2 ripe avocados
2 red chillies, seeded
1 garlic clove
1 shallot
30ml/2 tbsp olive oil, plus
extra to serve
juice of 1 lemon
salt
fresh flat leaf parsley, to garnish

SERVES 4

1 Halve the avocados, flick out the stones, using the point of a sharp knife, and use a dessert spoon to scoop the flesh into a large bowl.

2 Mash the flesh well, using a potato masher or a large fork, so that the avocado is a fairly smooth consistency.

3 Finely chop the chillies, garlic clove and shallot, then stir into the mashed avocado with the olive oil and lemon juice. Add salt to taste and mix well.

4 Spoon the mixture into a serving bowl. Drizzle over a little more olive oil and scatter with flat leaf parsley leaves. Serve immediately. Guacamole will not keep for very long but can be prepared up to 8 hours in advance and stored in the fridge, sprinkled with lemon juice and covered with clear film.

TOFFEE ONION RELISH

° ° °

Slow, gentle cooking reduces the onions to a soft, caramelized relish.
It makes a tasty addition to many barbecue menus.

2 Heat the butter and oil together in a large saucepan. Add the onions and sugar and cook very gently for 30 minutes over a low heat, stirring occasionally, until reduced to a soft rich brown toffeed mixture.

3 Roughly chop the capers and stir them into the toffee onions. Allow to cool completely.

4 Stir in the chopped fresh parsley and add salt and ground black pepper to taste. Cover with clear film and chill in the fridge until ready to serve.

INGREDIENTS

3 large onions
50g/2oz/4 tbsp butter
30ml/2 tbsp olive oil
30ml/2 tbsp light muscovado sugar
30ml/2 tbsp pickled capers
30ml/2 tbsp chopped fresh parsley
salt and freshly ground black pepper

SERVES 4

1 Peel the onions and halve them vertically, through the core, using a sharp knife. Slice them thinly.

PARSLEY BUTTER

· · ·

*This butter, or one of the variations below, makes a subtle accompaniment to
barbecued food, particularly fish with a delicate flavour.*

INGREDIENTS
115g/4oz/¹⁄₂ cup softened butter
30ml/2 tbsp parsley, finely chopped
2.5ml/¹⁄₂ tsp lemon juice
cayenne pepper
salt and freshly ground black pepper

SERVES 4

1 Beat the butter until creamy, then
beat in the parsley, lemon juice and
cayenne pepper, and season lightly.

2 Spread the butter 5mm/¹⁄₄ in thick
on to foil and chill, then cut into shapes
with a knife or fancy cutter.

3 Alternatively, form the butter into
a roll, wrap in clear film or foil and
chill. Cut off slices as required.

Variations
LEMON OR LIME BUTTER
Add 15ml/1 tbsp finely grated
lemon or lime rind and 15ml/
1 tbsp juice to the butter.

HERB BUTTER
Replace the parsley with
30ml/2 tbsp chopped mint,
chives or tarragon.

GARLIC BUTTER
Add 2 crushed garlic cloves
to the butter with 15–30ml/
1–2 tbsp chopped parsley.

ANCHOVY BUTTER
Add 6 anchovy fillets, drained of
oil and mashed with a fork, to the
butter. Season with pepper only.

MUSTARD BUTTER
Add 10ml/2 tsp English mustard
and 30ml/2 tbsp chopped chives
to the butter.

These butters will keep in
the fridge for several days,
and will also freeze, wrapped
in clear film or foil to avoid
any loss of flavour.

BASIL AND LEMON MAYONNAISE

This fresh mayonnaise is flavoured with lemon and two types of basil. Serve as a dip with potato crisps or crudités, or with salads and jacket potatoes.

INGREDIENTS

2 size 1 egg yolks
15ml/1 tbsp lemon juice
150ml/¼ pint/⅔ cup olive oil
150ml/¼ pint/⅔ cup sunflower oil
handful of green basil leaves
handful of opal basil leaves
4 garlic cloves, crushed
salt and freshly ground black pepper

SERVES 4

1 Place the egg yolks and lemon juice in a blender or food processor and process them briefly together.

2 In a jug, stir the two oils together. With the machine running, pour in the oil very slowly, a drop at a time.

3 Once half the oil has been added the remainder can be incorporated more quickly. Continue processing to form a thick, creamy mayonnaise.

4 Tear both types of basil into small pieces and stir into the mayonnaise with the crushed garlic and seasoning. Transfer to a serving dish, cover and chill until ready to serve.

MELLOW GARLIC DIP

Two whole heads of garlic may seem too much but, once cooked, the taste is sweet and mellow.
Serve with crunchy bread sticks and potato crisps.

2 When cool enough to handle, separate the garlic cloves and peel. Place on a chopping board and sprinkle with salt. Mash the garlic with a fork until puréed.

3 Place the garlic in a large bowl and stir in the mayonnaise, yogurt and wholegrain mustard. Mix well.

INGREDIENTS

2 whole garlic heads
15ml/1 tbsp olive oil
60ml/4 tbsp mayonnaise
75ml/5 tbsp Greek-style yogurt
5ml/1 tsp wholegrain mustard
salt and freshly ground black
pepper

SERVES 4

1 Slice the tops from the heads of garlic, using a sharp knife. Brush with olive oil and wrap in foil. Cook on a medium-hot barbecue or oven-grill for 25 minutes, turning occasionally.

4 Check the seasoning, adding more salt and pepper to taste, then spoon the dip into a serving bowl. Cover and chill in the fridge until ready to serve.

CREAMY AUBERGINE DIP

*Spread this velvet-textured dip thickly on to slices of French bread toasted on the barbecue,
then top with slivers of sun-dried tomato to make wonderful Italian-style crostini.*

INGREDIENTS

1 large aubergine
30ml/2 tbsp olive oil
1 small onion, finely chopped
2 garlic cloves, finely chopped
60ml/4 tbsp chopped fresh parsley
75ml/5 tbsp crème fraîche
red Tabasco sauce, to taste
juice of 1 lemon, to taste
*salt and freshly ground black
pepper*

SERVES 4

3 Peel the aubergine and mash the flesh with a large fork or potato masher to make a pulpy purée.

4 Stir in the onion and garlic, parsley and crème fraîche. Add Tabasco, lemon juice, and season to taste. Serve warm.

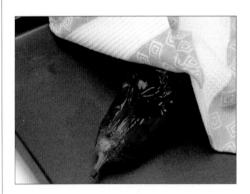

1 Cook the whole aubergine on a medium barbecue or grill for about 20 minutes, turning occasionally, until the skin is blackened and the aubergine soft. Cover the aubergine with a clean dish towel and set aside to cool for about 5–6 minutes.

2 Heat the oil in a frying pan and cook the chopped onion and garlic for 5 minutes, until soft but not browned.

FAT-FREE SAFFRON DIP

· · ·

*Serve this mild dip with fresh vegetable crudités – it is particularly good with
florets of cauliflower, asparagus tips and baby carrots and corn.*

INGREDIENTS

15ml/1 tbsp boiling water
small pinch saffron strands
200g/7oz/scant 1 cup fat-free
fromage frais
10 fresh chives
10 fresh basil leaves
salt and freshly ground black
pepper

SERVES 4

1 Pour the boiling water into a bowl
and add the saffron strands. Leave to
infuse for 3 minutes.

2 Beat the fromage frais in a large
bowl until smooth. Stir in the infused
saffron liquid with a wooden spoon.

Cook's Tip

If you don't have any saffron, add
a squeeze of lemon or lime juice.

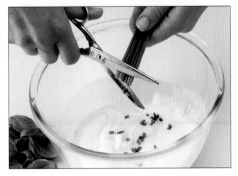

3 Snip the chives into the dip. Tear
the basil leaves into small pieces and
stir them in. Mix thoroughly.

4 Add salt and freshly ground black
pepper to taste. Serve the dip with fresh
vegetable crudités, if liked.

SPICY YOGURT MARINADE

Use this marinade for chicken, lamb or pork, and marinate the meat, covered and chilled,
for 24–36 hours to develop a mellow spicy flavour.

INGREDIENTS

5ml/1 tsp coriander seeds
10ml/2 tsp cumin seeds
6 cloves
2 bay leaves
1 onion, quartered
2 garlic cloves
5ml/2in piece fresh root ginger,
roughly chopped
2.5ml/½ tsp chilli powder
5ml/1 tsp ground turmeric
150ml/¼ pint/⅔ cup natural
yogurt
juice of 1 lemon

SERVES 6

1 Spread the coriander and cumin seeds, cloves and bay leaves over the bottom of a large frying pan and dry-fry over a moderate heat until the bay leaves are crisp.

2 Leave the spices to cool, then grind coarsely with a pestle and mortar.

3 Finely chop the onion, garlic and ginger in a blender or food processor. Add the ground spices, chilli, turmeric, yogurt and lemon juice.

Cook's Tip
Garnish the finished dish with fresh coriander leaves and slices of lemon or lime.

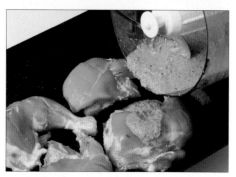

4 If you are marinating chicken joints or large pieces of meat, make several deep slashes to allow the flavours to penetrate. Arrange the pieces in a single layer and pour over the marinade. Cover and leave in the fridge to marinate for at least 24 hours.

ORANGE AND GREEN PEPPERCORN MARINADE

This is an excellent light marinade for delicately flavoured whole fish such as sea trout, bass or bream. The beauty of the fish is perfectly set off by the softly coloured marinade.

INGREDIENTS

1 red onion
2 small oranges
90ml/6 tbsp light olive oil
30ml/2 tbsp cider vinegar
30ml/2 tbsp green peppercorns in brine, drained
30ml/2 tbsp chopped fresh parsley
salt and sugar

FOR 1 MEDIUM-SIZE FISH

1 With a sharp knife, slash the fish 3–4 times on each side.

2 Cut a piece of foil big enough to wrap the fish and use to line a large dish. Peel and slice the onion and oranges. Lay half the slices on the foil, place the fish on top and cover with the remaining onion and orange.

3 Mix the remaining marinade ingredients and pour over the fish. Cover and leave to marinate for 4 hours, occasionally spooning the marinade over the fish.

4 Fold the foil loosely over the fish and seal the edges securely. Bake on a medium barbecue for 15 minutes for 450g/1lb, plus 15 minutes over.

GINGER AND LIME MARINADE

∘ ∘ ∘

This fragrant marinade will guarantee a mouth-watering aroma from the barbecue. Shown here on prawn and monkfish kebabs, it is just as delicious with chicken or pork.

INGREDIENTS

3 limes
15ml/1 tbsp green cardamom pods
1 onion, finely chopped
2.5cm/1in piece fresh root ginger,
grated
1 large garlic clove, crushed
45ml/3 tbsp olive oil

SERVES 4–6

3 Mix all the marinade ingredients together and pour over the meat or fish. Stir in gently, cover and leave in a cool place to marinate for 2–3 hours.

4 Drain the meat or fish when you are ready to cook it on the barbecue. Baste the meat occasionally with the marinade, while cooking.

1 Finely grate the rind from one lime and squeeze the juice from all of them.

2 Split the cardamom pods and remove the seeds. Crush with a pestle and mortar or the back of a heavy-bladed knife.

SUMMER HERB MARINADE
o o o

*Make the best use of summer herbs in this marinade. Try any combination of herbs, depending
on what you have to hand, and use with veal, chicken, pork, lamb or salmon.*

INGREDIENTS

*large handful of fresh herb sprigs,
e.g. chervil, thyme, parsley, sage,
chives, rosemary, oregano
90ml/6 tbsp olive oil
45ml/3 tbsp tarragon vinegar
1 garlic clove, crushed
2 spring onions, chopped
salt and freshly ground black
pepper*

SERVES 4

3 Place the meat or fish in a bowl
and pour over the marinade. Cover
and leave to marinate in a cool place
for 4–6 hours.

4 Drain the meat or fish when you
are ready to cook it on the barbecue.
Use the marinade to baste the meat
occasionally while cooking.

1 Discard any coarse stalks or
damaged leaves from the herbs, then
chop them very finely.

2 Add the chopped herbs to the
remaining marinade ingredients in a
large bowl. Stir to mix thoroughly.

DESSERTS

At the end of a barbecue it's a lovely idea to use the lingering fire

to make a delicious fruity dessert. You can cook fruit to melting

tenderness by wrapping it in foil, including sugar, spices and a sprinkling

of liqueur in the parcel. To grill fruit, cut it into chunks and spear it

on skewers, or just lay large slices on the grill rack. Sprinkle it with

sugar to caramelize in the heat. The aroma is intoxicating: even those

who thought they couldn't eat another bite will be beguiled by it.

Accompany barbecued fruit with a buttery, spicy sauce, crisp toasted

brioche or freshly made griddle cakes – and perhaps a scoop of whipped

cream or ice cream – to make a perfect end to the meal.

CHAR-GRILLED APPLES ON CINNAMON TOASTS

° ° °

This simple, scrumptious dessert is best made with an enriched bread such as brioche,
but any light sweet bread will do.

INGREDIENTS

4 sweet, dessert apples
juice of ½ lemon
4 individual brioches or muffins
60ml/4 tbsp melted butter
30ml/2 tbsp golden caster sugar
5ml/1 tsp ground cinnamon
whipped cream or Greek-style
yogurt, to serve

SERVES 4

2 Cut the brioches or muffins into thick slices. Brush the slices with melted butter on both sides.

4 Place the apple and brioche slices on a medium-hot barbecue and cook them for about 3–4 minutes, turning once, until they are beginning to turn golden brown. Do not allow to burn.

1 Core the apples and use a sharp knife to cut them into 3–4 thick slices. Sprinkle the apple slices with lemon juice and set them aside.

3 Mix together the caster sugar and ground cinnamon in a small bowl to make the cinnamon sugar. Set aside.

5 Sprinkle half the cinnamon sugar over the apple slices and brioche toasts and cook for a further minute on the barbecue, until the sugar is sizzling and the toasts are a rich golden brown.

6 To serve, arrange the apple slices over the toasts and sprinkle them with the remaining cinnamon sugar. Serve hot, with whipped cream or Greek-style yogurt, if liked.

PINEAPPLE WEDGES WITH RUM BUTTER GLAZE

Fresh pineapple is even more full of flavour when barbecued, and this spiced rum glaze makes it into a very special dessert.

INGREDIENTS

1 medium pineapple
30ml/2 tbsp dark muscovado sugar
5ml/1 tsp ground ginger
60ml/4 tbsp melted butter
30ml/2 tbsp dark rum

SERVES 4

3 Soak 4 bamboo skewers in water for 15 minutes to prevent them scorching on the barbecue. Push a skewer through each wedge, into the stalk, to hold the chunks in place.

4 Mix together the sugar, ginger, butter and rum and brush over the pineapple. Cook the wedges on the barbecue for 4 minutes; pour the remaining glaze over the top and serve.

1 With a large, sharp knife, cut the pineapple lengthways into four wedges. Cut out and discard the central core.

2 Cut between the flesh and skin, to release the skin, but leave the flesh in place. Slice the flesh across and lengthways to make thick chunks.

Cook's Tip

For an easier version, simply remove the skin and then cut the whole pineapple into thick slices and cook as above.

210

BAKED BANANAS WITH SPICY VANILLA FILLING

Bananas are ideal for barbecue cooking as they bake in their skins and need no preparation at all. This flavoured butter adds richness; children may prefer melted chocolate, jam or honey.

INGREDIENTS

4 bananas
6 green cardamom pods
1 vanilla pod
finely grated rind of 1 small orange
30ml/2 tbsp brandy or orange juice
60ml/4 tbsp light muscovado sugar
45ml/3 tbsp butter
crème fraîche or Greek-style yogurt, to serve

SERVES 4

1 Place the bananas, in their skins, on a hot barbecue and leave for 6–8 minutes, turning occasionally, until they are turning brownish-black.

2 Meanwhile, split the cardamom pods and remove the seeds. Crush lightly in a pestle and mortar.

3 Split the vanilla pod lengthways and scrape out the tiny seeds. Mix with the cardamom seeds, orange rind, brandy or juice, muscovado sugar and butter into a thick paste.

4 Using a sharp knife, slit the skin of each banana, then open out the skin and spoon in a little of the paste. Serve with a spoonful of crème fraîche or Greek-style yogurt, if liked.

ORANGES IN MAPLE AND COINTREAU SYRUP

*This is one of the most delicious ways to eat an orange, and a luxurious way to round off
a barbecued meal. For a children's or alcohol-free version, omit the liqueur.*

INGREDIENTS

*20ml/4 tsp butter, plus extra,
melted, for brushing
4 medium oranges
30 ml/2 tbsp maple syrup
30ml/2 tbsp Cointreau or Grand
Marnier liqueur
crème fraîche or fromage frais,
to serve*

SERVES 4

2 Remove some shreds of orange
rind, to decorate. Blanch these, dry
them and set them aside. Peel the
oranges, removing all the white pith
and catching the juice in a bowl.

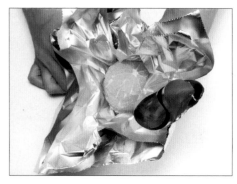

4 Tuck the baking foil up securely
around the oranges to keep them in
shape, leaving the foil open at the top.

1 Cut four double-thickness squares
of baking foil, large enough to wrap
each of the oranges. Brush the centre
of each square of foil with plenty of
melted butter.

3 Slice the oranges crossways into
thick slices. Reassemble them and place
each orange on a square of baking foil.

5 Mix together the reserved orange
juice, maple syrup and liqueur and
spoon the mixture over the oranges.

6 Add a knob of butter to each
parcel and close the foil at the top to
seal in the juices. Place the parcels on
a hot barbecue for 10–12 minutes,
until hot. Serve with crème fraîche or
fromage frais, topped with the reserved
shreds of orange rind.

NECTARINES WITH MARZIPAN AND MASCARPONE

∘ ∘ ∘

A luscious dessert that no one can resist – dieters may prefer to use low-fat soft cheese or ricotta instead of mascarpone.

INGREDIENTS

4 firm, ripe nectarines or peaches
75g/3oz marzipan
75g/3oz/5 tbsp mascarpone cheese
3 macaroon biscuits, crushed

SERVES 4

1 Cut the nectarines or peaches in half and remove the stones.

2 Divide the marzipan into eight pieces, roll into balls, using your fingers, and press one piece of marzipan into the stone cavity of each nectarine half.

Cook's Tip

Either nectarines or peaches can be used for this recipe. If the stone does not pull out easily when you halve the fruit, use a small, sharp knife to cut around it.

3 Spoon the mascarpone cheese on top of the fruit halves. Sprinkle the crushed macaroon bicuits over the mascarpone cheese.

4 Place the half-fruits on a hot barbecue for 3–5 minutes, until they are hot and the mascarpone starts to melt. Serve immediately.

BARBECUED STRAWBERRY CROISSANTS

The combination of crisp barbecued croissants, ricotta cheese and sweet strawberry conserve makes for a deliciously simple, sinful dessert, which is like eating warm cream cakes!

INGREDIENTS

4 croissants

115g/4oz/½ cup ricotta cheese

115g/4oz/½ cup strawberry conserve or jam

SERVES 4

3 Top the ricotta with a generous spoonful of strawberry conserve and replace the top half of the croissant.

4 Place the filled croissants on a hot barbecue and cook for 2–3 minutes, turning once. Serve immediately.

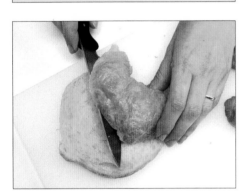

1 On a chopping board, split the croissants in half and open them out.

2 Spread the bottom half of each croissant with a generous layer of the ricotta cheese.

Cook's Tip

As an alternative to croissants, try scones, brioches or muffins, toasted on the barbecue.

GRIDDLE CAKES WITH MULLED PLUMS

° ° °

*These delectably light little pancakes are fun to make on the barbecue. They are served with
a rich, spicy plum sauce.*

INGREDIENTS

500g/1¼ lb red plums
90ml/6 tbsp light muscovado sugar
1 cinnamon stick
2 whole cloves
1 piece star anise
90ml/6 tbsp apple juice
cream or Greek-style yogurt,
to serve

FOR THE GRIDDLE CAKES
50g/2oz/½ cup plain flour
10ml/2 tsp baking powder
pinch of salt
50g/2oz/½ cup fine cornmeal
30ml/2 tbsp light muscovado sugar
1 egg, beaten
300ml/½ pint/1¼ cups milk
30ml/2 tbsp corn oil

SERVES 6

1 Halve, stone and quarter the
plums. Place them in a flameproof pan,
with the sugar, spices and apple juice.

Cook's Tip

If you prefer, make the
griddle cakes in advance, on
the hob, and then simply heat
them for a few seconds on the
barbecue to serve with the plums.

2 Bring to the boil, then reduce the
heat, cover the pan and simmer gently
for 8–10 minutes, stirring occasionally,
until the plums are soft. Remove the
spices and keep the plums warm on
the side of the barbecue.

3 For the griddle cakes, sift the
plain flour, baking powder and salt
into a large mixing bowl and stir in
the cornmeal and muscovado sugar.

4 Make a well in the centre of
the ingredients and add the egg, then
beat in the milk. Beat thoroughly with
a whisk or wooden spoon to form a
smooth batter. Beat in half the oil.

5 Heat a griddle or a heavy frying
pan on a hot barbecue. Brush with the
remaining oil, then drop tablespoons
of batter on to it, allowing them to
spread. Cook the griddle cakes for
about a minute, until bubbles start
to appear on the surface and the
underside is golden brown.

6 Turn the cakes over and cook the
other side for a further minute, or until
golden. Serve the cakes hot from the
griddle with a spoonful of mulled
plums and cream or yogurt.

FRUIT KEBABS WITH CHOCOLATE FONDUE

Fondues are always lots of fun, and the delicious ingredients used here – fresh fruit, chocolate and marshmallow – mean that this recipe will be a popular choice with children and adults alike.

2 Mix together the butter, lemon juice and ground cinnamon and brush the mixture generously over the fruits.

3 For the fondue, place the chocolate, cream and marshmallows in a small pan and heat gently, without boiling, stirring continuously until the mixture has melted and is smooth.

INGREDIENTS

2 bananas
2 kiwi fruit
12 strawberries
15ml/1 tbsp melted butter
15ml/1 tbsp lemon juice
5ml/1 tsp ground cinnamon

FOR THE FONDUE
225g/8oz plain chocolate
120ml/4fl oz/½ cup single cream
8 marshmallows
2.5ml/½ tsp vanilla essence

SERVES 4

1 Peel the bananas and cut into thick chunks. Peel the kiwi fruit and quarter them. Thread the bananas, kiwi fruit and strawberries on to four wooden skewers. (Soak the skewers in water for 15 minutes beforehand to prevent them scorching on the barbecue.)

4 Cook the kebabs on a medium-hot barbecue for about 2–3 minutes, turning once, or until the fruit is golden. Stir the vanilla essence into the fondue. Empty the fondue into a small bowl and serve at once, with the fruit kebabs.

SPICED PEAR AND BLUEBERRY PARCELS

This fruity combination makes a delicious dessert for a hot summer's evening.
You could substitute other berry fruits for the blueberries if you prefer.

INGREDIENTS

4 firm, ripe pears
30ml/2 tbsp lemon juice
15ml/1 tbsp melted butter
150g/5oz/1¼ cups blueberries
60ml/4 tbsp light muscovado sugar
freshly ground black pepper

SERVES 4

3 Cut four squares of double-thickness foil, large enough to wrap the pears, and brush them with melted butter. Place two pear halves on each, cut sides upwards. Gather the foil up around them, to hold them level.

4 Mix the blueberries and sugar together and spoon them over the pears. Sprinkle with black pepper. Seal the edges of the foil over the pears and cook on a fairly hot barbecue for 20–25 minutes.

1 Peel the pears thinly. Cut them in half lengthways. Scoop out the core from each half, using a teaspoon and a sharp kitchen knife.

2 Brush the pears with lemon juice, to prevent them from discolouring.

Cook's Tip

To assemble in advance, line with a layer of greaseproof paper, as the acid in the lemon juice may react with the foil and taint the flavour.

FRESH FIGS WITH VANILLA CREAM

o o o

The ripeness of the figs will determine their cooking time. This is an ideal recipe for a barbecue because it is prepared on the barbecue and left to stand until you are ready to eat.

INGREDIENTS
450ml/³/4 pint/scant 2 cups dry white wine
75g/3oz/¹/3 cup clear honey
50g/2oz/¹/4 cup caster sugar
1 small orange
8 whole cloves
450g/1lb fresh figs
1 cinnamon stick
sprigs of fresh mint, or bay leaves, to decorate

FOR THE VANILLA CREAM
300ml/¹/2 pint/1¹/4 cups double cream
1 vanilla pod
5ml/1 tsp caster sugar

SERVES 6

1 Put the wine, honey and caster sugar in a heavy saucepan and heat gently on the barbecue or hob until the sugar dissolves.

2 Stud the orange with the cloves and add to the syrup with the figs and cinnamon. Cover and simmer very gently for 5–10 minutes until the figs are tender. Transfer the contents of the pan to a serving dish and leave to cool.

3 Put 150ml/¹/4 pint/²/3 cup of the cream in a small saucepan with the vanilla pod. Bring almost to the boil, then leave to cool and infuse for 30 minutes. Remove the vanilla pod and mix the flavoured cream with the remaining cream and sugar in a bowl. Whip lightly. Transfer to a serving dish.

4 Decorate the figs with mint or bay leaves and serve with the vanilla cream.

Baked Apples in Honey and Lemon

. . .

Tender baked apples with a classic flavouring of lemon and honey make a simple dessert.
Serve with custard or a spoonful of whipped cream, if you wish.

INGREDIENTS

4 medium cooking apples
15ml/1 tbsp honey
grated rind and juice of 1 lemon
15ml/1 tbsp butter, melted

SERVES 4

1 Remove the cores from the apples, leaving them whole. Cut four squares of double-thickness baking foil, to wrap the apples, and brush with butter.

2 With a cannelle or sharp knife, cut lines through the apple skin at regular intervals.

3 Mix together the honey, lemon rind, juice and butter in a small bowl.

4 Spoon the mixture into the apples and wrap in foil, sealing the edges securely. Cook on a hot barbecue for 20 minutes, until the apples are tender

POACHED PEARS IN MAPLE AND YOGURT SAUCE

° . . °

This elegant dessert is easier to make than it looks – poach the pears on the hob or barbecue
when you cook the main course, and have the cooled syrup ready to add just before serving.

INGREDIENTS

6 firm pears
15ml/1 tbsp lemon juice
250ml/8fl oz/1 cup sweet white
wine or cider
thinly pared rind of 1 lemon
1 cinnamon stick
30ml/2 tbsp maple syrup
2.5ml/¹⁄₂ tsp arrowroot
150ml/¹⁄₄ pint/²⁄₃ cup strained
Greek-style yogurt

SERVES 6

1 Peel the pears, leaving them whole and with stalks. Brush with lemon juice to prevent them discolouring. Use a potato peeler or small knife to scoop out the core from the base of each pear.

2 Place the pears in a wide, heavy pan and pour over the wine, with enough cold water to almost cover the fruit. Add the lemon rind and cinnamon stick, and bring to the boil on the hob or, using a flameproof pan, on the barbecue. Reduce the heat, cover and simmer for 30 minutes, or until tender. Lift out the pears carefully.

3 Boil the remaining liquid, uncovered, until reduced to about 120ml/4 fl oz/¹⁄₂ cup. Strain and add the maple syrup. Blend a little of the liquid with the arrowroot. Return to the pan and cook, stirring, until thick and clear. Allow to cool.

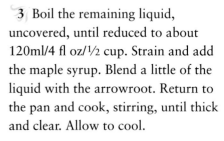

4 Slice each pear, leaving the slices attached at the stem end, and fan out on serving plates. Stir 30ml/2 tbsp of the cooled syrup into the yogurt and spoon around the pears. Drizzle the pears with the remaining syrup and serve immediately.

CHOCOLATE MINT TRUFFLE FILO PARCELS

These exquisite little parcels are utterly irresistible: there will be no leftovers. The use of fresh mint in the recipe gives a wonderfully fresh flavour.

2 Cut the filo pastry sheets into 7.5cm/3in squares and cover with a damp cloth to prevent them drying out.

3 Brush a square of filo with melted butter, lay on a second sheet, brush again and place a spoonful of filling in the middle of the top sheet. Bring in all four corners and twist to form a purse shape. Repeat to make 18 parcels.

4 Place the filo parcels on a griddle or baking sheet, well brushed with melted butter. Cook on a medium-hot barbecue for about 10 minutes, until the filo pastry is crisp. Leave to cool, then dust lightly with sifted icing sugar and then with sifted cocoa powder.

INGREDIENTS
15ml/1 tbsp very finely chopped fresh mint
75g/3oz/³/4 cup ground almonds
50g/2oz plain chocolate, grated
115g/4oz/¹/2 cup crème fraîche or fromage frais
2 dessert apples, peeled and grated
9 large sheets filo pastry
75g/3oz/¹/3 cup butter, melted
15ml/1 tbsp icing sugar, to dust
15ml/1 tbsp cocoa powder, to dust

MAKES 18 PARCELS

1 Mix the chopped fresh mint, almonds, grated chocolate, crème fraîche or fromage frais and grated apple in a large mixing bowl. Set aside.

Outdoor
Entertaining

———❖———

Everything tastes better out of doors, and picnics – whether in the

garden, at the seaside or in a grassy meadow – are a great pleasure both

to organize and to take part in, as long as the weather is kind. If you

have a portable barbecue you can take it along with you and make the

food twice as exciting, but take care that you light it in a safe place and

clear up carefully afterwards. Food for barbecuing can be transported

in its marinade, all ready to be popped on to the grill. Pack interesting

dips into plastic boxes, and take pittas or prepared vegetables to go with

them. Homemade quiches and pies will also help to satisfy healthy

outdoor appetites. This section also offers inspirations for special

summer meals and garden parties at home, including some original

and delicious ideas for party drinks.

VEGETABLES WITH TAPENADE AND HERB AIOLI

A beautiful platter of summer vegetables served with one or two interesting sauces makes a really appetizing and informal starter, which is perfect for picnics as it can all be prepared in advance.

INGREDIENTS

2 red peppers, cut into wide strips
30ml/2 tbsp olive oil
225g/8oz new potatoes
115g/4oz green beans
225g/8oz baby carrots
225g/8oz young asparagus
12 quails' eggs
fresh herbs, to garnish
coarse salt, for sprinkling

FOR THE TAPENADE
175g/6oz/1½ cups stoned black olives
50g/2oz can anchovy fillets, drained
30ml/2 tbsp capers
120ml/4fl oz/½ cup olive oil
finely grated rind of 1 lemon
15ml/1 tbsp brandy (optional)
freshly ground black pepper

FOR THE HERB AIOLI
5 garlic cloves, crushed
2 egg yolks
5ml/1 tsp Dijon mustard
10ml/2 tsp white wine vinegar
250ml/8fl oz/1 cup light olive oil
45ml/3 tbsp chopped mixed fresh herbs, such as chervil, parsley and tarragon
30ml/2 tbsp chopped watercress
salt and freshly ground black pepper

SERVES 6

1 To make the tapenade, finely chop the olives, anchovies and capers and beat together with the oil, lemon rind and brandy, if using. (Alternatively, lightly process the ingredients in a blender or food processor.)

2 Season with pepper and blend in a little more oil if the mixture seems very dry. Transfer to a serving dish.

3 To make the aïoli, beat together the garlic, egg yolks, mustard and vinegar. Gradually blend in the olive oil, a drop at a time, whisking well until thick and smooth.

4 Stir in the mixed herbs and watercress. Season with salt and pepper to taste, adding a little more vinegar if necessary. Cover with clear film and chill until ready to serve.

Cook's Tip
Any leftover tapenade is delicious tossed with pasta or spread on to warm toast. If you are making this dish as part of a picnic, allow the vegetables to cool before packing in an airtight container. Pack the quails' eggs in their original box.

5 Brush the peppers with oil and grill on a hot barbecue or under a hot grill until just beginning to char.

6 Cook the potatoes in a large pan of boiling, salted water until tender. Add the beans and carrots and blanch for 1 minute. Add the asparagus and cook for a further 30 seconds. Drain the vegetables. Cook the quails' eggs in boiling water for 2 minutes.

7 Arrange all the vegetables, eggs and sauces on a serving platter. Garnish with fresh herbs and serve with coarse salt, for sprinkling.

CRUDITES

Serve a colourful selection of raw vegetables as a quick and easy accompaniment
to apéritif drinks or as a refreshing starter for summer meals.

RAW VEGETABLE PLATTER

INGREDIENTS

2 red or yellow peppers, sliced
lengthways
225g/8oz fresh baby corn,
blanched
1 chicory head (red or white),
trimmed and leaves separated
175–225g/6–8oz thin asparagus,
trimmed and blanched
small bunch radishes, trimmed
175g/6oz cherry tomatoes
12 quail's eggs, boiled for
3 minutes, drained, refreshed and
peeled
aioli or tapenade,
for dipping

SERVES 6–8

Arrange a selection of prepared
vegetables, chosen from the list above,
on a serving plate with your chosen
dip. Keep covered until ready to serve.

TOMATO AND CUCUMBER SALAD

INGREDIENTS

1 medium cucumber, peeled and
thinly sliced
30ml/2 tbsp white wine vinegar
90ml/3fl oz/1/3 cup crème fraîche or
soured cream
30ml/2 tbsp chopped fresh mint
4 or 5 ripe tomatoes, sliced
salt and freshly ground black
pepper

SERVES 4–6

Place the cucumber in a bowl, sprinkle
with a little salt and 15ml/1 tbsp of the
vinegar and toss with 5 or 6 ice cubes.
Chill for 1 hour to crisp, then rinse,
drain and pat dry. Return to the bowl,
add the cream, pepper and mint and
stir to mix well. Arrange the tomato
slices on a serving plate, sprinkle with
the remaining vinegar, and spoon the
cucumber slices into the centre.

Cook's Tip

Any leftover vegetables can
be used in soups or stir-fries,
even if they have already
been dressed.

CARROT AND ORANGE SALAD

INGREDIENTS

1 garlic clove, crushed
grated rind and juice of 1 unwaxed
orange
30–45ml/2–3 tbsp groundnut oil
450g/1lb carrots, cut into very fine
julienne strips
30–45ml/2–3 tbsp chopped fresh
parsley
salt and freshly ground black
pepper

SERVES 4–6

Rub around a bowl with the garlic
clove, leaving the clove in the bowl.
Add the orange rind and juice, and
season with salt and freshly ground
pepper. Whisk in the groundnut oil
until blended, then remove the garlic
clove. Add the carrots and half of the
fresh parsley and toss well to mix.
Garnish with the remaining parsley.

AIOLI

Put 4 peeled garlic cloves (more or less can be added, to taste) in a bowl with a pinch of salt, and crush with the back of a spoon. Add 2 egg yolks and beat for 30 seconds with an electric mixer until creamy. Beat in 250ml/8fl oz/ 1 cup extra virgin olive oil, drop by drop. As the mixture thickens, the oil can be added in a thin stream. Thin the sauce with lemon juice, if necessary, and season to taste. Chill for up to 2 days; bring to room temperature and stir before serving.

TAPENADE

Put 200g/7oz stoned black olives, 6 anchovy fillets, 30ml/2 tbsp capers, rinsed, 1 or 2 garlic cloves, 5ml/1 tsp fresh thyme, 15ml/1 tbsp Dijon mustard, the juice of half a lemon, freshly ground black pepper and, if

FROM TOP LEFT: raw vegetable platter with aïoli, carrot and orange salad, tomato and cucumber salad.

you like, 15ml/1 tbsp brandy in a food processor and process for about 15–30 seconds until smooth, scraping down the sides of the bowl. With the machine running, pour in 60–90ml/4–6 tbsp extra virgin olive oil to make a smooth paste. Store in an airtight container.

FALAFEL

· · ○

*These North African fritters are traditionally made using dried broad beans, but chick-peas are
more easily available. Serve in warmed pitta bread, with salad and garlicky yogurt.*

INGREDIENTS

150g/5oz/¾ cup dried chick-peas
1 large onion, roughly chopped
2 garlic cloves, roughly chopped
*60ml/4 tbsp roughly chopped fresh
parsley*
5ml/1 tsp cumin seeds, crushed
5ml/1 tsp coriander seeds, crushed
2.5ml/½ tsp baking powder
*salt and freshly ground black
pepper*
oil for deep frying

SERVES 4

1 Put the chick-peas in a large bowl
and cover with plenty of cold water.
Leave to soak overnight.

2 Drain the chick-peas and cover
with fresh water in a saucepan. Bring
to the boil and boil rapidly for 10
minutes. Reduce the heat and simmer
for about 1 hour, or until soft. Drain.

3 Place in a food processor with the
onion, garlic, parsley, cumin, coriander
and baking powder. Season to taste.
Process to form a firm paste.

4 Shape the mixture into walnut-size
balls, using your hands, and flatten
them slightly. In a deep pan, heat
5cm/2in oil until a little of the mixture
sizzles on the surface. Fry the falafel
in batches until golden. Drain on
kitchen paper and serve.

Cook's Tip
Although they can be fried
in advance, falafel are at their
best served warm. Wrap them in
foil or pack them in an insulated
container to take them on picnics,
or keep them warm on the edge
of the barbecue until needed.

HUMMUS BI TAHINA

∘ ∘ ∘

Blending chick-peas with garlic, lemon and oil makes a deliciously creamy purée to serve as a dip with crudités or warmed pitta bread.

INGREDIENTS

150g/5oz/³⁄₄ cup dried chick-peas
juice of 2 lemons
2 garlic cloves, sliced
30ml/2 tbsp olive oil, plus extra to serve
150ml/¹⁄₄ pint/²⁄₃ cup tahini paste
salt and freshly ground black pepper
cayenne pepper, to serve
flat leaf parsley, to garnish

SERVES 4–6

1 Put the chick-peas in a large bowl and cover with plenty of cold water. Leave to soak overnight.

2 Drain the chick-peas and cover with fresh water in a pan. Bring to the boil and boil rapidly for 10 minutes. Reduce the heat and simmer for about 1 hour, or until soft. Drain.

3 Process the chick-peas to a purée in a food processor. Add lemon juice, garlic, oil, cayenne pepper and tahini and blend until creamy.

4 Season the chick-pea purée with plenty of salt and freshly ground black pepper and transfer to a serving dish. Drizzle the purée with olive oil and sprinkle lightly with cayenne pepper. Serve the dip garnished with a few flat leaf parsley sprigs.

Cook's Tip

If you do not have time to soak dried chick-peas, canned chick-peas can be used instead. Allow two 400g/14oz cans and drain them thoroughly.

TOMATO AND CHEESE TARTS

*These crisp little tartlets look impressive but are actually very easy to make.
They are best eaten fresh from the oven.*

INGREDIENTS

3 sheets filo pastry
1 egg white
175g/6oz cream cheese
handful fresh basil leaves
4 small tomatoes, sliced
*salt and freshly ground black
pepper*

MAKES 12

1 Preheat the oven to 200°C/400°F/
Gas 6. Brush the sheets of filo pastry
lightly with egg white and cut into
24 × 10cm/4in squares.

2 Layer the squares in twos, in
12 bun tins. Spoon the cream cheese
into the pastry cases. Season with
ground black pepper and top with
fresh basil leaves.

3 Arrange the tomatoes on the tarts,
season and bake for 10–12 minutes,
until the pastry is golden. Serve warm.

Cook's Tip
Use halved cherry tomatoes
for the tarts, if you prefer.

Tandoori Chicken Sticks

These aromatic chicken pieces are traditionally baked in the special clay oven known as a tandoor. They are equally delicious served hot or cold, and make irresistible barbecue food.

INGREDIENTS

450g/1lb boneless, skinless chicken breasts

FOR THE CORIANDER YOGURT
250ml/8fl oz/1 cup natural yogurt
30ml/2 tbsp whipping cream
½ cucumber, peeled, seeded and finely chopped
15–30ml/1–2 tbsp fresh chopped coriander or mint
salt and freshly ground black pepper

FOR THE MARINADE
175ml/6fl oz/¾ cup natural yogurt
5ml/1 tsp garam masala or curry powder
1.5ml/¼ tsp ground cumin
1.5ml/¼ tsp ground coriander
1.5ml/¼ tsp cayenne pepper (or to taste)
5ml/1 tsp tomato purée
1–2 garlic cloves, finely chopped
2.5cm/1in piece fresh root ginger, finely chopped
grated zest and juice of ½ lemon
15–30ml/1–2 tbsp fresh chopped coriander or mint

MAKES ABOUT 25

2 To prepare the marinade, place all the ingredients in a food processor and process until smooth. Pour into a shallow dish.

3 Freeze the chicken breasts for 5 minutes to firm them, then slice in half horizontally. Cut the slices into 2cm/¾ in strips and add to the marinade. Toss to coat well. Cover with clear film and chill for 6–8 hours or overnight.

4 Drain the chicken pieces and arrange on a rack, scrunching up the chicken slightly to make wavy shapes. Cook on a hot barbecue for 4–5 minutes until brown and cooked through, turning once. Alternatively, arrange on a foil-lined baking sheet and cook under a hot grill. Serve hot, threaded on cocktail sticks or short skewers, with the yogurt dip. For a picnic, cool and pack into a box.

1 For the coriander yogurt, combine all the ingredients in a bowl. Season, cover and chill until ready to serve.

HAM PIZZETTAS WITH MELTED BRIE AND MANGO

These individual little pizzas are topped with an unusual but very successful combination of smoked ham, Brie and juicy chunks of fresh mango.

INGREDIENTS

225g/8oz/2 cups strong white flour
10g/¼ oz sachet easy-blend dried yeast
150ml/¼ pint/⅔ cup warm water
60ml/4 tbsp olive oil

FOR THE TOPPING
1 ripe mango
150g/5oz smoked ham, sliced wafer-thin
150g/5oz Brie cheese, diced
12 yellow cherry tomatoes, halved
salt and freshly ground black pepper

SERVES 6

1 In a large bowl, stir together the flour and yeast, with a pinch of salt. Make a well in the centre and stir in the water and 45ml/3 tbsp of the olive oil. Stir until thoroughly mixed.

Cook's Tip

It's important to flatten out the dough rounds quite thinly and to cook them fairly slowly, or they will not cook evenly. To save time, you could use a 300g/11oz packet of pizza dough mix.

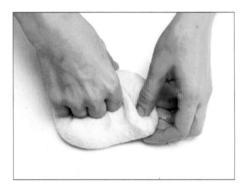

2 Turn the dough out on to a floured surface and knead it for about 5 minutes, or until smooth.

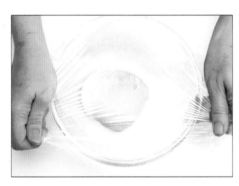

3 Return the dough to the bowl and cover it with a damp cloth or oiled clear film. Leave the dough to prove in a warm place for about 30 minutes or until the dough is doubled in size and springy to the touch.

4 Divide the dough into six and roll each piece into a ball. Flatten out with your hand and use your knuckles to press each piece of dough to a round of about 15cm/6in diameter, with a raised lip around the edge.

5 Halve, stone and peel the mango and cut it into small dice. Arrange with the ham on top of the pizzettas. Top with cheese and tomatoes and sprinkle with salt and ground black pepper.

6 Drizzle the remaining oil over the pizzettas. Place them on a medium-hot barbecue and cook for 8 minutes, until golden brown and crisp underneath.

OYSTER AND BACON BROCHETTES

Six oysters per person make a good starter, served with the seasoned oyster liquor to trickle over the skewers. Alternatively, serve nine per person as a main course, accompanied by a cool salad.

INGREDIENTS

36 oysters
18 thin-cut rashers rindless streaky bacon
15ml/1 tbsp paprika
5ml/1 tsp cayenne pepper
freshly ground black pepper
celery leaves and red chillies, to garnish

FOR THE SAUCE

½ red chilli pepper, seeded and very finely chopped
1 garlic clove, crushed
2 spring onions, very finely chopped
30ml/2 tbsp finely chopped fresh parsley
liquor from the oysters
juice of ¼–½ lemon, to taste
salt and freshly ground black pepper

SERVES 4–6

2 Push the knife in and cut the muscle, holding the shell closed. Tip the liquor into the bowl. Cut the oyster free. Discard the drained shells.

3 For the sauce, mix the chilli, garlic, spring onions and parsley into the oyster liquor and sharpen to taste with lemon juice. Season with salt and pepper and transfer to a serving dish.

4 Cut each bacon rasher across the middle. Season the oysters lightly with paprika, cayenne and freshly ground black pepper and wrap each one in half a bacon rasher, then thread them on to skewers. Cook on a hot barbecue for about 5 minutes, turning frequently, until the bacon is crisp and brown. Garnish with celery leaves and red chillies and serve with the sauce.

1 Open the oysters over a bowl to catch their liquor for the sauce. Wrap your left hand (if you are right-handed) in a clean dish towel and cup the deep shell of each oyster in your wrapped hand. Work the point of a strong, short-bladed knife into the hinge between the shells and twist firmly.

TURKEY ROLLS WITH GAZPACHO SAUCE

This Spanish-style recipe uses quick-cooking turkey steaks, but you could also cook veal escalopes in the same way.

INGREDIENTS

4 turkey breast steaks
15ml/1 tbsp red pesto
4 chorizo sausages
15ml/1 tbsp olive oil
salt and freshly ground black
pepper

FOR THE GAZPACHO SAUCE
1 green pepper, chopped
1 red pepper, chopped
7.5cm/3in piece cucumber
1 medium tomato
1 garlic clove
45ml/3 tbsp olive oil
15ml/1 tbsp red wine vinegar

SERVES 4

1 To make the gazpacho sauce, place the peppers, cucumber, tomato, garlic, 30ml/2 tbsp of the olive oil and the vinegar in a food processor and process until almost smooth. Season to taste with salt and ground black pepper.

2 If the turkey breast steaks are quite thick, place them between two sheets of clear film and beat them with the side of a rolling pin, to flatten them slightly.

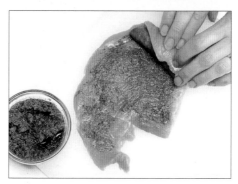

3 Spread the red pesto over the turkey, place a chorizo on each piece and roll up firmly.

4 Slice the rolls thickly and thread them on to skewers. Brush with olive oil and cook on a medium barbecue for about 10–12 minutes, turning once. Serve with the gazpacho sauce.

CHICKEN, MUSHROOM AND CORIANDER PIZZA

Shiitake mushrooms add an earthy flavour to this colourful pizza, while fresh chilli and chilli-flavoured olive oil give it a hint of spiciness. Cook the pizza on the barbecue or in the oven.

INGREDIENTS

45ml/3 tbsp olive oil
350g/12oz skinned chicken breast fillets, cut into thin strips
1 bunch spring onions, sliced
1 fresh red chilli, seeded and chopped
1 red pepper, cut into thin strips
75g/3oz fresh shiitake mushrooms, sliced
45–60ml/3–4 tbsp chopped fresh coriander
1 pizza base, about 25–30cm/10–12in diameter
15ml/1 tbsp chilli oil
150g/5oz mozzarella cheese
salt and freshly ground black pepper

SERVES 3–4

2 Pour off any excess oil, then set aside to let the chicken mixture cool.

3 Stir the fresh coriander into the cooled chicken mixture in the wok.

4 Brush all over the pizza base with the chilli oil.

5 Spoon over the chicken mixture and drizzle over the remaining olive oil.

1 Heat 30ml/2 tbsp olive oil in a wok or large frying pan. Add the chicken, spring onions, chilli, red pepper and mushrooms and stir-fry over a high heat for 2–3 minutes until the chicken is firm but still slightly pink inside. Season to taste.

6 Grate the mozzarella cheese and sprinkle it over the pizza base. Cook the pizza on a medium-hot barbecue for 15–20 minutes, until the base is crisp and golden and the cheese is bubbling. Serve the pizza immediately.

MEDITERRANEAN QUICHE

∘ ∘ ∘

This quiche forms the ideal base for a hearty picnic feast. The strong Mediterranean flavours of tomatoes, peppers and anchovies complement the cheese pastry beautifully.

INGREDIENTS

FOR THE PASTRY
225g/8oz/2 cups plain flour
pinch of salt
pinch of dry mustard
115g/4oz/½ cup butter, chilled and
diced
50g/2oz Gruyère cheese, grated
salt and freshly ground black
pepper

FOR THE FILLING
50g/2oz can anchovy fillets, drained
50ml/2fl oz/¼ cup milk
30ml/2 tbsp French mustard
45ml/3 tbsp olive oil
2 large Spanish onions, peeled and
sliced
1 red pepper, very finely sliced
3 egg yolks
350ml/12fl oz/1½ cups double
cream
1 garlic clove, crushed
175g/6oz sharp Cheddar cheese,
grated
2 large tomatoes, thickly sliced
30ml/2 tbsp chopped fresh basil, to
garnish

SERVES 6–8

1 To make the pastry, place the flour, salt and mustard in a food processor, add the butter and process the mixture until it resembles fine breadcrumbs.

2 Add the Gruyère cheese and process again briefly. Add enough iced water to make a stiff dough: the dough will be ready when it forms a ball. Wrap the dough in clear film and chill in the fridge for at least 30 minutes.

3 Meanwhile, make the filling. Soak the anchovies in the milk for about 20 minutes to make them less salty. Pour off the milk. Heat the olive oil in a frying pan and cook the onions and red pepper until they soften.

4 In a bowl, beat the egg yolks, cream, garlic and Cheddar cheese together; season with salt and pepper.

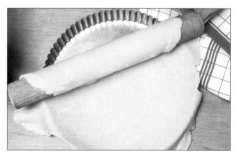

5 Preheat the oven to 200°C/400°F/ Gas 6. Roll out the chilled pastry and line a 23cm/9in loose-based quiche tin. Spread the mustard over and chill in the fridge for a further 15 minutes.

6 Arrange the tomatoes in a layer in the pastry crust. Top with the onion and pepper mixture and the anchovy fillets. Pour over the egg mixture. Bake for 30 minutes. Serve warm or at room temperature, sprinkled with fresh basil.

Cook's Tip
Leave the quiche in its tin if you are packing it for a picnic.

CHICKEN AND APRICOT FILO PIE

*The filling for this pie has a Middle Eastern flavour – minced chicken combined with apricots,
bulgur wheat, nuts and spices. It both looks and tastes spectacular.*

INGREDIENTS

75g/3oz/½ cup bulgur wheat
75g/3oz/6 tbsp butter
1 onion, chopped
450g/1lb minced chicken
50g/2oz/¼ cup ready-to-eat dried
apricots, finely chopped
25g/1oz/¼ cup blanched almonds,
chopped
5ml/1 tsp ground cinnamon
2.5ml/½ tsp ground allspice
50ml/2fl oz/¼ cup Greek yogurt
15ml/1 tbsp snipped fresh chives,
plus extra to garnish
30ml/2 tbsp chopped fresh parsley
6 large sheets filo pastry
salt and freshly ground black
pepper

SERVES 6

1 Preheat the oven to 200°C/400°F/
Gas 6. Put the bulgur wheat in a large
bowl with 120ml/4fl oz/½ cup boiling
water. Allow the wheat to soak for 5
minutes, until the water is absorbed.

2 Heat 25g/1oz/2 tbsp of the butter
in a pan and fry the onion and chicken
until pale golden. Stir in the apricots,
almonds and bulgur wheat and cook
for a further 2 minutes. Remove from
the heat and stir in the cinnamon,
allspice, yogurt, chives and parsley.
Season to taste with salt and pepper.

3 Melt the remaining butter. Unroll
the filo pastry and cut into 25cm/10in
rounds. Keep the pastry rounds covered
with a clean, damp dish towel to
prevent them from drying out.

4 Line a 23cm/9in loose-based flan
tin with three pastry rounds, brushing
each with butter as you layer them.
Spoon in the chicken mixture and
cover with three more pastry rounds,
brushed with melted butter as before.

5 Crumple the remaining rounds
and place on top of the pie. Brush with
any remaining butter. Bake the pie for
about 30 minutes, until the pastry is
golden brown and crisp. Serve the pie
hot or cold, garnished with fresh chives.

CHICKEN WITH FRESH HERBS AND GARLIC

A whole chicken can be roasted on a spit on the barbecue. This marinade keeps the flesh moist and delicious and the fresh herbs add summery flavours.

INGREDIENTS

1.75kg/4½ lb free-range chicken
finely grated rind and juice of 1 lemon
1 garlic clove, crushed
30ml/2 tbsp olive oil
2 fresh thyme sprigs
2 fresh sage sprigs
90ml/6 tbsp unsalted butter, softened
salt and freshly ground black pepper

SERVES 4

1 Season the chicken well. Mix the lemon rind and juice, crushed garlic and olive oil together and pour them over the chicken. Leave to marinate in the fridge for at least 2 hours.

Cook's Tip

If roasting the chicken in the oven, preheat the oven to 230°C/450°F/ Gas 8 and reduce the heat to 190°C/375°F/Gas 5 after 10 minutes. If you are roasting a chicken to serve cold, cooking it in foil helps to keep it succulent – open the foil for the last 20 minutes to brown the skin, then close it as the chicken cools.

2 Place the herbs in the cavity of the bird and smear the butter over the skin. Season well. Cook the chicken on a spit on the barbecue for 1½–1¾ hours, basting with the marinade, until the juices run clear when the thigh is pierced with a skewer. Leave the bird to rest for 15 minutes before carving.

PEPPER STEAK

This easy, rather indulgent, bistro classic can be put together in a matter of minutes for an intimate summer supper in the garden. The creamy sauce helps to balance the heat of the pepper.

INGREDIENTS

30ml/2 tbsp black peppercorns
2 fillet or sirloin steaks, about
225g/8oz each
15g/½ oz/1 tbsp butter
10ml/2 tsp olive oil
45ml/3 tbsp brandy
150ml/1/4 pint/²/3 cup whipping
cream
1 garlic clove, finely chopped
salt, if necessary

SERVES 2

1 Place the black peppercorns in a sturdy polythene bag. Crush the peppercorns with a rolling pin or steak hammer until they are crushed to medium-coarse pepper.

2 Put the steaks on a chopping board and trim away any excess fat, using a sharp kitchen knife. Press the pepper firmly on to both sides of the meat, to coat it completely.

3 Melt the butter with the olive oil in a heavy frying pan over a medium-high heat. Add the meat and cook for 6–7 minutes, turning once, until cooked to your liking. Transfer the steaks to a warmed platter or plates and cover to keep warm.

4 Pour in the brandy to de-glaze the frying pan. Allow the brandy to boil until it has reduced by half, scraping the base of the frying pan, then add the whipping cream and garlic. Bubble gently over a low-medium heat for about 4 minutes or until the cream has reduced by about one-third. Stir any accumulated juices from the meat into the sauce, taste and add salt as necessary. Serve the steaks hot, with the sauce.

PORK WITH MARSALA AND JUNIPER

Sicilian marsala wine gives savoury dishes a rich, fruity and alcoholic tang. The pork is fully complemented by the flavour of the sauce in this quick and luxurious dish.

INGREDIENTS
25g/1oz dried cep or porcini mushrooms
4 pork escalopes
10ml/2 tsp balsamic vinegar
8 garlic cloves
15g/¹/₂ oz/1 tbsp butter
45ml/3 tbsp marsala
several rosemary sprigs
10 juniper berries, crushed
salt and freshly ground black pepper

SERVES 4

1 Put the dried mushrooms in a large bowl and just cover with hot water. Leave to stand for 20 minutes to allow the mushrooms to soak.

2 Brush the pork with 5ml/1 tsp of the vinegar and season with salt and pepper. Put the garlic cloves in a small pan of boiling water and cook for 10 minutes until soft. Drain and set aside.

3 Melt the butter in a large frying pan. Add the pork and fry quickly until browned on the underside. Turn the meat over and cook for 1 minute more.

4 Add the marsala, rosemary sprigs, drained mushrooms, 60ml/4 tbsp of the mushroom water, the garlic cloves, juniper berries and the remaining balsamic vinegar.

5 Simmer gently for 3–5 minutes until the pork is cooked through. Season lightly and serve hot.

STUFFED ROAST LOIN OF PORK

. . .

This recipe uses fruit and nuts as a stuffing for roast pork in the Catalan style. It is full of flavour and is very good served cold, making an excellent centrepiece for a summer buffet or a picnic.

INGREDIENTS

60ml/4 tbsp olive oil
1 onion, finely chopped
2 garlic cloves, chopped
50g/2oz/1 cup fresh breadcrumbs
4 ready-to-eat dried figs, chopped
8 stoned green olives, chopped
25g/1oz/¼ cup flaked almonds
15ml/1 tbsp lemon juice
15ml/1 tbsp chopped fresh parsley
1 egg yolk
900g/2lb boned loin of pork
salt and freshly ground black
pepper

SERVES 4

1 Preheat the oven to 200°C/400°F/ Gas 6, or prepare the barbecue. Heat 45ml/3 tbsp of the oil in a pan, add the onion and garlic, and cook gently until softened. Remove the pan from the heat and stir in the breadcrumbs, figs, olives, almonds, lemon juice, chopped fresh parsley and egg yolk. Season to taste with salt and ground black pepper.

2 Remove any string from the pork and unroll the belly flap, cutting away any excess fat or meat to enable you to do so. Spread the stuffing over the flat piece and roll it up, starting from the thick side. Tie at intervals with string.

3 Pour the remaining olive oil into a roasting tin and put in the pork, or arrange on the spit of the barbecue. Roast for 1 hour and 15 minutes, or until the juices run clear from the meat.

4 Remove the pork from the oven or the spit and, if serving hot, let it rest for 10 minutes before carving into thick slices. If serving cold, wrap the meat in foil to keep it moist until you carve it.

LAMB CASSEROLE WITH GARLIC AND BEANS

This recipe has a Spanish influence and makes a substantial meal, served with potatoes.
Broad beans add colour and texture to the dish.

INGREDIENTS

45ml/3 tbsp olive oil
1.5kg/3–3½ lb lamb fillet, cut
into 5cm/2in cubes
1 large onion, chopped
6 large garlic cloves, unpeeled
1 bay leaf
5ml/1 tsp paprika
120ml/4fl oz/½ cup dry sherry
115g/4oz shelled fresh or frozen
broad beans
30ml/2 tbsp chopped fresh parsley
salt and freshly ground black
pepper

SERVES 6

3 Add the garlic, bay leaf, paprika and sherry. Season to taste and bring to the boil. Cover and simmer gently for 1½ hours, until tender.

4 Add the broad beans to the casserole and cook for a further 10 minutes. Stir in the chopped fresh parsley just before serving.

1 Heat 30ml/2 tbsp olive oil in a large flameproof casserole. Add half the meat and brown well on all sides. Transfer to a plate. Brown the rest of the meat in the same way and remove from the casserole.

2 Heat the remaining oil in the pan, add the onion and cook for about 5 minutes until soft. Return the meat to the casserole.

RED MULLET WITH LAVENDER

Cook a fish dish with a difference by adding lavender to red mullet for a wonderful aromatic flavour. Sprinkle some lavender flowers on the coals too, to give a delightful perfumed ambience.

INGREDIENTS

4 red mullet, scaled, gutted and cleaned
30ml/2 tbsp olive oil

FOR THE MARINADE
45ml/3 tbsp fresh lavender flowers or 15ml/1 tbsp dried lavender leaves, roughly chopped
roughly chopped rind of 1 lemon
4 spring onions, roughly chopped
salt and freshly ground black pepper

SERVES 4

1 Place the fish in a shallow dish. Mix the ingredients for the marinade and pour over the fish. Cover the fish with clear film and leave in the fridge to marinate for at least 3 hours.

2 Remove the fish from the marinade and brush it with olive oil. Cook the fish on a hot barbecue for about 10–15 minutes, turning once and basting with olive oil as it cooks.

SALMON STEAKS WITH OREGANO SALSA

* * *

This combination of salmon with piquant tomato works incredibly well. The barbecue gives the salmon an exquisite flavour. Served hot or cold, this is an ideal dish for a summer lunch.

INGREDIENTS

15ml/1 tbsp butter
4 salmon steaks, about 225g/8oz each
120ml/4fl oz/½ cup white wine
freshly ground black pepper

FOR THE SALSA
10ml/2 tsp chopped fresh oregano, plus sprigs to garnish
4 spring onions, trimmed
225g/8oz ripe tomatoes, peeled
30ml/2 tbsp extra virgin olive oil
2.5ml/½ tsp caster sugar
15ml/1 tbsp tomato purée

SERVES 4

1 Butter four squares of double-thickness baking foil. Put a salmon steak on each and add a little wine and a grinding of ground black pepper. Wrap the salmon steaks loosely in the squares, sealing the edges securely. Cook on a medium-hot barbecue for 10 minutes, until just tender. If serving the steaks hot, keep them warm.

2 Put the chopped fresh oregano in a food processor and chop it very finely. Add the spring onions, tomatoes and remaining salsa ingredients. Pulse until chopped but not a smooth purée.

3 Serve the salmon hot or cold with the salsa, garnished with a sprig of fresh oregano.

HERBAL PUNCH

This refreshing party drink will have people coming back for more, and it is an original non-alcoholic choice for drivers and children.

INGREDIENTS

450ml/³⁄4 pint/2 cups honey
4 litres/7 pints water
450ml/³⁄4 pint/2 cups freshly
squeezed lemon juice
45ml/3 tbsp fresh rosemary leaves,
plus extra to decorate
1.5kg/3¹⁄2 lb/8 cups sliced
strawberries
450ml/³⁄4 pint/2 cups freshly
squeezed lime juice
1.75 litres/3 pints/7¹⁄2 cups
sparkling mineral water
ice cubes
3–4 scented geranium leaves

SERVES 30 PLUS

1 Combine the honey, 1 litre/ 1³⁄4 pints/4 cups water, one-eighth of the lemon juice and the fresh rosemary leaves in a saucepan. Bring to the boil, stirring, until the honey is dissolved. Remove from the heat and allow to stand for about 5 minutes. Strain into a large punch bowl and leave aside to cool.

2 Press the strawberries through a fine sieve into the punch bowl, add the rest of the water and lemon juice, and the lime juice and sparkling mineral water. Stir gently to combine the ingredients. Add the ice cubes just 5 minutes before serving, and float the geranium and rosemary leaves on the surface.

MINT CUP

o o o

Mint is a perennially popular flavouring and this delicate cup is a wonderful mixture with an intriguing taste. It is the perfect summer drink to serve with meals outdoors.

INGREDIENTS

handful fresh mint leaves
15ml/1 tbsp sugar
crushed ice
15ml/1 tbsp lemon juice
*175ml/6fl oz/³⁄4 cup grapefruit
juice*
*600ml/1 pint/2¹⁄2 cups chilled
tonic water*
*mint sprigs and lemon slices,
to decorate*

SERVES 4–6

1 Crush the mint leaves with the sugar and put into a jug. Fill the jug to the top with crushed ice.

2 Add the lemon juice, grapefruit juice and tonic water. Stir gently o combine the ingredients and decorate with mint sprigs and slices of lemon.

STRAWBERRY AND MINT CHAMPAGNE

This is a simple concoction that makes a bottle of champagne or sparkling white wine go much further. It tastes very special on a hot summer's evening.

INGREDIENTS
500g/1¼lb strawberries
6–8 fresh mint leaves
1 bottle champagne or sparkling
white wine
fresh mint sprigs, to decorate

SERVES 4–6

2 Strain through a fine sieve into a large bowl. Half fill a glass with the mixture and top up with champagne or sparkling wine. Decorate with a sprig of fresh mint.

1 Purée the strawberries and fresh mint leaves in a food processor.

MELON, GINGER AND BORAGE CUP

Melon and ginger complement each other magnificently. If you prefer, you can leave out the powdered ginger – the result is milder but equally delicious.

INGREDIENTS
½ large honeydew melon
1 litre/1¾ pints/4 cups ginger beer
powdered ginger, to taste
borage sprigs with flowers,
to decorate

SERVES 6–8

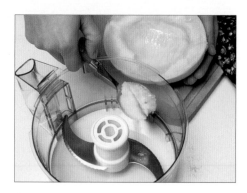

1 Discard the seeds from the half melon and scoop the flesh into a food processor. Blend the melon to a purée.

2 Pour the purée into a large jug and top up with ginger beer. Add powdered ginger to taste. Pour into glasses and decorate with borage.

INDEX